Our Place

Changing the Nature of Alberta

Kevin Van Tighem

RMB

RMB | Rocky Mountain Books Ltd.
rmbooks.com
@rmbooks
facebook.com/rmbooks

Cataloguing data available from Library and Archives Canada
ISBN 978-1-77160-203-7 (paperback)
ISBN 978-1-77160-242-6 (electronic)

Book design by Jessica Chan
Moose in Lake at Sunset © hinzundkunz

Printed and bound in Canada by Friesens

Distributed in Canada by Heritage Group Distribution and in the US by Publishers Group West

For information on purchasing bulk quantities of this book, or to obtain media excerpts or invite the author to speak at an event, please visit rmbooks.com and select the "Contact Us" tab.

RMB | Rocky Mountain Books is dedicated to the environment and committed to reducing the destruction of old-growth forests. Our books are produced with respect for the future and consideration for the past.

We acknowledge the financial support of the Government of Canada through the Canada Book Fund and the Canada Council for the Arts, and of the province of British Columbia through the British Columbia Arts Council and the Book Publishing Tax Credit.

"I think today that most of our people – I don't say this unkindly – feel that the greatest achievement in life is to take as much as possible out of the land and convert it into money. If the resources are poorer and their bank account is richer, then they are satisfied. But that is not leaving ... Alberta better than we found it."

—*Grant MacEwan, former mayor of Calgary and lieutenant-governor of Alberta*

"You were my brother. You shoulda taken care of me just a little ... I coulda been a contender."

—*Marlon Brando,* On The Waterfront

"I have faith in a better future, because I have faith that most human beings want to do the right thing."

—*Lois Hole, former lieutenant-governor of Alberta*

"It isn't enough to recognize the land. Does the land recognize you?"

—*Narcisse Blood, Blackfoot elder and teacher*

Acknowledgments

These writings, for the most part, belong to others; I'm just the scribe. Countless people contributed in different ways to the making of the essays, articles and stories gathered here. I'm deeply and humbly grateful to every person who agreed to be interviewed, who shared their personal and professional knowledge and who offered me anecdotes and insights that, ultimately, are theirs and not mine. You will find their names as you read; these are the good people who make places real and writing possible. I can't thank them enough for their friendship and generosity.

This book is based on previously published material. Some appeared in earlier collections, now out of print; the rest has never appeared in book form before. I wish to acknowledge and thank the publications who carried the original versions: *Alberta Views, Alberta Outdoorsmen, Borealis, Bugle, Calgary Herald, Canadian Geographic, Environment Views, Event, Highline, Nature Canada, Outdoor Canada, Outdoor Edge, Trumpeter, Western Sportsman* and *Wolf International*.

I've been very fortunate to work with fine editors whose talents helped refine both this material and, over the years, my writing ability. That list includes Margaret Chandler, James Little, Evan Osenton, David Stalling, Red Wilkinson, Lynn Zwicky and, now, Peter Norman. Bruce Masterman and Gail Van Tighem read through a working draft of this book and offered valuable advice, which I am happy to say I took.

I will be eternally grateful to my late father, Jack Van Tighem, for immersing me in wild nature from an early age, and to my late mother, Eileen Van Tighem, for her deep wisdom, support and the courage to grant me freedom to roam, err, learn and become. My treasured wife, Gail, and our children, Corey, Katie and Brian, have extended the gift of family, love and shared discovery through my whole life. I've been exceptionally blessed. Those six people remain the best friends and finest companions I could ever have hoped for; this body of work is dedicated to them.

And to the prairies, hills, mountains, streams, wild things and people of this home place – thanks for so many seasons of joy, inspiration, discovery and meaning. May we prove worthy of you.

Introduction

We might be born into history, but that truth rarely dawns on us until a few decades have sneaked by. When we look back in midlife, it becomes disconcertingly clear that, while blithely assuming history belonged to earlier generations, we were actually living it ourselves. I suppose that's the point where one begins to feel old. Each lifetime becomes part of tomorrow's story of what was – and what might have been but wasn't.

Alberta's history only goes back to 1905, technically speaking, because that's when the province acquired a name and boundaries. This place's earlier written history begins in the 1800s, when Europeans brought paper and ink with them across the prairies and began to record their version of events here where the plains end and the mountains begin.

Our deepest history is in the oral traditions of the indigenous people who occupied this place for many generations before pushy newcomers decided to name it after a foreign queen's daughter. Many of those oral traditions, unfortunately, failed to survive the 20th century's war on Canada's indigenous cultures, a passive but nonetheless deadly war waged with the Indian Act, residential schools and prejudices so deeply entrenched that many of us weren't even aware that we were (and in too many cases still are) infected by them.

The Alberta idea is a colonial one, invented by strangers from away. The place itself had no need for a name, a set of boundaries or the British tradition of representational government under a foreign constitution; it was doing just fine without them. But history flows in one direction, and this is what history has given to this part of the planet. The imposition of foreign ideas on a native place meant that nothing could go on the way it had before. The story had changed, and changing its story always changes a place.

And it has changed in profound ways; it's changing even now. We can feel virtuous in our regret for what might have been, blaming those who came before us, but considering the dramatic changes that have unfolded in our generation, to do so is to deny our shared culpability. In any case, today and tomorrow remain our responsibility.

If this collection has a central purpose, it is to understand and consider some of these changes to Alberta's nature and to consider how best to manage our way into a future that respects this unique place on Earth and rewards those who love it. Fortunately, many of us do love this place; we have lived here so long that it has become more than just an address – it's who we are. Four generations in, its history belongs as much to the newcomers as to those whose roots go deeper. We all occupy the same home, now. Dysfunctional family that we might sometimes seem to be, we've got some things to figure out if we hope to keep the place together.

Cultural history and natural history cannot be viewed in isolation of one another. The stories of a place and of its people are indivisible even if reductionist science assigns one to the realm of geography and the other to that of history; they are simply the same home place viewed through different windows.

Nature is comprised of ecosystems; ecosystems, by definition, are about connections and consequence. American preservationist John Muir wrote: "When we try to pick out anything by itself, we find it hitched to everything else in the Universe." Needless to say, that includes us. Place shapes us; we shape place. Each defines the other.

So this is our home: a bit run down, a bit worse for wear, but still structurally sound. Even the broken bits are part of our family album. We should still have hopes for it in spite of our failures and regrets and the things we'd rather not talk about. Our home place is the product of choices – both good and bad. Choices we have yet to make will determine what it will yet become – either by continuing to try and force land, water and wildlife to adapt to our whims, or by evolving a sustaining culture in which we can become truly native to this unique and precious part of the only known living planet.

This book is a collection of works going back three decades. Most have been edited or lightly revised, and I've added updating footnotes where it most seemed essential. For the most part, though, each essay and story speaks in the voice of the younger man who wrote it and remains anchored in the time it was written. Even though places like the Little Smoky, for which I once expressed a desperately hopeful kind of optimism, have now been left ravaged by a generation whose stubborn sense of entitlement trumped its duty of stewardship, I have left that early optimism to stand in contrast to what we allowed to happen. Thankfully, other tales turned out happier – the Whaleback and, just west of the Alberta boundary, the

Columbia River wetlands were both saved by the efforts of caring people determined to ensure they would be as much a part of our future as our past. We haven't left all the best behind. And we could still choose to restore much of what has been lost in the land – and in ourselves.

That will depend on whether our better selves can triumph over the seeming relentlessness of history's trajectory. Those who invaded, exploited and compromised one of the finest places on planet Earth might have been, for the most part, before our time, but we do tend to carry on their ways: blindness to the real nature of this place, obsession with prosperity over sustainability, impatience with anything that might constrain ambition. I offer this book of chronicles, reflections and polemics as a personal contribution to our shared challenge of sustaining what is best of the west that defines us – by finding the best of what exists within us.

It's never too late to try and get it right. This place is worth it. So are we.

CHAPTER 1

The Back Trail

From Wild to Weeds (1996)

Dad stopped the car abruptly to point out the first deer he had ever spotted east of Calgary. It was 1965; I was 12. Three doe mule deer stood staring at us far out in a field of barley stubble. We stared at those exotic creatures in amazement. Real deer, way out on the prairie; who would have imagined it?

We probably should have been less surprised than we were; ecological change so defines Alberta's story that different generations have entirely different ideas of what is normal here. Home is a moving target.

Dad and Mom had both grown up in Strathmore, a farming town in southern Alberta. Dad hunted sharp-tailed grouse in the brushy pastures north of town. Mom went fishing with her father on the Bow River near Carseland. It was a dry and windy country back when the Siksika hunted bison there, but by my parents' time irrigation was well on the way to transforming the region into something more pastoral. New thickets of cottonwood, willow and saskatoon followed the long lines of ditches across the gently undulating contours of what once had been prairie grassland and now grew wheat, barley and forage crops.

Through the 1960s and 1970s Dad took his kids back to the Strathmore area each fall. We hunted introduced Hungarian partridges and ring-necked pheasants on the farms of friends and relatives. The shrub tangles and poplar groves that grew along the edges of the irrigation ditches by then seemed like jungles to me. By my early teens those riparian thickets had grown extensive enough for deer to follow the irrigation canals up out of the Bow River valley and make themselves at home on the uplands. Poplars that had not yet sprouted when Dad was young were towering veterans, many of them 30 metres tall. One day I pointed out a blue jay to Dad; he was as amazed as he had been by the deer a few years earlier.

Hunting that irrigation country year after year fed what became for me a deep and lasting passion for the land and its wildlife. When the opportunity arose, I studied botany and geography in university, the way one strives to know the one he loves.

My parents' reminiscences about the prairies of their youth had already given me a sense of how much Alberta's prairies had changed in barely two human lifetimes. I had seen many changes in the farmland east of Calgary during my own few decades: the arrival of deer, then woodpeckers, blue jays, foxes, even the occasional moose. But it was the university library, with its books and journals rich in historical and ecological information, that fully opened my eyes to how much change those familiar everyday fields had known in the past century. The more I learned, the more I realized that the nature of my home place might be something quite different from what I could see around me.

One fall in the late 1970s, as my now-aging father and I came home from another day afield, we saw fields of stubble burning north of the Trans-Canada highway. Long lines of flame flickered orange in the fading evening, scrolling out across the contours of a sprawling barley field. I'd been studying about the role that wildfire and other natural disturbance processes had played in shaping the ecology of the primeval prairie, and suddenly, in the growing darkness when things grow strange, the eyes of my imagination saw past the familiar irrigation country, back to the wild prairie of only a few decades ago.

In my mind's eye I saw an endless, rolling mosaic of needle-grass, blue grama, western wheatgrass and a hundred other species of low-growing grasses, herbs and shrubs stretching unbroken beneath a sky unmarred by jet trails. Great patches of that landscape were blackened where lightning and indigenous hunters had lit fires and let them run in the wind. Thousands of bison peppered the plains, grazing on succulent new grass that had sprouted from earlier burns. The hissing prairie wind was full of their mutter and grumble and the sweet-pungent odour of dung.

A pack of wolves sauntered along the edge of the herd, watching for weakness. Eagles, ravens and magpies fed on the last remains of an old bull nearby. Endless lines of migrating waterfowl – geese, ducks and cranes – filled the sky overhead. The prairie echoed with their gabble. Far to the south, a line of gold marked the foliage of cottonwoods along the Bow River where grizzly bears foraged among the ripened saskatoon berries and chokecherries ...

The sudden glow of street lamps illuminating a concrete overpass jarred me back to the present; we were arriving home to Calgary, a city that had already grown to hold more people than lived in the entire province of Alberta when I was born. I think it was that abrupt return to reality that led me to see, for the first time, the province of my birth as a strange place – where people view landscape change as normal rather than strange and upsetting, where many native plants and animals fade toward oblivion while introduced weeds and exotic species thrive – a province whose landscapes are the product no longer of place but of engineering and error.

What has happened to this west we call home? How can we know it better? What part of our identity derives from its true nature – or are we more at one with the weeds?

Two centuries ago, the people who lived here understood natural forces of destruction and renewal as the way of the world. The Blackfoot peoples got their colloquial name from the fact that their moccasins were usually blackened with char ash from prairie fires. When fires burned or rivers flooded in the spring, the indigenous people didn't worry about damage and loss. They simply got out of the way and waited for the renewal they knew would follow. Death and life and death and life; the landscape's patterns recorded a constantly shifting story of loss and renewal.

Alberta's ecosystems depend now as they depended then on natural cycles and periodic disturbances to keep them vital.

Floods fertilize and water riparian (river-bottom) areas, renewing stands of cottonwood and sandbar willow. Wet weather refills wetlands; dry spells expand shorelines. Waterfowl thrive during the wet years, while shorebirds benefit from the dry. Fires and insect outbreaks stimulate the growth of new forage for grazing animals and maintain a constantly shifting mosaic of vegetation ranging from shadowy old forests to shrubby young woodlands.

Alberta's indigenous peoples understood those natural forces; that was simply how the world was. Nothing nature did was bad; it was all part of the cycles of change that sustained life and diversity. Fire, flood, drought and weather melded and moulded a distinctive ecological mosaic – the unique living map of this place on Earth. June mornings were filled with birdsong and the hum of fecund life – living music; an organic symphony of place and being.

I n 1754 change arrived. It wore a white face, side whiskers and, no doubt, a bemused expression. That year Anthony Henday, the first European to describe what would someday become Alberta, looked west from near modern-day Carstairs and saw what he described as the "Shining Mountains" arrayed along the western horizon. Then he turned back east to report to his fur trade superiors, setting in motion forces that would rearrange the face of this landscape at a pace and on a scale greater than anything that had ever come before.

The Hudson's Bay Company and North West Company soon established fur trading outposts along the Athabasca and North Saskatchewan rivers. Indigenous people adapted to new opportunities by trapping fur animals for trade and hunting meat to supply the newcomers. By the time ranchers began to speculate on Alberta grass in the late 1800s, the West had become a place of plunder and slaughter. Death no longer led to rebirth.

Beavers were the first resource to attract the get-rich-quick enthusiasm of European capitalists. The fur trade's approach was to trap an area out, and then move on to new killing grounds. As a result, beavers were almost extirpated by the late 1800s. As beaver populations crashed, their dams washed out. Wetlands shrank and streams became more flood-prone. There was no circle of life under the rules of the new economy – just plunder.

The growing numbers of fur traders, prospectors, missionaries and other European frontiersmen relied on indigenous people to supply them with big game, ducks, geese, grouse and other game. First Nations and Metis hunters, already exceptionally skilled, became deadly once equipped with modern firearms. By the beginning of the 20th century uncontrolled slaughter by European and indigenous hunters had virtually wiped out most accessible game populations to feed growing towns, mining camps, logging camps and other outposts. Elk survived only in a few small herds that ranged the upper Brazeau and Kananaskis valleys. Bull and cutthroat trout were fished out of accessible streams. Whooping cranes and trumpeter swans no longer nested in the aspen parkland. Bison were only memories.

Canada's minister of the interior, worried that tourists to the nation's new park at Banff might be disappointed by the lack of wildlife, commissioned a study by a Mr. W.F. Whitcher. After conducting a cursory investigation, most of which took place in Banff's beer parlours, Whitcher concluded that Native people and market hunting had nearly wiped out game. He recommended the government kill off predators to save the survivors. In reality, however, predator populations were already depleted by strychnine poisoning, traps and unregulated hunting.

By the dawn of the 20th century Alberta's wildlife wealth was devastated. Even the natural processes that had once sustained wildlife were under assault by government efforts to prevent prairie and forest fires, limit spring flooding and eradicate predators. A growing flood of aggressive colonists was spilling across the land. Few, if any, of those newcomers had any way of understanding the ecosystems to which they were laying claim. Their religious and cultural beliefs assured them that indigenous people had nothing to teach them and that nature was an adversary to be overcome. They extirpated wildlife for food and to make the land safe for crops and cattle, and they sank plough blades into the living earth and turned it upside down.

A growing stillness settled across a land that, only a few decades earlier, had teemed with life.

꿷

I t was the Canadian Pacific Railway that kicked off the first great wave of landscape change. Upon its arrival in Alberta in 1883, the big steel rail suddenly made the journey west less daunting for hopeful settlers. Here on the treeless plains and chinook-warmed foothills, they could lay claim to a homestead and build new lives as farmers and ranchers.

Those hopeful settlers didn't see their work as an assault on the new land's ecosystems; they saw it as putting fertile soil to its God-intended use of producing crops for human consumption. In trying to replace nature's ill-disciplined and wasteful natural fecundity with well-ordered agricultural landscapes, however, they had to fight nature. The same natural forces that give life to Alberta's natural ecosystems made it hard to settle and cultivate the land. Fires burned fields, fences and homes. Droughts bred grasshoppers and left crops to wither and soil to blow away. Wet cycles made the soil too wet for machinery. Floods killed livestock, damaged buildings and wreaked havoc on towns and cities.

The 20th century, consequently, saw a progression of government, industry and community initiatives to eliminate those processes of ecological renewal. Fire control, dams, wetland drainage and irrigation were among the chief methods.

By the 1930s, thanks to cultivated fields and a spreading gridwork of roads that created barriers to windblown flames, big prairie fires were pretty much a thing of the past. In the foothills and northern forests, though, fire control was more difficult. Big forest fires burned through parts of Alberta in 1910, 1919 and the dry 1930s, renewing the lodgepole pine forests, fescue meadows and sheep winter ranges that had always been sustained by periodic wildfires, but scaring the newcomers badly. By the 1950s, consequently, government had made it a priority to build fire lookouts and good roads into remote forests so fire crews could detect fires early and respond quickly. The growing use of aircraft to water bomb remote blazes also helped turn the tide toward effective fire control in forested areas.

As prairie fires became less frequent, aspen forests spread south and east into areas that had formerly been grassland. The late Stettler-area naturalist Lloyd Lohr describes the landscape around his farm as his grandfather saw it when homesteading in the area in 1900: "There were groves of trees, but there was a lot of grass and a lot of sloughs. There'd be a slough and then a circle of willows and then maybe some bigger poplars around it.... but prairie fires came through every spring and sometimes in the fall ... They would burn up to these bushes, burn the grass and then they would kill the sapling trees around the ring. And the bigger trees in the middle, they'd stay. So it kept it under control that way."

Today, their spread no longer inhibited by frequent fires, dense aspen forests surround the Lohr farm. White-tailed deer, once nonexistent, are everywhere. Native prairie birds like upland sandpipers, Sprague's pipits and sharp-tailed grouse, part of the fabric of Lloyd's boyhood, are rare. Starlings, savannah sparrows, ruffed grouse and Hungarian partridges – species better suited for life in the new landscape – have replaced them.

Settlers welcomed floods and droughts no more than fires. Floods were a problem from the start, since many Alberta towns and cities were sited where trails crossed creeks and rivers. Calgary, Rockyford, Okotoks, High River, Red Deer and Lethbridge all had to deal with spring floodwaters that washed away buildings, livestock and the occasional hapless human.

Spring floods too often gave way to summer droughts. Farmers who had watched vast quantities of water pouring off the landscape in May and June had to contend with hot sun, cloudless skies and moisture-sucking winds during July and August, when their growing crops most needed water.

Alistair Crerar, executive director for the now-defunct Environment Council of Alberta, once wrote: "Water in a dry land has a mythic emotive power that moves civil engineers to visions and irrigation farmers to poetry. The absence or shortage of water is so searing, so terrifying, that anything that promises to prevent or avoid it is accepted without question."

As towns grew and farms proliferated, demand for control of Alberta's undisciplined streams and rivers increased. From 1950 on, governments built a series of huge dams to tame Alberta rivers for irrigation water supply, power and flood control. In the late 1960s the immense W.A.C. Bennett Dam in British Columbia even tamed the mighty Peace River.

The reservoirs behind those big dams are of little value to native fish or wildlife. They fill and drain at all the wrong times. Few plants or animals can adapt to the backwards ecosystems of man-made reservoirs, so the windswept expanses of water upstream from dams usually support only bottom-feeding or deepwater fish and, along their eroded shorelines, exotic weeds. In addition to the formerly wildlife-rich river valleys lost under the reservoirs, many hundreds of kilometres of wildlife habitat downstream from Alberta's dams has also been damaged by changes to the rivers' natural cycles.

R unning parallel with the control of fire and water in Alberta was an expansion of cultivated farmland. Land not growing crops was considered "unimproved" in a province founded by farmers; most of Alberta's former grasslands have now been "improved" for agriculture. By the 1970s it was already difficult to find native grassland in the most fertile parts of the province – the aspen parkland ecoregion that extends from Lloydminster to Edmonton and south to Drumheller and High River. Today, ecologists who have studied aerial photography and satellite images of Alberta estimate that less than 5 per cent of central Alberta's original fescue grassland survives. Less than half of the drier grassland types farther south have escaped the plough.

Periodically through much of the 20th century, governments provided programs and subsidies to drain wetlands in order to grow more grains and other crops. The result was a steady, irreversible loss of the most productive habitat for waterfowl, amphibians and other wildlife, and further changes to the movement of water across the prairie and parkland landscapes. Gradually the rich mosaic of low-lying sedge marshes, sprawling wetlands, shortgrass ridge tops and mixed-grass uplands that once typified prairie Alberta has given way to a checkerboard of monocultures that feed no bison, shelter no pipits and provide habitat for only a few common wildlife species.

By the 1970s irrigation farming had spread across most of the region between Calgary, Medicine Hat and the Milk River Ridge. Today, Alberta has more than two-thirds of all the irrigated farmland in Canada – more than 625,000 hectares. Rivers like the lower Bow and Oldman run so nearly dry in summer that fish sometimes die, but the once-dry uplands are lush and green with exotic crops watered by an intricate network of canals and pipelines.

The irrigation projects and farms of the early part of this century essentially moved riparian habitats onto the uplands as leaky ditches gradually enabled shrub tangles and woodlands to spread across a land where the buffalo once roamed. Blackbirds, orioles, deer, pheasants and other animals that could adapt to these linear habitats thrived in the new irrigation farming landscapes. The rest – animals like wolves, elk, burrowing owls and upland sandpipers that depend on fires, floods, native vegetation or isolation – vanished or became rare.

During the oil boom of the 1980s, the Alberta government

poured hundreds of millions of dollars into projects to make irrigation canals more efficient. This meant, among other things, killing off the poplar forests and brush tangles that lined the leaky old canals. As farms grew larger and farmers moved to town, many of the old farmsteads with their windbreaks and shelter belts vanished too. Few parts of Alberta have seen as much ecological change as irrigation country. The loss of both the original natural diversity and the temporary riparian habitats of the early irrigation era continues today. Offsetting the losses, to some degree, are the increased number of artificial wetlands created by some irrigation districts. Birds like glossy ibis and black-crowned night heron – once unknown in Alberta – have spread north from the US to take up residence in these productive wetlands. Northern birds like white pelicans, double-crested cormorants and terns have been able to shift southward to nest on islands in large irrigation reservoirs like McGregor Lake. For the most part, however, southern Alberta's prairies are biological disaster areas; even the ghosts are dead.

Prosperity is a mixed blessing. A temporary spike in world oil prices in the 1980s upended Alberta's traditionally frugal and cautious culture and shifted political control from the farm kitchens of the province to the boardrooms of Calgary and Edmonton. Flush with new wealth, the government began looking for ways to further diversify the province's economy. One consequence: the control of nature and remaking of landscapes spread north into the northern forests, by way of government subsidies to the pulp and paper industry. Already sliced by hundreds of thousands of kilometres of oil industry exploration cutlines, northern forests, muskegs, wetlands and river meadows quickly sprouted a network of roads connecting clearcut expanses of scarified (ploughed) soil planted to commercial tree species.

Logging, unlike the fires that are the primary and best force for forest renewal, leaves the landscape without phosphorus-rich ash and the abundant standing and fallen dead wood that provide habitat for native vegetation as well as ants, beetles and other animals. Instead, it removes the woody material and leaves soils damaged both by compaction under haul roads and by scarification in the logged sites. The industrialization of northern Alberta is incrementally eliminating sensitive species like caribou, marten and boreal wood warblers, while creating the patchwork, disturbed landscapes favoured by weedy species like white-tailed deer, coyote, cowbird and starling.

The 20th century was barely half over before many people in North America awakened to the realization that wilderness, many native wildlife species and the clean water and air that we had previously taken for granted were disappearing. Even oil-rich, optimistic Albertans began to see their province as a place of endangered species and vanishing natural ecosystems. Organizations like the Alberta Wilderness

Association and the Federation of Alberta Naturalists became active in promoting the need for nature conservation.

Public support for conservation was widespread in Alberta by the 1980s, even if that support wasn't reflected by government policies – the provincial government had long been more responsive to industry lobbyists than to the grassroots. Much of the public support, in fact, arose in reaction to the hasty industrialization of the province, which was fuelled by the province's windfall oil revenues of the late 1970s and early 1980s. Battles over the Oldman River Dam, northern pulp mills and industrial tourism development in Banff National Park awakened more and more Albertans to the fact that they could no longer take their province's natural wealth for granted.

By the 1990s even Alberta's development-obsessed government could no longer ignore widespread public demand to protect what remained of Alberta's original wild beauty. Even so, the few small patches of landscape that finally gained recognition through the province's notorious "Special Places" program remained open to many of the industrial uses that most parks and protected areas elsewhere prohibit. Even if they had been properly protected, however, the question of restoring their ecological vitality would have been perplexing. After a century of constant change, expanding settlement and the control of nature, few Albertans can begin to imagine what our ecosystems should look like under natural conditions, or how to restore the natural processes needed to rebuild our province's original diversity and resilience. Even among many who value nature, its natural forces of renewal, like fire, floods and large predators, are more often seen as problems than as part of the solution. But failure to restore natural fire and flood regimes – and to value forest insect outbreaks, bring back wild predators and improve livestock grazing patterns – will certainly ensure that even the best-protected areas become degraded and unnatural over time.

の

A nimals poorly adapted to eluding human predators were the first to decline as human numbers increased through the late 1800s and early 1900s. Later in the 20th century, with better wildlife regulations and more public concern for conservation of game animals, some of those animal species recovered. Deer, for example, once virtually eradicated south of the Red Deer River, are now abundant throughout the province. Trumpeter swans, beavers and even whooping cranes are more numerous than in the first half of the last century.

However, even as Alberta began to conserve and restore animals once threatened by uncontrolled hunting, we continued to erase their habitat directly through agricultural expansion, the growth of cities and the expansion of industries like forestry, and to change it indirectly by putting out fires, draining wetlands and altering the flows of rivers and streams with dams and diversions.

Today, much of the province remains green, but fewer kinds of plants contribute to it. The total number of animals remains high, but most are domestic or weedy species. Ecologically,

Alberta has become a faded facsimile of itself.

Hope and inspiration are scarce commodities for an ecologist looking at the post-frontier west. Humans are more numerous than ever before; our mark is everywhere. Compounding our sheer numbers are a scarcity of ecological literacy and a collective obsession with prosperity rather than sustainability.

Even so, Albertans can still restore the best of our home place. Most of us, after all, love the place and mean to stay. Science has given us deeper insights into the workings of nature than ever before in human history. History has taught us practical lessons about what doesn't work, and what just might. And for all the losses ignorance and haste have wrought, much of this land's original living wealth survives. It isn't too late.

Since Anthony Henday, generations of outsiders have flowed into Alberta, leaving home behind and imposing foreign ambitions on a landscape they did not know or recognize. Even many of those who lived here already have lost their way through generations of cultural loss and disenfranchisement. The time has come to understand the nature of this wounded place we call home, and to put that understanding to work in restoring its health and diversity. Western historian Wallace Stegner insisted optimistically, against all evidence, that the North American west could yet "create a society to match its scenery." That was more than half a century ago; we haven't managed it yet.

What Happened to the Forests? (2015)

In the mid-1940s, Alberta's economy faced bigger challenges than today. The Second World War had hit hot on the heels of the 1930s drought and depression. Farms had stayed fallow, and spending was flat. A few folks were making money from oil, but nobody had any reason to expect that industry to amount to much.

But those bad times were ultimately good for our forests.

The drought of the 1930s hadn't just dried up farmers' fields and sloughs. The hot, dry weather ramped up the forest fire hazard in the foothills and front ranges of the Rockies. Between 1931 and 1936, fires burned through an average of 47,000 acres a year – almost four times more than in the 1920s. In 1936 a massive fire from BC burned through the Highwood and Sheep River valleys. Lack of roads and equipment combined with inexperienced firefighters and penny-pinching bureaucrats made battling the blaze a nearly hopeless endeavour. Freddy Nash, the forest ranger in the Highwood, got on the phone to head office to raise the alarm. Instead of a crew to hold the fire back, he got a scolding for wasting money on an expensive long-distance call.

Unable to cope with the costs of fire protection, in 1947 the province worked out a deal with the federal government establishing the Eastern Rockies Forest Conservation Board. The feds' interest was water: the forests of western Alberta yield most of the water for southern Alberta and Saskatchewan and part of Manitoba. The provincial government's was money: the new board came with a $6.3 million federal grant (more than $80 million in today's dollars) and ongoing operational funds.

It was the start of a golden era. The ERFCB administered our headwater forests for more than two decades, the same period in which Alberta's baby boomers were growing up. Many families used ERFCB-financed roads and campgrounds to access green, healthy forests, sparkling trout streams and wilderness hunting grounds. Photo albums across the province are filled with family memories rooted in those carefully stewarded and much-loved forests.

The ERFCB was established in part to "conserve, develop, maintain and manage the forests in the Area with a view to obtaining the greatest possible flow of water in the Saskatchewan River and its tributaries." The board subsequently moved to the idea of optimum rather than maximum water production in light of the flooding and stream damage that would arise if they just managed for the "greatest possible flow of water." Chief forester W.R. Hanson said the board was responsible for protection and maintenance of watershed values, restoration where damage had occurred and improvement where possible.

The ERCFB researched forest hydrology, mapped important ecological and watershed features, put strict restrictions on logging, repaired damage from cattle and brought a host of other enlightened practices to western Alberta's forests. Archived correspondence from that era shows the board's determination to protect watershed health. Provincial bureau-crats wanted to log protected forests; the ERCFB said no. And that was that … for a while.

By the 1970s, when the ERCFB's initial 20-year term expired, Alberta was flush with oil money. Peter Lougheed's confi-dent young government had just come into power, and there was little appetite in Alberta for federal involvement. Senior bureaucrats in the Alberta Forest Service and other resource departments doubtless advised against renewing the board's tenure; they were tired of restrictions on their ambitions.

The ERCFB was officially disbanded in 1971. The Alberta Forest Service assumed jurisdiction over the forested public lands of western Alberta. The Forest Service was – and still is – managed by bureaucrats who see forests primarily as sources of pulp and lumber. Although the department's responsibilities included recreation, fisheries protection and watershed health, logging got all the attention; everything else was a sideline.

Fast-forward to today. Provincial campground maintenance has been privatized by an uninterested Forest Service. Clearcuts checker the foothills. Motorized recreational vandalism has filled creeks with eroded banks and silted beds while leaving the uplands scarred by eroding runoff gullies. Destructive floods pour off the damaged landscape more often, and streams grow shallower and warmer each summer.

Wealth can make a province smug and careless. Those of us who grew to love the Alberta foothills during the ERCFB's golden era are horrified anew each time we return to see what negligence has wrought in those green hills that yield virtually all our water and once provided the finest of outdoor recreation.

But change is once more in the wind. In the wake of its most destructive and expensive spring flood ever, Alberta got hit with a drop in oil revenues that once again has raised sustainability questions. Crisis, as they say, is a time of dangerous opportunity.

One such opportunity would be to tap into the wisdom of hindsight and rethink the administration of our precious headwater forests. The Alberta Forest Service has proven itself incompetent at protecting the public interest. It has to go. Alberta needs a new conservation board to restore and protect our forested watersheds as well as the ERCFB once did.

Our Best Stories (2015)

Henry Stelfox arrived in Alberta during one of the worst winters in our history – the endless cold and deep, drifting snows of 1906–07. That winter, by some estimates, killed more than half the cattle in the province, a devastating setback for many hundreds of settlers who had preceded the tall Englishman here. Stelfox and his wife eventually settled near Rocky Mountain House and raised nine kids. He ranched cattle, cut wood, dabbled in real estate and bought furs as the family adapted to the challenge of making a living in a young and not particularly prosperous province.

Farther south, that same killing winter set events in motion that helped Aubrey Cartwright start up his D Ranch on Pekisko Creek. Disheartened by their losses, some of the small homesteaders in the area decided to sell out. Cartwright and his partner consolidated some of those small holdings into a large ranch. His son Jim eventually passed it on to Gordon and John Cartwright.

"I remember as a young boy asking my father how much land we owned," Gordon Cartwright said recently. "My father took care to explain that no man could truly own land; the deed or lease by which we held the land was really our covenant to look after it."

The Cartwrights looked after it well. Faced with the prospect of a major gas field development in their green, well-watered landscape, the Cartwright brothers joined their neighbours in a costly but ultimately successful effort to head it off. They then arranged for their leased pasturelands to be included in a new, protected Heritage Rangeland. On his deeded land, Gordon locked in his family's tradition of responsible steward-ship by registering a conservation easement with the Southern Alberta Land Trust Society. The easement ensures the land can never be broken or subdivided.

Henry Stelfox created a conservation legacy too – not the least by passing on his stewardship ethic to grandkids devoted to forest conservation, landscape health, wildlife and fisheries. Stelfox believed in public service as a duty, not a sinecure. He signed on as the region's game warden and travelled the upper Clearwater River country, keeping an eye on wildlife conditions and making sure hunters and anglers stuck to the rules. His work brought him into contact with Cree, Chippewa and Stoney Nakoda people who lived in those remote foothills and he soon became their advocate to Edmonton and Ottawa.

When the government insisted that Stelfox accept payment for his services, he quit. It was against his principles to accept money for serving the public interest – an interesting contrast to the expense account and severance scandals we hear about too often in these later years. He continued to write about and promote conservation and played a key role in organizing the Alberta Fish and Game Association – helping turn hunters and anglers into a force for conservation rather than exploitation.

The Cartwrights and Stelfoxes are the stuff of which Alberta was made: principled, hard-working people whose love of their new home places led them to choose stewardship over greed. They gave themselves to Alberta rather than taking all they could from it.

Aritha Van Herk popularized the idea that Alberta's culture is defined by its mavericks – larger-than-life risk-takers who grabbed our sprawling natural landscapes and shook fortunes out of them. It's an attractive creation myth for those invested in resource exploitation; as such it's been widely misappropriated to support a vision of this place founded on greed and exploitation. From elsewhere in the country, Alberta is too often viewed as a land of rednecks in pickup trucks. Visit the foothills on a May long weekend, and that stereotype might not seem far from the mark. At least until the latest downturn in oil and gas prices, anyone could come here from away and become an instant "Albertan" with a pickup truck, a monster home, a ball cap and an attitude.

But that version of Alberta leaves out the Stelfoxes and Cartwrights whose quiet work and self-sacrifice not only built our province but preserved much of it from the reckless exploitation that continues to deplete its natural wealth and mar its landscapes and watercourses. It omits conservationists like Kerry Wood and Grant MacEwan who gave us a very different set of stories about what Alberta is and who Albertans are. Lois Hole and Jeanne Lougheed, champions of the arts, cultural heritage and philanthropy, don't contribute much to the greed-based story of Alberta – but they too are among the real Albertans who define us at our best. This place we love has never lacked for people who love it back; they just don't get much airtime now that the forces of greed have grabbed the microphone.

"In the Beginning, there was the Word," it says in the Book of Genesis. Who controls the word controls the story – and a culture is the product of stories. As Alberta struggles once again to shape a sustainable future in the face of yet another greed-fuelled economic bust, it might be well to revisit the stories by which we define ourselves. Our best stories – our true genesis stories – don't derive from a maverick tradition; they come from caring stewards of the land. We have lots of those stories. They have much to teach us.

CHAPTER 2

Better Conversations

We Need to Talk. Differently. (2015)

An abandoned road in Jasper National Park winds through the forests and meadows behind Annette and Edith lakes. It used to be the main drive connecting Jasper Park Lodge to the bridge at Old Fort Point and the town of Jasper, but it fell into disuse after the government bridged the Athabasca River at a more convenient location as part of a project to run a tourist road up the Maligne River valley to Medicine Lake.

The original road is cracked and pitted but still, for the most part, intact. Its unconventional-looking asphalt has a dense, sandy texture. In very hot weather, the road surface becomes soft enough to hold boot impressions until the next warm spell softens it again. The road isn't, in fact, surfaced with asphalt; it was paved with bituminous sand brought into the park by train from the Athabasca tar sands northeast of Edmonton.

As a kid growing up in Calgary, a few hundred kilometres south of that tar road, I learned about the tar sands in Grade 8. Someday, we were told, somebody might figure out how to get oil out of them.

Somebody did. In recognition of their new economic status, the deposits of gooey muck got renamed "oil sands." The term "tar sands," although the historically authentic name for a material so gummy it can pave a road, became loaded up with negative symbolism. Good resource capitalists say "oil sands." Hippie tree-huggers say "tar sands."

Words are meant to be tools; when loaded, however, they become weapons.

Former prime minister Stephen Harper knew this well. It's why he didn't allow public servants to have public conversations. Journalists got carefully scripted answers in a one-way conversation where the language was controlled by political staffers. One never heard the term "tar sands" from the Harper PMO. One did, however, hear "terrorist" in reference to environmental groups. It was a useful word for marginalizing citizens concerned about rapid tar sand exploitation and for diverting attention away from serious questions whose answers might threaten the profits of the large corporations whose donations got that government elected.

Who controls the words, controls the conversation. For every idealist trying to get the conversation right, there is someone else trying to spin it toward their interests. That's why we need to pay attention to words, and who is using them.

When rivers flood, water managers and land developers call for better control rather than more responsible land use. When fires burn, foresters talk about destruction rather than the ecological renewal of fire-dependent landscapes. Vested interests steer public conversations toward their preferred outcome by describing natural processes with words like damage, destruction, emergency and control – rather than toward the kind of ecological literacy and serious reflection that might challenge orthodoxy.

The Bow River and its tributaries flooded in the spring of 2013. Water management engineers took control of the conversation before basements were even bailed out. We heard about the need to better control the rivers to prevent future floods. Conveniently, that kind of conversation leads to expensive engineering projects as profitable to engineering firms as they are destructive to rivers. Once the problem was defined, the conversation became about where to build flood control structures, not whether we really understood the problem. When acting premier Jim Prentice, hoping for Calgary votes during an election campaign, announced a flood control dam on the Elbow River near Springbank, a real estate developer in Bragg Creek began lobbying instead for a dam farther upstream, near McLean Creek. The conversation had already been framed around the need to tame the river; now the only question was where to send the dam builders.

But floods don't come from rivers. They come to rivers. They come from landscapes. The headwaters of the Oldman, Bow, Red Deer and North Saskatchewan rivers are fragmented, vandalized remnants of what was once a green, living sponge that released groundwater gradually through the seasons. Clean, cold groundwater springs sustained healthy streams, native fisheries and rich riparian wildlife habitats. Now, thanks to clearcut logging, off-road vehicle vandalism and a network of gas well roads, pipelines and other linear disturbances, water runs off the landscape rapidly each spring rather than soaking into the water table. Land abuse gives us worse floods and, ironically, worse droughts. Repairing the land is the only responsible and sustainable way to reduce the risk of bigger future problems.

That's the conversation we didn't have ... because dam engineers chose the words we ended up using to define the problem and its solutions.

And of course there is the question of the floodplain, where rivers store spring runoff and trap the mud and sand those high flows carry. The floodplain is part of the river, but only in the spring runoff season. There would be little or no flood damage if there were fewer valuable structures on the floodplain. But that's not a conversation that turns short-term profits or makes politicians popular, so we got steered into a dialogue that leads, ironically, to further destruction.

Two years after the flood of 2013, the winter snows melted early and the June rains passed us by. Instead of floods, in 2015 western Canada got fires. In 2016 the drought deepened; fires even burned into Fort McMurray. Predictably, the public conversation was about hectares of forest destroyed, crews and machines deployed to "fight" the fires, and the need to head off such disasters in the future. We could have managed some of those fires differently – recognizing them as natural processes that help landscapes adapt to climate change – but that would have required choosing different words and having different conversations than the ones the forest industry was quick to steer us toward.

Floods and fires are natural processes. They keep nature vital, diverse and functioning. They are not problems; they are, in fact, essential. They don't destroy nature; they renew it. It's how we talk about them, and what that leads us to do or not do, that is the problem. In a crowded world worried about sustainability, where species blink out as public debt grows and places we love become increasingly compromised by failure, it should be obvious that we've been having the wrong conversations.

Having the right conversation calls for more of us to shout down the vested interests who are always so quick to tell us what we should talk about. Oil billionaires want us to talk about oil sands because oil sounds like jobs. Tar is something mucky and hard to clean up. But those are, in fact, tar sands. Call them what they are and we can have the more challenging, better conversations that boreal Alberta and our future sustainability need and deserve.

Floods are only a problem when we get in their way. Under normal circumstances, spring floods scour out deep pools for fish, deposit fertile silt and life-giving water across green riparian floodplains and renew valley-bottom forests – and then the rivers stay cold and full through the subsequent months because water that didn't add to spring flood levels continues to seep out of springs and wetlands from healthy water tables under green, living headwater landscapes. We should be talking about this – not about more dams and bank-armouring.

Fires are a problem if you are in the business of turning trees into wood products, or if you were irresponsible enough to build structures in forested landscapes without bothering to protect them properly. In nature, fire is a force for renewal and diversity – replacing old trees with new saplings; creating dead spars that feed woodpeckers and house bats; regenerating willows and poplars that feed moose, beavers and caterpillars; opening up winter ranges for bighorn sheep and elk and the predators that eat them. We should be talking about this – not about destruction.

If the only language we have for natural events is the language of disaster, then all our conversations will lead to an ever more intense war against nature. But a war against nature is, ultimately, a war against our very selves. That sort of war can only be lost. Like the abandoned ribbon of tar sand that winds through Jasper National Park, it's a road that leads nowhere.

We really need to talk.

Differently.

༚

Facebook Post

April 21, 2016. Calgary.

Every species of tree in Calgary was leafed out today, and on the way home the sky was smudged with regional forest fire smoke. All this before the end of April. Enjoying the new world this month, but only by ignoring the panicked voice in the back of my head saying "we dithered too long; we're acting too late; we're going too slow ..."

Save the Beetles? (2014)

Two hard winters in a row mean that our latest crisis in the forest – the mountain pine beetle outbreak – may be winding down.

That would be too bad.

Hyperventilating headlines to the contrary, mountain pine beetles may well be the best thing that's happened in the woods in a long time. But you won't hear that from Alberta Agriculture and Forestry or from the forest industry. Their story – and they got it out there first – is that the recent population eruption of this native bark beetle is a disaster that has to be stopped before it destroys our forests.

Their preferred method of stopping beetles is aggressive clearcutting. Shades of Vietnam: "We had to destroy the village in order to liberate it."

Crisis rhetoric to the contrary, pine beetle populations have always erupted from time to time. The wildlife-rich Kootenay River valley west of Banff, for example, was hit by beetles in the 1940s. That's why it's wildlife-rich: by killing off the old pine trees, the beetles created countless grassy openings and freed up young spruce trees and aspens to grow freely. The resulting forest mosaic was far better for deer, bears and other wildlife than the dense old pine stands of earlier years.

Southwestern Alberta and the Cypress Hills had a beetle outbreak in the mid-1980s. Many forest stands in and around

Waterton Lakes National Park lost up to 90 per cent of their lodgepole pines. Parks Canada came under heavy pressure from the Alberta government to let loggers into the park to cut infected trees. Fortunately, the feds said no. Outside the park, however, emergency logging left sprawling clearcuts along the foothills north to Crowsnest Pass.

A decade later, curious about the long-term effects of the pine beetle infestation, I compared sites inside the park that had been left to nature with sites outside the park that had been salvage-logged to save the forest.

The sites inside the park were lush and thriving. Douglas fir and white spruce that had been seedlings when the beetles killed the pine were bushy and tall. Openings in the woods were full of shrubs and herbaceous cover. Woodpeckers were abundant, enjoying the bounty of insects in standing dead trees. Fallen pine trees provided shelter for red-backed voles, pine martens and other wildlife. All that new habitat diversity, where before there had been a near-monoculture of aging pines, teemed with wildlife – from grizzly bears and elk to lazuli buntings, hummingbirds, flying squirrels, various species of warblers and flycatchers. The birdsong was almost deafening.

Nearby salvage-logged areas, on the other hand, were a mess. Poorly laid out emergency logging roads were now rutted with off-road vehicle tracks and full of non-native weeds like knapweed. Erosion gullies ran into clearcuts that had been planted back to lodgepole pine – as if somehow the Forest Service hadn't figured out that the best defence against future mass beetle attacks might be a forest containing at least some trees the beetles don't eat. Only a few common wildlife species were abundant; the great variety of more uncommon species that I had found in the unlogged forests was absent. The forest hadn't been saved; it had been savaged.

While the foresters who try to control the pine beetle narrative are always ready to help nature, that help seems always to involve chainsaws and feller-bunchers. It's easy to see how sawmills benefit; the benefits to nature are considerably less clear.

The simple truth that almost no forester will ever state is that forests benefit far more from mountain pine beetle outbreaks than from industrial-scale logging.

Our changing western climate no longer favours dense, water-hungry forests of lodgepole pine. As mild winters and summer dry spells become more frequent, mountain pine beetles survive and thrive better than in the early 20th century. Their population eruptions are simply nature's form of climate change adaptation. Once the beetles have boomed and busted, what remains behind is a more diverse and drought-tolerant forest with healthier trees and abundant wildlife.

In fact, given that most of the water in our rivers comes from snow, beetle-attacked forests may also play a vital role in increasing our future water supply. Researchers have found that sublimation of snow trapped in the canopy of a dense, healthy forest can reduce water yield by as much as 60 per cent. The open canopies of beetle-modified forests trap more water in the snowpack while also shading those snowdrifts in the spring, so that the increased water supply comes slowly – unlike the massive, short-lived floods that pour off exposed clearcuts where foresters have "saved" the forest from beetles.

Mountain pine beetles enhance biodiversity, help our forests adapt to a changing climate and improve water supplies. The only reason we think our native beetles are a problem is because loggers told us they are. In conservation, as in politics, it's always wise to consider the source of the story and what they stand to gain.

The forest, if it could talk, would tell a very different tale.

It's All about Us (1994)

What a mess we have made of things.

Some might argue that human awareness is more a curse than a blessing. Our ability to think, reason and plan might seem unprecedented in the living world, but it too often manifests in a sort of species self-absorption. Our collective obsession with human matters seems hard-wired to the exploitation, degradation and pollution of the natural environment. We make it all about us.

Others say that we can yet develop a healthy relationship with the world if we change our point of focus. They call for humans to replace anthropocentricity – a focus on the needs, wants and self-interest of the human animal – with what the late ecologist Stan Rowe described as biocentrism, or eco-centrism. Dr. Rowe called for humans to adopt an ethic that would place the good of the ecosystem above the self-interest of people.

We certainly need to make choices that sustain ecosystems, even when those choices seem inconvenient. But the idea that we can do this by substituting eco-centrism for anthropocentrism is, I believe, neither logical nor ecological.

Eco-centrists like Dr. Rowe point to a widespread tendency to see ourselves as the centre of the living universe, rather than merely a part of it, as evidence that our world view is flawed. On the other hand, saying that every living thing is, in fact, at the centre of the universe might come closer to the truth. To a giant liver fluke – a translucent parasite that lives inside elk livers – the entire universe exists to serve the interests of liver flukes. To a limestone rock, the universe exists to create limestone rocks. To a human being, the universe exists for humans.

That the universe exists to serve the self-interest of every living thing is true and provable. John Muir once wrote: "When we try to pick out anything by itself, we find it hitched to everything else in the Universe." That is the nature of life: a web of relationships and consequence ultimately connects all things. Any point in that web can be considered its centre. Humans are unique among living creatures only in that we strive to understand this.

Arguing against anthropocentricity denies a fundamental principle of ecology. In a functioning ecosystem, each organism or entity acts – to the extent that it can – in the interests of its self and its family. The remarkable thing about ecosystems is how they integrate the self-interests of a vast diversity of living things into a greater, interdependent whole. The determined self-centredness of each individual animal or plant ultimately strengthens and sustains the ecosystem.

A coyote kills other animals to sustain its own life. Other animals flee and hide from the coyote to sustain their own lives. The interaction strengthens both by selecting for the most effective predator and the most elusive prey. Predation – the ongoing conflict between competing self-interests – thus becomes a cooperative function. It is good for both hunter and hunted and, by extension, for the ecosystem of which they are elements.

The human conundrum is that our species' self-interest seems consistently to be out of whack. Much of what we do to advance our own interests disrupts, degrades and harms the ecosystems of which we are elements, rather than strengthening them. This is why Stan Rowe and other ecological thinkers argue that we need to be less self-centred (anthropocentric) and more focused on the needs of ecological systems and the ecosphere as a whole (eco-centric).

This is correct as far as it goes. But self-interest is an ecological *sine qua non*. It's in our wiring; we cannot just turn it off.

If the very nature of life won't let us rise above self-absorption, then, perhaps what we need is a better definition of "self."

༚

I recall visiting the Calgary Zoo one day when our family was young. The kids spent a long time staring at a massive Siberian tiger. They were overwhelmed by its tiger-ness. It was a magnificent specimen in a large open-air enclosure where it could exercise, find privacy, stalk passersby and live a generally satisfactory existence – certainly as good as any zoo tiger could hope to enjoy.

But this tiger had never stalked and killed a wild deer. It had never waded a reedgrass swamp or smelled the resin-scented wind sweeping in off the Aldan Platcau. The grass it bedded down in was Kentucky bluegrass, a tame hay species. The trees that shaded it were black poplars, endemic to North America. It had been born in a zoo, grown to maturity and would die in a zoo without ever killing a thing.

Was this a tiger? Is a species merely the translation of chromosomes into a creature of a certain shape and behaviour? Is that all there is to being a tiger?

It might be closer to the truth to say that a tiger without its habitat is barely a tiger at all. It's merely a biological facsimile. In the absence of its native habitat, an important part of what makes a tiger whole is missing. A real tiger is genetic potential interacting with environmental context over time. In fact, that is a reasonable definition of any creature. In the zoo, the context is not tiger context; thus, for all its impressive appearance, the animal there was something less than a tiger.

In the early 20th century, fish culturists began removing rainbow trout from their natural stream habitats to propagate them in hatcheries. Natural selection in those stream environments had produced fish whose lives were completely integrated with seasonal cycles of flood and spate and warmth and cold, and with other animals that shared those streams. As wild fish they had spawned, fed and sheltered within the all-encompassing, unique and dynamic ecosystem of which they were part.

Reared in hatcheries, the descendants of those trout continued to look like rainbow trout. However, captive-breeding under controlled conditions rewired them as fish that fed aggressively, clustered in large groups, and sought refuge from danger in open water rather than in sheltered places. They had adapted to their new context: the hatchery pond. They no longer needed knowledge of flood cycles, predators and stream structure. Like zoo tigers, they had become convincing counterfeits of themselves.

When fisheries managers stocked those hatchery fish back into the same streams where their ancestors had lived, they no longer fit. They weren't stream trout; they were hatchery trout. Behaviour that had served them well in fish tanks worked against their survival in natural streams. No longer integrated with their natural habitats, most died.

Complex brains and opposable thumbs aside, we humans are animals subject to the same natural laws that govern other animals. By definition, then, we are ecological beings: products of and, ultimately, parts of greater ecosystems. Can one be a human being without that context, or is one just unfulfilled potential and maladaptation?

S ome of our most powerful and poignant literature is rooted in other people's nostalgia. W.O. Mitchell's great novel *Who Has Seen the Wind*, Harper Lee's *To Kill a Mockingbird* and Mark Twain's *Huckleberry Finn* each derive from different childhoods lived in different landscapes. For all those differences, each connects deeply for readers nostalgic about their own childhoods lived in other places. There is something about growing up in a place that bonds us to it. We recognize the power of that bonding experience whenever we find it in art and literature; we react strongly to the emotional power of self-discovery. Nostalgia represents a gut-level, passionate reminder of those place-bonding experiences that helped to create our knowledge of ourselves: genetic potential meeting environmental context through time.

An individual is not merely a name, or a biologically produced prototype of some generic species. Who else can one be, if not the sum and product of every smell one has ever smelled, every experience, every person and place one has ever known, and every decision one has ever made? Each of us is constantly becoming, because our environment constantly adds to who we are, how we know ourselves, how we are known.

Had I been conceived in a test tube and raised through parturition, weaning, walking and puberty inside a box, would I still be the same person? History has recorded cases of individuals kept isolated and captive through their developmental years. They became impaired and incomplete. They had all the human genes but they had been deprived of the environmental influences that those genes needed in order fully to develop the individual.

One cannot view oneself in isolation of one's environment. Similarly we cannot consider families, communities, nations and the human race as a whole except in the context of our collective environments. We are where we live, we are how we live; we are our environment. We are not separate; we are wholly integrated.

If a tiger in a cage is not a whole tiger, and a trout in a hatchery pond is no longer a real trout, then are humans confined to synthetic environments still human? That's where most of us live, after all. It might be that the most essential and missing piece of our humanness lies somewhere beyond the end of the asphalt.

The Europeans who colonized North America brought with them not merely a disdain for indigenous people and their ways of knowing; they brought a Cartesian approach to knowledge based on isolating the subjects of study rather than integrating them, and a Judeo-Christian religious tradition that sets humans apart from all Creation. Several decades later, few question a dysfunctional Western world view that sets our individual, community and species self-interest apart from the ecosystems that, ultimately, give us our context as a species. We have become so good at dis-integrating nature's integrated systems that we've become our own lab rats. Just as a giant liver fluke sees no need for the brain and heart that sustain the liver, we see no real need for many other organisms. Yet without the elk's brain, the liver fluke cannot survive, because the elk will die. Taken a step further, without windswept grassland slopes and sheltering pine forests, the liver fluke cannot exist because those keep its host alive through each long northern winter. Without the forest fires that maintain that winter range, the fluke might cease to exist. These are secrets no liver fluke has ever suspected. Fortunately for the species, no liver fluke has ever been able to extinguish fires or subdivide elk winter range either.

If one cannot define the liver fluke without including those other things, neither can one define a human without including all that connects with her or him. Identity is much more than skin deep; it reaches out to everything else.

Anthropocentrism is not the problem. We just need to work on the "anthro" part a bit more. There is nothing wrong with stating that all the world exists for the benefit of humankind – just as it does for tigerkind and troutkind. But humankind, by definition, is the whole world in which it exists. That world – in its wholeness and well-being – makes us human. We have little choice but to sustain the world's ecosystems, because they make us whole.

Anthropocentrism becomes dysfunctional only when humans try to isolate themselves from all else. Anthropocentrism becomes healthy, on the other hand, when we see ourselves as connected to, dependent upon and, ultimately, defined by all else that exists. Healthful anthropocentrism would make one agonize over any decision that might reduce the natural diversity, aesthetic integrity and long-term health of the natural ecosystems that are the source of our very identities.

It makes sense to look out for one's own self-interest. It makes sense to want a better standard of living, and to protect one's family from adversity and danger. It makes sense because every living organism does so. Through this determined self-interest organisms integrate, paradoxically, into complex, diverse, mutually sustaining ecosystems.

Humans have conscience, consciousness, intelligence, future-orientation – an entire awareness system that makes us different, we assume, from all other living creatures. This uniqueness has tricked us into setting ourselves apart from the rest of Creation. We gaze across a gulf of our own making, filled with a deep yearning for wholeness.

Those same attributes that make us unique among animals, however, can also offer a solution to the mess we have wrought of the world we love. Drawing upon them, we can discover that our self-interest – in a species whose consciousness integrates the entirety of existence and draws upon the entirety of existence to understand itself – demands that we cherish, value, respect and nurture all that gives us life, meaning and identity.

Nature defines us. To abuse nature should be understood not as exploiting something outside of ourselves but as what it is: self-abuse.

Eco-centrism is not ecological. It denies the logic of self-interest by which every living thing exists. Anthropocentrism – if we could get it right – might in fact be the solution rather than the problem. What we need, however, is a better anthropocentrism based on the simple truth that, just as caged tigers and a hatchery trout are not truly tigers or trout without the living ecosystems that are their proper contexts, neither can human beings ever be truly human if we fail to sustain the living ecosystems that are not merely our home places, but our very selves.

Conservation without Party Colours (2014)

Almost 50 species of wildlife are considered at risk in Alberta. Some formerly common species, such as the burrowing owl and sage grouse, after thriving here for millennia, may be wiped out completely within this decade. Every population of caribou in northern and western Alberta is in trouble. Even barn swallows, once common, are classed as a species of concern.

If that weren't evidence enough that nature is under siege, a Global Forest Watch report released last winter showed that almost two-thirds of the Alberta landscape is fragmented by roads, cultivation and development to the point where wildlife are displaced. That's an area of 410,000 square kilometres, three times the size of England. The prairie region has fared worst: only 12 per cent remains capable of sustaining native wildlife. Wetlands are vanishing – up to 70 per cent are gone already – and watersheds are so stressed that the Alberta government no longer issues new water-use licences in the Oldman and Bow River watersheds.

Alberta's economic prosperity has been achieved, to a large degree, at the expense of nature – ironic, considering that so many Albertans profess to love wildlife and the outdoors. If this province's natural diversity, wildlife, lakes, streams and clean air are going to be more than just a fond memory, it's time to get serious about conserving the environment.

Waterton Lakes National Park was set aside for nature in a less crowded era, back in 1895. Canada's government, in establishing the park, essentially embraced the idea that nature could best be protected by strong government regulations and by taking land out of the commercial marketplace. That model of conservation served the park well through much of the 20th century; Waterton became known for its thriving wildlife populations, clean streams and diverse, pristine ecosystems.

A century later I became Waterton's first conservation biologist. My job was to monitor the park's ecological health, diagnose any conservation problems and then advise how to solve them. By the late 20th century, serious strains were starting to develop in many parks, including Waterton. For one thing, the science of landscape ecology had developed to the point where nobody could delude themselves any more with the idea that natural systems stop at park boundaries. Grizzly bears, sandhill cranes, trumpeter swans, bull trout and other vital elements of Waterton's protected ecosystem actually relied more on the private ranches outside the park than on the park itself. That was partly because the most productive land, and the best for wildlife, had been left outside the park, where it could be put to work producing cows, timber and other economic resources. The other reason was because the park was a popular tourism destination; wildlife enjoyed more peace and quiet on adjacent ranches whose owners strictly limited access.

The biggest threat to the park that my colleagues and I identified in the 1990s was, ironically, the park itself. As a tourism and outdoor recreation destination, the national park created real estate market value adjacent to its boundaries. Land that, for most of the 20th century, had been used profitably for cattle ranching was now worth much more if subdivided and sold for recreational second homes and tourist resorts. In 1997 real estate speculators wanted to subdivide a large forested area right on the national park boundaries. Access would have been from a park road. I worked with lawyers to put in place a regulatory access closure to cut off access from inside the park. It was the kind of approach that made sense from inside the traditional conservation paradigm of protecting nature through laws and restrictions. Given the economics and politics of land development, however, it wasn't likely to work for long.

Then, at the 11th hour, just as the County of Cardston was poised to approve the development, the Nature Conservancy of Canada brokered the purchase of the land by private citizens who valued nature and understood what was at stake. The NCC is a national land trust organization that works essentially as a realtor for nature – facilitating market transactions that protect biodiversity-rich private land from nature-unfriendly development. Their last-minute intervention adjacent to Waterton Lakes National Park demonstrated that, in a free market, conservation buyers are sometimes willing to pay more to keep ecologically important land in its natural state than real estate promoters can come up with to develop it.

That was the beginning of a remarkable conservation initiative – the Waterton Front Project – that saw the Nature Conservancy of Canada mobilize $50 million of private money in the ensuing decade and a half to protect over 100 square kilometres of ranchland adjoining the park. Major funders included the W. Garfield Weston Foundation and John and Barbara Poole, but many other Canadians anted up smaller amounts to buy protection for the area's rich biodiversity and open spaces in the face of competing economic pressures.

Grizzly bears, sandhill cranes and trumpeter swans thrive in the Waterton Front today because of ranching. Ranching persists as an economic land use because of private conservation investments. And none of it would have happened if government had not set aside a national park in this spectacular corner of the province more than a century ago. The traditional conservation approach of setting aside public parks and establishing laws to protect them secured the core park area and also established the value proposition – that wilderness in southwestern Alberta is worthy of protection. However, when the economic law of supply and demand put the adjacent land at risk, the inadequacy of that traditional conservation approach became clear. Fortunately, the marketplace helped to save it.

We often associate the political left with conservation of the environment and the political right with its exploitation. But as Waterton demonstrates, that stereotypical view is oversimplified: what is likely to serve Alberta best is a collaborative approach to conservation that transcends political partisanship.

Preston Manning, for one, is not persuaded that early 20th-century prescriptions involving government regulation and saving wildlife in public parks will work in the 21st century. "Are the public policies and the direction we've been going in achieving conservation objectives and can they continue to do [so] under increasing pressure of growing populations?" he asks. "If the answer is no or that we're not satisfied, that gives you a case for looking at the provision of ecological goods and services through market mechanisms.

"I don't think we're making a lot of progress on conservation. I think governments and government policy are as likely part of the problem as part of the solution, so I'm more inclined to look at other mechanisms."

Manning is widely recognized as a voice for the libertarian right. He is the son of evangelical preacher and long-time Alberta premier Ernest Manning, a co-founder of the Reform Party and an early mentor to Stephen Harper – likely the most anti-environment prime minister Canada has ever had. If the right is anti-environment, then one might expect Manning to be among those most fervently promoting nature-exploiting economic policies.

But Manning spends a surprising amount of time thinking about how to protect and restore the environment – from a conservative perspective. Pointing out that "conservation" and "conservative" are derived from the same root word, he insists that conservatives are missing the boat by buying into the common belief that concern for the environment is not a conservative value.

Conservatives, Manning asserted in a 2010 *Globe and Mail* op-ed, are arguably "in the best position to provide fresh start leadership on the environmental front ... applying the core concepts of fiscal conservatism ... to living within our means ecologically and balancing the ecological budget ... and most importantly, harnessing market mechanisms to the task of environmental protection and conservation as the 'signature contribution' of conservatives to environmental and economic sustainability."

When I interviewed Manning four years after publication of his article, he was frustrated by the lack of uptake from the federal and provincial Conservatives. "The difficulty with governments at the political level, both Edmonton and Ottawa, is that their strategists tend to conceptualize issues as either shield or sword. The sword issues being the ones you're willing to invest your political capital on and go out and crusade for, and the shield issues being ones where you've kind of given up before you start. And unfortunately for a number of conservative regimes, healthcare reform and the environment get conceptualized that way [as shield issues] so it's hard to get proactive approaches."

His concern is shared by former federal environment minister Jim Prentice. Widely touted as a leading contender for future leadership of the Conservative Party, Prentice recently rebuked the Harper government for undermining Canada's environmental reputation with changes to environmental legislation and failure to follow through on commitments to regulate greenhouse gas emissions from the oil and gas sector. "We should not cede this ground to others or allow ourselves to be portrayed as indifferent to the world around us," he said at the March 2014 annual Manning Networking Conference. "I can say from hard experience: we can't ever again allow ourselves as a country to be off-footed, and be caught in a circumstance where we are following rather than leading."

Conservative thinkers might call for environmental leadership, but their political parties appear deaf to the point of obtuseness. Under Harper, the federal Conservatives have proclaimed environmental groups to be one step removed from terrorist organizations. Far from embracing carbon taxes – a form of full-cost accounting consistent with conservative principles – Harper's insider government used the small print in budget bills to rewrite the Fisheries Act, the Canadian Environmental Assessment Act and other environmental legislation. By exempting resource industries from environmental due diligence, Harper virtually ensured that resource industries can continue to externalize the environmental costs of doing business, with citizens eventually swallowing the environmental losses and footing the cleanup costs. At the same time, the government has directed Revenue Canada to audit the books of public interest organizations that traditionally speak up for the environment on behalf of Canadians.

While Stephen Harper's hyperpartisan, development-focused government seems to ignore conservative environmental thinkers, Alberta's Progressive Conservative government might be paying a bit more attention.

The 2009 Alberta Land Stewardship Act (ALSA) was a response to widespread criticism that Alberta's unplanned and overheated resource development, a product of laissez-faire policies during the Klein years, was unsustainable and would lead to massive future environmental costs. Environmental degradation was also contributing to a growing social licence issue that worked against efforts to move Alberta oil and gas to global markets. The ALSA mandates regional planning to balance competing resource development, conservation and other land use pressures. One regional plan – for the Athabasca drainage, where rapid tar sands development has created the most urgent need for land use planning – has already been completed. Public consultation on the second plan, for the densely populated, water-poor and biologically impaired South Saskatchewan region, was completed in spring 2014.

Land use planning doesn't appear in Manning's conservative songbook, smacking as it does of government intervention in the joyous anarchy of the free market. But the ALSA also includes a regulatory framework for "Conservation and Stewardship Tools." The new legislation provides for government to develop new market-based instruments, invest public funds directly into environmental stewardship, modify tax regimes to promote conservation outcomes, and expand the use of conservation easements to protect wildlife habitat. This section of the act goes directly to Manning's call to create markets for environmental goods and services. If market forces are already helping protect nature in places like the Waterton Front through private land transactions, government should be able to build on this model by creating carbon markets, transferrable development credits and other new trade mechanisms that mobilize market forces to secure critical habitat for endangered species, restore wetlands, hold back floodwaters and sequester carbon in soils and vegetation.

The basic premise behind creating markets for environmental goods and services is that those who benefit from environmental goods (such as wildlife or open spaces) and services (such as groundwater recharge or carbon sequestration) should be able to buy those goods and services from private property owners. More simply put, a farmer who spots a burrowing owl in her pasture shouldn't go home panicking about new restrictions on her land use – instead, she should see the prospect of new profits either through public conservation subsidies or by payments from private interests concerned about endangered prairie wildlife. If an oil company nearby can only get surface access to native prairie by investing in tangible conservation of the wildlife that depends on it, ALSA enables a regulatory regime that could let the company pay an annual premium to that farmer so she can keep doing what she has been doing to make the place attractive to owls. Everyone, arguably, would win.

If more restrictive regulations – favoured by the left-leaning side of the political spectrum – were the only tool available to keep owls around, a farmer who managed his grassland well enough to attract owls to it might end up feeling punished, rather than rewarded, by success. There's a bumper sticker for that kind of perverse incentive: "Shoot. Shovel. Shut up." It doesn't lead to conservation.

But getting markets for environmental goods and services right is a tricky proposition. There's plenty of room for misfires and unintended consequences.

Some of our greatest historical conservation successes actually arose from taking nature out of the marketplace. It was the ban on commercial sale of dead animals that brought waterfowl, deer and other animals back from the brink of eradication in the early 20th century. That's why the Alberta Fish and Game Association views discussions about environmental goods and services markets suspiciously. If one of the new market approaches involved letting ranchers charge a fee for hunting public wildlife on their private land, for example, it could motivate landowners to kill off native hawks, wolves and other predators or to plough up native grassland to grow feed crops for trophy game. Martin Sharren, executive vice-president of the AFGA, recently wrote that any move toward paid hunting would lead to "the erosion of public support for wildlife management as a whole, not to mention having a disastrous effect on the world-class hunting opportunities Albertans have in their own province."

❧

Harvey Locke acknowledges Preston Manning's sincerity and intellect, but he doesn't buy the idea that the solution to all our environmental challenges should be sought in the marketplace.

Those who consider the Liberal Party to be as endangered a species in Alberta as the burrowing owl had to rethink their assumptions after the 2012 federal by-election in Calgary Centre, in which Locke came a close second to the Conservative candidate. An internationally renowned environmentalist who mobilized a successful 1990s campaign to put the brakes on commercial development in Banff National Park, Locke went on to co-found the Yellowstone to Yukon Conservation

Initiative and has recently become a prominent spokesperson for the Nature Needs Half movement, which calls for reserving at least half of the Earth's lands and waters for biodiversity conservation.

Over coffee in Canmore recently, Locke argued that conservative libertarians, in making a near-religion of Adam Smith's invisible hand, have discounted nature. "There's a passage in the New Testament that says 'Render unto Caesar that which is Caesar's, and render unto God that which is God's.' My concern is that monetizing things that you didn't create or add any value to is a false activity.

"That isn't to say there isn't something we can do with market mechanisms. Biodiversity offsets, for example: if the idea is that I'm generating this impact here to generate wealth for me and society, and I have an ability to offset that somewhere else to prevent harm to something of equal or greater value to the environment or society, then I think that's an important and worthwhile conversation. What I don't like is if that gets reduced to some kind of overly simple metrics – for example, I damage 100 acres, so I have to protect 100 acres. It needs to be at the level of values: What are the values that we are trying to save or offset? With biodiversity, the value we're trying to save is the full suite of all naturally occurring organizations and the natural processes that maintain them in a given system. That's not easy to work out in a market context, but it's a worthwhile conversation we need to have.

"This idea that we can monetize the Commons feels to me like it's masking the fundamental truth, which is that humanity has to learn to live within its ecological means. To put it in a market context and to keep going with the market approach avoids that basic challenge. People who are trying to use market mechanisms for the environment are not being devious. They're smart people trying to do something good. I just think it has a very limited potential for success if you don't ask the bigger questions about where society is going in relation to its environmental context."

Locke argues that wrong-headed solutions to environmental challenges originate from flawed thought models. The common "triple bottom line" model, of three interlocking circles representing economy, environment and societal well-being, is one of those thought models. A more realistic way to present those relationships, in Locke's view, is as three concentric circles. The largest, outside circle is the environment. Within that circle is a smaller one representing society, and embedded in that one is a smaller circle for the economy.

"The way I approach it is like this: The environment is the context for all life on Earth. Everything that happens, happens within that. Society is a subdivision of the environment, wholly and completely dependent on the environment for everything. And within society is the economy, wholly dependent on society. They're subsets. The big show is the environment.

"Why don't we start talking about this relationship we're in? We're in a relationship with the natural world, and right now we're in an abusive relationship with that world. We need to ask what nature needs from this relationship, and nature needs at least half to be protected in an interconnected way, to function. That's what every study shows us. That is why we have national parks and wilderness areas."

Progressives such as Locke have long argued for more parks and regulations to protect wildlife, waters and natural habitats from commercial exploitation. Libertarian conservatives such as Manning, however, rarely look for governments to put land out of reach from resource companies. Still, Manning agrees that parks are valuable.

"I think there's a place for parks," he told me, "but I think we have to be careful about having parks be a substitute for conservation, to assume that if we barricade off a few hundred thousand acres in the north that we've somehow done our duty to conserve the land ... The bigger challenge is how to live with the land, with the water, with the air in an integrated fashion, not an isolated fashion. So while I see a place for parks to preserve the pristineness of some areas, our bigger problem is how to live with the land and the watersheds when there are all kinds of people there who are going to put demands on it. I think that's the bigger challenge, and you don't want the creation of parks to be seen as a substitute – as if we've done our duty [there], and now we can do whatever we feel like where we are."

Just as Locke is correct in pointing out that the environment that sustains all life on Earth is too complex and all-embracing to be conserved by simply turning it into a bundle of marketable goods and services, Manning scores an important point when he points out that biodiversity, water and air need to be conserved everywhere, not just in protected landscapes, and that that requires new thinking about private lands conservation. And that's the important point: they're both right. No single point of view and no single set of conservation tools will deliver meaningful conservation results in this crowded, complicated century.

Where people put partisanship aside in the cause of conservation, the results can exceed anyone's expectations. This past winter I was invited to the annual "eat and greet" dinner event hosted by the Nature Conservancy of Canada for those involved in the Waterton Front. I found an eclectic group gathered at the Twin Butte community hall – ranchers, young biologists, well-heeled urban investors, government bureaucrats. Scratch anyone in the room and you might come up with a Wild Roser, a PC, a Green or a Liberal. But nobody was scratching anyone; instead the place was abuzz with cheerful conversation among people who, only a decade earlier, had only talked about, not with, one another.

In the 15 years since that first conservation land transaction on the Waterton Front, an unusual social synergy has emerged. Now that they know one another and are united by a common cause, the same rural-urban, producer-investor, non-partisan mix of people has teamed up on stewardship projects too. They work together to hand-pull non-native weeds, install electric fences and stronger doors on granaries to keep bears out of temptation, and even install "deadstock" bins where ranchers can deposit stillborn calves and other dead livestock rather than leave the remains out on the range, where they might attract wolves and grizzlies.

The dinner chatter was not about politics; it was about conservation – a cause that transcends partisan divides and, clearly, can build new kinds of community.

Later that night, as I drove home on Alberta's Cowboy Trail – Highway 22 – moonlight glistened on snow-covered grassland where the road curved through the massive Waldron Ranch, north of Lundbreck. Most of that ranch is privately owned, so even though it is vitally important for several at-risk Alberta wildlife species, it will never be set aside as a protected park. But I could drink in the magic of its moonlit landscape, untroubled by worries about what the future might bring to it, because I had just learned that based on the success of the Waterton Front, the Nature Conservancy of Canada had secured a conservation easement on most of the Waldron's 12,357 hectares of pristine foothills landscape. With protected public lands to the west, it is now one of the largest conservation holdings in western Alberta – more proof of what is possible when people define themselves around what they care for, rather than what their politics are.

The Waterton Front serves as a model for an approach to environmental conservation that draws from all sides of the political spectrum. Conservation, far from being a cause owned by one particular political philosophy, can and should be the great social cause of the 21st century that breaks down partisan divides and mobilizes a full range of approaches to keep nature whole and vital into the future. The consequences of failure are too great, and the rewards of success too important, for Albertans to settle for anything less.

CHAPTER 3

By the Water

Olden Days Creek (1991)

Dad used to tell me about the olden days, when he and my grandfather fished remote streams in the far, lonely valleys of the Rocky Mountains. His tales were tinged with regret that the kind of fishing they had enjoyed in those days was long gone. By the time I got my first fishing rod, new roads penetrated into the back of beyond. Anglers were everywhere. I grew up nostalgic for days I had never known, regretting the fate that waited to place me on this Earth until other people's boots had tracked up every stream bank.

In the olden days one could be alone on trout streams where the water was as pure as the air, and cold as ice. The valleys were wild and seldom visited by humans. Streams teemed with trout. They were easy to catch. There were moose in the meadows and the possibility of a grizzly around every bend. In the olden days, a determined angler could still find pools that no other fisherman had ever seen.

I pored over Dad's maps in a forlorn search for lonely creeks that other anglers, by some miracle, might have overlooked. I insisted to Dad that there still must be some olden day creeks left out there somewhere. We certainly checked out all the possibilities. It was a search that enriched my boyhood summers. Still, by the time I grew up and left home, I had come to believe that fishing for undisturbed populations of native trout had become the stuff of legend.

Even so, I never quite surrendered the belief that somewhere, temporarily forgotten, there must yet be one or two little bits of yesterday. Faith, Mom used to tell me, eventually will be rewarded ...

One summer, I decided to follow up on a fishing story I had heard a decade earlier. Map in hand, I drove down a woods road far from the highway. At length I pulled off and parked where the map showed a small meadow stream – the headwaters of a well-known river – not too far off the road. There was no sign of running water anywhere; just lodgepole pines and heat haze. Stepping out into an eager swarm of hungry mosquitoes, I donned waders and vest and set off into the resin-scented shade of the forest.

Sunbeams pierced the forest canopy and dappled the forest floor. It was late morning. Few birds sang, but somewhere ahead I could hear the plaintive "Quick! Three beers!" cry of an olive-sided flycatcher: beaver pond music. I was in the right place.

After a few hundred metres of forest shadow and deadfall, I emerged into a long, narrow meadow of sedge and reedgrass. Halfway across the meadow a meandering line of willows marked the course of Olden Days Creek.

Several trout darted away downstream as I stepped to the edge of the stream. The creek was clear and sleek, eddying against the willow tangles and feeling its way into the sedge marsh and out again. A submerged jungle of sedge, undulating gently, stretched out in the direction of the current.

The fleeing trout vanished into the watery tangle, and the stream was suddenly empty, winking innocently in the sunshine.

I stepped back from the edge. Hands already shaking from excitement, I tied on a bucktail caddis. On the first cast several trout appeared magically and raced each other for my fly. So began one of the finest days fishing in my life.

The creek was full of native west-slope cutthroat trout, deep-bodied and richly patterned with orange and salmon markings. Most were in the 15- to 25-centimetre range. I soon found that my biggest challenge today would be keeping the eager little fellows off the hook long enough to allow the bigger trout to bite. The big ones were barely 30 centimetres long, but in a stream only a metre wide, catching one felt like hooking a beaver. I caught many.

That was the first of several visits to a stream time seems to have forgotten. I have yet to see another angler there.

Olden Days Creek, I learned during my long hours of trying to learn its secrets, is more stable than many other mountain streams. It flows at the bottom of a long, wide valley. In late June its meadows are marsh, with treacherous little beaver runs waiting to submerge the unwary angler. The marshy valley floor absorbs the spring runoff, protecting the stream channel from high flows that might otherwise damage it.

Later in the summer, springs seep from the banks along the valley, maintaining the stream's flow by discharging water trapped by the porous forest soils. From creekside, all that is visible is green meadow, old-growth spruce and pine, and the tops of the surrounding mountains. I knew that loggers had been busy in some parts of the valley, but Olden Days Creek, so far, showed no sign of having noticed them.

One evening I picked up the kids after work and we headed out to explore Olden Days Creek more thoroughly. The stream winds through beaver ponds and marshes and loses itself in a deep floodplain lake before fanning through a vast plain of waving reeds. A few hundred metres farther the stream emerges again, meandering through more sedge meadows and willow. On foot, quagmire and marsh had turned me back time and again. This time we had the canoe on the roof of the van.

I carried the canoe down the forested slope to the water-meadow, two little life-jacketed figures bobbing along behind me. Leaving them seated beside each other on the canoe, I went back for paddles and gear. A snipe winnowed above the meadow. A moose stood stock still a few hundred metres upstream, watching as I loaded the kids into the canoe.

We launched the canoe beside an ancient beaver dam over-grown with swamp birch and willows. The kids chattered excitedly, then became silent as we drifted toward the spot where the water pours over the dam into a fast little chute.

"I don't want to go over that waterfall, Daddy," said Katie, the 4-year-old.

"Hang on," I replied.

The canoe teetered on the brink of the chute, then tilted and slid into the tailrace. I steered us into a long bay where the creek widened and shallowed, then lost itself into the dark water of a small lake.

Something laughed.

"What's that?" said 5-year-old Corey.

"A loon."

The loon watched us impassively as we skimmed the marly shallows. Pondweeds gave way to inky black where the bottom dropped suddenly away.

"It's deep," said Katie, mournfully. She sat very stiff and straight, a little hand clenching each gunwale.

The loon disappeared. The kids watched for it to surface again. I tied on a nymph fly and fed line out over the edge. The loon played peekaboo with us as we trolled the drop-off.

The valley turned gold as the sun dropped lower in the sky. At length I conceded that this was not the day I would prove my theory about this lake holding big trout. I brought in the line and set us on a course for the outlet, another shallow, marl-bottomed bay.

"Look for leeches," I said.

"What are they?"

"Black wormy things that suck your blood if you fall in."

"I don't like this place," Katie muttered.

"There's one!" shouted Corey.

Katie said, very softly, "Yuck."

We drifted quietly along. The kids leaned over the gunwales and watched the leeches and water bugs. Schools of minnows squirted off to the side or hung suspended like silver slivers in the crystal water. Ahead, tall jointed stems of water rushes formed a jungle wall where the stream widened and disappeared into a wide marsh.

Out of the corner of my eye I saw movement. For a moment my heart nearly stopped; it looked like the biggest fish I had ever seen. Then I realized it was a beaver swimming underwater. I pointed him out to the kids.

The beaver's big feet kicked up puffs of marl with each stroke. His eyes were clearly visible as we veered closer to him; he twisted his body and went burrowing away from us into the reeds.

"Look," I said. "You can see where he is. The reeds are waving."

Waving, clattering reeds marked the beaver's course, like a slow wind twisting its way through the marsh.

Then we slipped into the marsh ourselves. The reeds closed around the canoe. The channel vanished. The only clues to the direction of flow were grasses and leaves all strung out in one direction and the movement of bits of debris along the bottom. It was too shallow to paddle, so I used the paddles to pole the canoe through the rattling reeds.

At length, open water appeared ahead. We emerged into an open pond that lay along an old beaver dam. Water poured through a gap.

Landing, I lifted the kids out one by one, then pulled the canoe up on the dam. We stretched the stiffness out of our legs and looked around. As far as the eye could see there was only marsh, forest and mountains – all lit with the rich, golden glow of a Rocky Mountain sunset. No jet trails, no roads, no sound except the whine of mosquitoes and the singing of yellow-throats and Lincoln's sparrows.

For a moment I stood still, caught by an unexpected sensation of timelessness. Nothing so much as hinted that this was the late 20th century, or that we were not the first people to visit this place. I half expected to see my grandfather's salt-and-pepper cap showing above the willows. Looking around, however, all I saw was two small faces looking up impatiently at their bemused father.

I got the kids comfortable on the grass and then crept over to within casting distance of the outlet. Spilling through the gap in the old dam, the stream roared straight into a willow tangle, eddying out into another long, meandering reach.

On my first cast, three trout flashed at the fly and one connected. As my rod tip began to dance there came a chorus of shouts: "Did you get one, Dad?"

"He's got a fish."

"I wanna see! I wanna see!"

I tried to hustle the trout out of the pool so it wouldn't disturb any others that might be there. It was stubborn, churning up the surface and diving deep into the undercut hole. Finally I got him up on the grass: a fat 33-centimetre cutthroat. I need not have worried about disturbing the pool; my next cast brought me a smaller fish that I released into the upstream pond. The next few casts brought fish swirling out of the depths, but it was a while before I hooked another. This one was a 36-centimetre beauty, and completed my limit.

We launched again and went boiling down through the pool into the lower stream. A few hundred metres farther, the creek spread out into another reed marsh even more extensive than the first, so I turned the canoe around. We headed back.

The shadows were deep and the evening grown chilly by the time we reached our original launch site. I stashed the canoe in the woods and ushered the kids up through the forest gloom.

Much later, we arrived home. The kids were full of stories for their mom. It was well past their usual bedtime before we could get them to sleep.

Later, I phoned my dad to tell him about our evening. I could have waited until our next visit, I suppose. But he and I had spent many days afield hunting for Olden Days Creek. I wanted to tell him that the kids and I had just been there, and it was every bit as good as the olden days he had described. Maybe even better.

ॐ

Facebook Post

April 13, 2016. Canmore.

I remember when I was a kid there was a story in the Calgary Herald about a kid catching a 29-inch bull trout in the Bow River at the foot of Bearspaw Dam. In my naïveté at the time, I thought that meant I should fish harder for the big bull trout that lived in the river. In reality, it was one of the last prairie-dwelling bull trout returning once again to be stymied by a dam that had been completed when I was 3. Bull trout are essentially gone from the Bow now, thanks to dam builders who blocked their spawning runs. The Oldman's prairie bull trout are mostly gone, thanks to the Three Rivers Dam. Bull trout no longer occur in the middle reaches of the Red Deer, thanks to the Dickson Dam. If Site C is built, the Peace may be next. But hey, bull trout were clearly an evolutionary mistake; they were meant to be electric toothbrushes. I suppose it's hard to get creation right when you have only seven days.

Clogged Arteries (1991)

"As one slips quietly down the last slack reaches of the Parsnip, the roar of the Finlay Rapids, a couple miles down the Peace, breaks upon the ear in a slow crescendo.... Ahead, and beyond the big shingle bar, fast water is playing strange tricks in the dancing mirage; it is of a new colour and it is moving from left to right, shearing off, as with a knife, the sluggish current of the Parsnip. And that is where the Peace is born ..."

—*R.M. Patterson*, Finlay's River (1968)

Today the birthplace of the mighty Peace River lies drowned beneath the still waters of British Columbia's largest artificial reservoir, Williston Lake.

The same year that R.M. Patterson's book about the wilderness rivers of BC's Rocky Mountain Trench was published, the floodgates closed on the 182-metre W.B. Bennett Dam, plugging one of Canada's greatest rivers. The dam drowned more than 1600 square kilometres of forest, rapids and fertile bottomland forever.

Almost half a century before Patterson first ventured up the Peace to its headwaters, Vivian Pharis's grandparents floated down the Parsnip into the Peace River. A few kilometres downstream they found their new home on the fertile river floodplain 30 kilometres above the Peace Canyon.

Pharis spent much of her childhood on their wilderness ranch. "It was the most beautiful ranch I have ever seen in the world," she says. "My grandmother had an acre of garden where she grew field corn, cucumbers, tomatoes – things we can't even grow here in Calgary. The hay grew four feet high – over my head when I was a little girl."

By the 1930s the Goldbar Ranch had its own post office and school, and a population of 30. "Many were the trappers who spent their summers at the ranch," says a local history book compiled in 1973. "They preferred the farm with its freedom, its jollity and its bounteous home cooked meals, to life in town."

In 1968 the ranch too disappeared under the flood.

"I think that was what turned me into an environmentalist," says Pharis. At the time she was a university undergraduate. Today she is president of the Alberta Wilderness Association, one of the province's longest-serving conservation groups. In the years since floodwaters erased her family's home, the AWA has fought and lost a series of battles to stop dams on other Alberta rivers. It failed to save the historic Kootenay Plains from a hydropower dam on the North Saskatchewan River in the early 1970s. A few years later, it tried and failed to stop the Dickson Dam from plugging the Red Deer. Nothing daunted, the AWA continues to fight an irrigation dam under construction on the Oldman River in southern Alberta. The association's efforts, thus far, have saved Alberta's Milk River from the dam builders.

The BC government only partially cleared the great forests of the Peace, Parsnip and Finlay rivers before filling the Williston Reservoir. "Some of those cottonwoods along the river were more than eight feet in diameter," says Pharis, "but they only took some of the best timber from the slopes."

Deadheads – sodden timber that has drifted loose from the flooded valley floor – remain a major hazard to boat travel on the reservoir today, and on other reservoirs dating from the same period.

∞

"Twenty years ago," admits Dr. Anthony Tawil, an engineer with Acres International, an engineering firm that represents Canada on the International Committee on Large Dams, "we didn't clear reservoirs. Now, that was an incredibly stupid way to operate, and we don't do that anymore. Now we clear them as a matter of course."

Flooded timber, farmland, homes and scenery, however, are only a few of the social and ecological costs of plugging living rivers with cement and fill. Some costs turn up many kilometres away, and years after the controversy surrounding the dam's construction has faded into history.

Several hundred kilometres downstream from the Bennett Dam, the Peace River meets the Athabasca River. There, in the far northeast corner of Alberta, the two rivers form one of the largest freshwater deltas in the world where they empty into

Lake Athabasca. Each year, swollen by runoff from melting snow and seasonal rains, the two mighty rivers flood over their banks, spilling across the delta. River silt enriches delta soils and floodwater replenishes shallow basins and marshes, raising the water table.

Too much flooding can turn the perched basins into open lakes and drown fertile shoreline areas. Too little, and they dry up. Under normal conditions the annual flooding cycle produces up to 19,000 kilometres of rich, well-vegetated shoreline throughout the delta. As many as 600,000 young ducks and geese fly south each year from the delta's mosaic ecosystem. Millions of muskrats remain behind. Almost 2,000 Cree and Metis people sustain themselves year-round on the delta's walleye, goldeye and pike populations, trapping thousands of muskrats each winter.

While the Williston Reservoir was filling behind the Bennett Dam, the massive spring floods that had sustained the delta for millennia suddenly dried up. Without the floods, perched bogs and ponds dried up. Productive wetland communities shrank, replaced by dry grassland and sedge. Open sedge meadows, in turn, dried up and gave way to dense willow thickets and spruce.

The prolonged drought devastated fish and wildlife populations.

Faced with a continuing environmental disaster, the BC government reluctantly joined the Alberta and federal governments to find a solution. The solution, predictably, employed more dam engineers and involved more damming: the governments built two weirs on major delta channels. The weirs hold back floodwaters from the undammed Athabasca River, partially compensating for the loss of spring flooding from the tamed Peace.

Although the artificial weirs restore flooding only to part of the delta, the Peace-Athabasca Delta Implementation Committee boasted in 1987 that the weirs had successfully restored a near-normal flooding cycle. Vegetation, muskrats, fish and waterfowl appeared to be responding to the restored rhythms of the delta. Wood bison in the delta's vast sedge meadows benefitted that winter too.

Yet this may be only a temporary solution. Another hydroelectric dam – temporarily deferred for economic reasons – waits in the wings. The Alberta government wants to build a dam on the Slave River rapids, below the delta. As the river backpools behind the dam, it will inundate critical bison ranges. The downstream effects of the proposed Slave River dam would impoverish the entire Mackenzie River valley.

M ost people, to the extent that they even think of dams as being hard on rivers, assume that the damage is confined to the area flooded by the reservoir. However, as the case of the Peace-Athabasca Delta shows, one large dam can radically alter a whole river. In his classic textbook *The Ecology of Running Waters*, Dr. H.B.N. Hynes says: "The influence of a large dam is … profound and it extends a long way downstream." It also extends well upstream, because a dam's reservoir changes the river's base level. That reduces its energy for many kilometres upstream, causing the river to deposit sediment and build up its floodplain. As the stream bed rises, flood risk also increases for streamside residents who might have thought their upstream location had spared them from the dam's impacts.

Government and industry build dams for many reasons. Hydropower, irrigation, water supply, flood control and lake level stabilization are among the most important. In every case, engineers promote dams as a means of controlling water resources. The problems hinge on the fact that a river is not merely a water resource: it is a living ecosystem driven by running water. Change the flow of water, and we change the whole system.

Hynes describes rivers as dynamic, complex ecosystems. River water changes as it flows down its channel, picking up dissolved minerals, sediments and heat. The flowing water erodes or deposits silt, sand and gravel in predictable patterns, depending on how fast the water flows and how much sediment it carries. Because water flows at different speeds in different parts of a channel, a natural river bed is a mosaic of habitats sustaining many species of algae, invertebrates and fishes.

Spring floods bring fresh deposits of sediment to replace those washed downstream. The floodwaters are stored temporarily on the floodplain, enriching it with silt and moisture. That sustains lush plant communities and a host of wildlife. The floodplain's trees and other vegetation, in turn, produce shade and food for stream life.

Running water is merely the common thread that binds the river ecosystem together. A river's ecological complexity is almost beyond comprehension. Hydraulic engineers can begin to predict a dam's impact on the water and its bed – although even here reality often surprises them – but they usually fail to predict the intense ecological damage dams inflict on downstream ecosystems.

In a 1987 study Stewart Rood, an ecologist at the University of Lethbridge, examined aerial photographs and measured forest stands along three small rivers in southern Alberta. He found that dams can ultimately destroy prairie Canada's most productive ecosystems.

Rood found that the Belly River – with only three small weirs that barely affect spring flooding – still has cottonwood forests as lush and abundant as they were a quarter of a century ago. The Waterton River, however, has 25 per cent fewer cottonwoods than it did before water engineers dammed it, in 1964, to supply water for irrigation farmers. Just a short distance away, the St. Mary River has fared even worse. Dammed in 1951 for irrigation water supply, the St. Mary has lost more than half its original cottonwood forest. Its valley is becoming a barren coulee.

The loss of riparian cottonwood forests is a serious matter on the dry plains of prairie Canada. The huge trees provide shade and shelter for deer and breeding habitat for orioles, raccoons, owls, herons and countless other species of wildlife. More than three-quarters of all prairie wildlife species depend on riparian habitats for part, or all, of their lives. Cottonwood leaves, shed by the billions each fall, provide organic debris that keeps rivers fertile and productive.

World Wildlife Fund Canada's Prairie Conservation Action Plan describes prairie riparian ecosystems as "some of the most threatened ecosystems in arid and semi-arid regions of the world." It predicts that, without remedial action, cottonwood habitats may disappear by the end of the next century.

Rood suspects the big trees are dying because government water engineers draw too much water out of the rivers every summer to meet the needs of irrigation farmers. Some prairie rivers run nearly dry in mid-July downstream of irrigation dams. Cheryl Bradley's research on the Milk River, however, suggests that the problem is more complex than that.

One of the most magnificent prairie wildernesses remaining in North America is along the Milk River canyon in southern Alberta. The river's headwaters are mostly in Montana. It swings north into Alberta near Lethbridge, then flows another 200 kilometres along the southern edge of the province. South of Medicine Hat, the river swings back into Montana. There it encounters the Fresno Dam.

Cheryl Bradley conducted painstaking studies of cottonwood

groves both upstream of the Fresno Dam, in Alberta, and downstream, in the USA. She found that cottonwoods sprout on the insides of meander bends where silt accumulates, year after year, while the river erodes the outsides of bends.

Spring floods make meander bends migrate, year after year, across the floodplain. In the process, old cottonwood stands fall victim to the hungry waters eroding the outside of each bend. The same waters, building the opposite point bars up, leave bands of maturing cottonwoods behind as point bars grow. Cottonwoods, over millennia, have adapted their life cycle to line up with the behaviour of the river; they release their seeds in late spring when prairie rivers are in full flood. That timing ensures that new generations of cottonwood trees will sprout on rich, wet, newly deposited silt that the flood-waters have spread across the point bars.

The whole floodplain is a living, dynamic system.

Below the Fresno Dam, Bradley found that cottonwood groves were aging. New seedlings were scarce. As old trees died, they were not being replaced. The forests were fading toward extinction.

A river's ability to carry silt in suspension depends on its ability to keep moving. When water piles up behind a dam, its silt load settles out. The water coming out of the dam is clean and hungry; the river promptly sets to work restoring its silt load. It does this by eroding the river bed.

Downstream from the Fresno Dam, the Milk River's

meanders no longer migrate. Instead, the river is slowly cutting downwards, entrenching itself in the channel it was following when the engineers who built the Fresno Dam closed its floodgates. Old cottonwoods are now high and dry as the water table follows the river downward. The new point bars that cottonwood seedlings rely upon have become rare and unreliable, choked with weeds and often dry just at the most critical season.

The dam, of course, has benefited farmers, who use the stored water to irrigate barley, alfalfa and other field crops in an area notorious for its unreliable summer rains. But the river, deprived of its silt, its seasonal cycles and much of its water, is no longer able to sustain its once-rich ecosystem.

To Nelbert Little Moustache, a Piikani elder from the Peigan Reserve on the Oldman River, the loss of floodplain cottonwoods is more than an ecological disaster. It is a cultural and religious sacrilege. The cottonwood tree is a central element of the spiritual traditions of the Blackfoot people. Already declining along every dammed river in western North America, some of the healthiest and most extensive stands of plains cottonwoods still thrive along Alberta's Oldman River. The potential loss of their sacred forest is one of many reasons why the Piikani continue, with Pharis's Alberta Wilderness Association, to wage an underdog battle against the Three Rivers Dam, currently nearing completion on the Oldman.

If the Oldman's cottonwoods die, the last healthy stands in Canada will be on the Milk River. And Alberta's water bureaucrats have already drafted plans to dam the Canadian reach of the Milk River. The plans are waiting on the shelf for the right political moment.

৩৫

The downstream ecological effects of dams aren't widely understood and, until recently, have not been important factors in motivating communities to rise against dam building. Most of the opposition to dams in Canada has centred on either the value of the areas those dams will flood, or the damage those dams will cause to fisheries. Plugging a river wreaks havoc on most fish populations.

Some big dams have created valuable cold-water fisheries on rivers where they didn't exist before, a fact that damming proponents are quick to point out. In the American southwest, for example, rivers like the Green and Columbia were once too muddy, volatile and warm for trout. Today, with predictable flows released from the cold bottom layers of reservoirs, these rivers have productive recreational fisheries. Their native fish species, however, are mostly either extinct or endangered because of the impact of dams and cold water on their habitats.

On balance, history has shown that large dams cause far more damage than good to river fisheries. Canada's Department of Fisheries and Oceans, in 1986, released an assessment of the likely impacts of Alcan's proposed Kemano Completion Project in British Columbia. The scientists reported that in 75 per cent of the 81 cases they studied, flow changes had hurt natural trout and salmon populations. They identified several different ways in which dams hurt fishes.

The most obvious impact – the one that killed the once awe-inspiring salmon runs of the Columbia River basin – is that dams physically block migrating fish. Salmon, bull trout and other species heading upstream to spawn in cold headwaters are doomed to frustration if they encounter a dam. Even in cases where engineers install fish ladders or electric companies trap spawners and truck them around the dam, few spawners get through. Young salmon, returning downstream, die when hydroelectric turbines grind them into fish food, or when nitrogen gas churned into the water in turbulent dam tailraces poisons them.

Dams change downstream water temperatures because, unlike natural lakes, most release cold, oxygen-poor water from the bottoms of their reservoirs. Sudden releases of cold water – a daily occurrence below most hydro dams – can kill food organisms, fish eggs and fish because of drastic shifts in water temperature and pressure. Dams cause upstream habitats to clog up with sediment that settles out of the ponded water. Blocked by the dams, fine gravels no longer enrich down-stream reaches; fishes there gradually lose their spawning beds. Some dams also pollute downstream river water because organic waste or heavy metals accumulate in the reservoirs.

The ecological costs of damming a river are staggering. So why do we build them?

M ore than half of Canada's large dams were built to generate power. Energy utility companies often call hydroelectricity – since it does not rely on burning fuels – "clean" energy. The great dams in the Columbia River basin and the more modern dams of Robert Bourassa's James Bay Project fall into this category. Ask the rivers, however. They know that no energy comes without an environmental cost. Far from being clean, hydroelectricity is ecologically one of the dirtiest energy sources available.

The Columbia River project, for example, destroyed some of the greatest salmon spawning runs in the world. Almost 80 per cent of the 748 kilometres of river that once flowed in Canada have vanished beneath reservoirs. Arrow Lakes reservoir flooded some of British Columbia's only Class 1 agricultural land. Thousands of square kilometres of the most productive forest land in BC have been lost forever and – as on the Peace – the dam builders left most of the trees standing, uncut.

Anthony Tawil agrees that Canadians have paid some high environmental prices for cheap hydropower. He argues, however, that there is little point in dwelling on the mistakes of the past. "Most publicity on dams is bad," he says. "Partly it's because in the past we have done some very destructive things. But partly it's because engineers have not done a good job of communicating. There have been some very beneficial results from dams."

Tawil cites flow regulation as a downstream benefit that improves the river environment. Spreading out a river's flow so that more water runs during the critical low-flow periods of midsummer and late winter can provide aquatic life with a more stable environment. It also produces recreational benefits throughout the year. Fluctuating flows caused by a network of hydropower dams on its headwaters nearly destroyed Alberta's Bow River while subjecting the city of Calgary to repeated winter ice jams and flooding. Since the 1950s the Bearspaw Dam, just upstream from Calgary, has regulated its flow. The Bow is now one of the most heavily used urban recreational rivers in Canada. Its rainbow trout fishery is world-famous. Flow regulation paid off for the Bow – but only because other dams had devastated it.

The International Committee on Large Dams is compiling a report that will assess both the benefits and disbenefits of large dams "to try to provide a more balanced view," according to Anthony Tawil.

The committee's report is not likely to sway Vivian Pharis. She points out that whatever benefits dams may deliver to consumers, on-stream dams inevitably hurt rivers and riparian ecosystems. She insists that water management should emphasize reducing water demand and using existing supplies as efficiently and frugally as possible. While she recognizes the need to divert some water from rivers into off-stream storage reservoirs – which deliver many of the same benefits with far fewer ecological costs – she remains adamantly opposed to damming rivers.

"We have lost rivers, valleys and ecosystems that should have been protected as national treasures," she says. "Maybe we didn't know enough about the environmental costs of big dams, back in the 1950s and '60s. But today we do."

Cliff Wallis, president of the Friends of the Oldman River, points out that decades of experience have shown that large dams don't even deliver the economic benefits that their proponents often boast about. "In the United States," he says, "water agencies have found that by investing in technologies that use water efficiently, they can increase available water supplies just as much, at a tenth of the cost."

Tim Palmer – an American journalist whose book *Endangered Rivers and the Conservation Movement* examines the history of dam building and river protection in the US – agrees. Most often, he says, the costs of building a dam vastly exceeded initial estimates, while proponents consistently overestimated economic benefits. Growth in demand for power and water has not matched projections. New technologies, growing costs and increased public commitment to conservation, according to Palmer, have turned the tide against large dams in the United States.

There is, simply, no need to waste money and rivers anymore.

Tom McMillan, Canada's former minister of the environment, has called for more sensitivity to the values of rivers, and new approaches to meeting society's water and power needs. In 1987 McMillan released a Federal Water Policy that states: "Canadians have tended to undervalue in-stream uses in their water management decisions, with very expensive long-term consequences. Canada's rivers are a priceless and irreplaceable part of our natural and cultural heritage."

Nonetheless, a century of freewheeling development and economic growth has left many Canadians with a sort of benign indifference that works against river protection. If we continue to demand cheap, abundant water and power, we cannot expect to save our surviving rivers.

John Thompson, a Calgary-based resource economist, points out the logical inconsistency that often undermines our efforts to protect rivers from ourselves. It does not show much serious commitment, he says, to leave the sprinkler on in the yard and the light on in the hall while we go canoeing all weekend, only to come home Sunday night and write an angry letter to a politician about the mismanagement of a favourite river.

The value of Canada's surviving wild rivers and riparian ecosystems derives not only from their ecological complexity, historical significance and intrinsic worth but, sadly, also from their rarity. Most Canadian rivers are already dammed. Work continues today on dams on Alberta's Oldman, Saskatchewan's Souris, and Quebec's La Grande. Government water developers may announce new dams soon for Alberta's Milk, North Saskatchewan and South Saskatchewan; Manitoba's Assiniboine and Nelson; and British Columbia's Stikine.

Peter Pearse, chairman of the 1984–85 Inquiry on Federal Water Policy, underscored the scarcity of free-flowing rivers in a 1984 speech to the Canadian Water Resources Association. He reminded the engineers gathered there that "the Fraser is the only major river in southern Canada that has escaped damming."

❧

Vivian Pharis has no photographs to remind her of her family's wilderness ranch on the upper Peace River. She shows photographs of Williston Lake reservoir instead: a vast expanse of steel-grey water stippled with floating logs and surrounded by vast clearcuts. There is a deadness to the pictures. The water no longer dances.

I asked her if she feels bitter about her family's loss. She shook her head.

"I suppose we didn't know then what we do now about the waste and damage that a big dam represents," she said. "The important thing is to recognize that we no longer have that excuse. And there are very few free-flowing rivers left in Canada today."

Today, in the waning years of the 20th century, our understanding of river ecosystems has barely begun to catch up with our technical capability to exploit them. Understanding and humility, if they come, will be too late for the hundreds of river reaches lost to reservoirs or forever impoverished by the subtler impacts of dams.

It is time to save the few that remain.[1]

---

1 Today, while the US has begun removing dams that should never have been built, Canada continues to build them. Site C, a dam that will flood another long reach of the Peace River, is under construction.

All Dried Out (2015)

The next drought appears to have begun. Most of western Canada was dry and parched this year, and a major El Niño event now threatens to keep us thirsty for at least another year or two.

Environment Canada's weather prognosticator, David Phillips, has pointed out the contrast between two years ago, when flooding swamped southern Alberta, and this year's record-breaking low rainfall and high temperatures. Describing it as "weather whiplash," Phillips said it "seems to be a common thing that we're seeing around the world, where normal doesn't exist anymore."

Actually, droughts are part of our normal; it's just that we tend quickly to forget the thirsty years once the rains return.

Ranchers in central Alberta, forced by lack of hay and water to sell their herds, might feel nostalgic for the wet 1950s when rain averaged well above normal. But they shouldn't. In the early 1950s many sloughs that float ducks today held no standing water. Rain fell, but the wet didn't persist.

University of Alberta ecologist Glynnis Hood analyzed air photos taken in the 1950s east of Edmonton. Most of the wetlands were dry. When she looked at air photos from 2002, however, she found 61 per cent more open water, even though that year was one of the driest on record. Barely half as much rain and snow fell in 2002 as in 1950.

The difference: beavers that had been trapped out in the mid-20th century had returned by 2002, rebuilt the wetlands and raised the regional water table. Even with much less water to work with, those hard-working rodents had kept the landscape wet.

The ability of beavers to keep land wet even when the rains are disappointing is no secret to long-time foothills ranchers. In the mid-20th century, the Cartwright family, who ranch along Pekisko Creek, went so far as to ask government problem-wildlife officers for live beavers they could release into their trapped-out valley. "Beavers now store water in all the small tributaries that used to dry up in summers," Gordon Cartwright says. "That helps to maintain the water table."

Dr. John Pomeroy, a leading Canadian hydrologist, says that many small beaver dams provide the same water storage benefit as one large engineered dam, but without the negative side effects. Beaver-built wetlands give landscapes "hydrological memory." The effect of stored water in beaver landscapes can persist up to six years – particularly meaningful since droughts rarely persist that long.

Lethbridge biologist Lorne Fitch says that beaver colonies are far more valuable, both for flood control and drought mitigation, than most people realize. Not only do beavers increase the amount of open water by almost 10 per cent in some drainages, he says, but they store five to ten times as much water underground. When beavers move into a stream, their dams can eventually increase stream flow up to 1,000 per cent. But since the dams can also make the effective floodplain up to 12 times as wide as it was before, the increased flows don't translate to bigger floods. It's the size of a stream's floodplain determines how fast its flood flows drain; beavers actually reduce down-stream flooding.

The ability of beavers to turn fast-draining valleys into spongy reservoirs is no recent discovery. Biologist Constance Hunt points out that southern Arizona's indigenous people used to weave barriers of seep willow, burrobrush and mesquite and anchor them to streamside trees to slow the streams and en-courage sediment deposition. These man-made beaver dams sustained the riparian fields where the people grew food crops – just one example of how indigenous cultures studied nature to sustain their societies.

Beaver management in Alberta's post-industrial culture, how-ever, is not about encouraging them to store more water. It's mostly about killing them.

Fur trappers alone kill more than 12,000 beavers a year. Thou-sands more die at the hands of government officers and contract trappers as "problem wildlife" when they plug road culverts or flood hayfields. Under Alberta's Wildlife Act, any private landowner can kill beavers on sight. Beavers aren't considered valuable allies against drought and flooding; they are treated as nuisances.

Many foothills streams whose broad floodplains were once liv-ing sponges storing precious water in beaver meadows are now incised into their floodplains for lack of the beaver colonies that kept those headwaters lush for millennia. Water drains fast in spring, sending punishing floods downstream, rather than seeping slowly into streams from the saturated ground upstream from beaver dams.

The loss of beaver landscapes may be part of the reason why the South Saskatchewan's natural river flow is now about 12 per cent lower than it was when measurements began half a century ago. The region's human population, in the meantime, has grown by over 900 per cent. Those diverging lines between water availability and water demand are never so apparent as when, once again, a drought cycle reduces the supply of snow and rain to our headwater basins.

Thousands of Alberta beavers will die in traps this winter. We may rue their absence when next summer's dry winds return again.

༚

Facebook Post

November 12, 2015. Canmore.

Every species of stream-dwelling trout native to Alberta is now classified as threatened. When fish stocks crash we are being sent a message. That isn't junk mail – it's a final notice. Land abuse and climate change are the crucial environmental issues of this generation.

A Matter of Timing (2014)

In October the smell of decomposing chlorophyll fills the forest as days grow shorter and frosts more frequent. The birdless woods go briefly yellow; then the wind takes the leaves away. Hunting season comes and the missing leaves reveal themselves on the forest floor, dry as cornflakes, frustrating hunters who hope to sneak up close to deer.

Bambi, according to author Felix Salten, was grateful for the timing of leaf fall: "O, how kind last year's leaves are! They do their duty so well and are so alert and watchful.... And they give warning in advance of every danger."

Our human tradition of hunting deer after harvest season aligns with each annual bounty of fallen leaves to make hunting more uncertain and the escape of our prey more likely. It's a matter of fortuitous timing – just one of thousands of overlapping events that make the natural world work.

Not all those fallen leaves end up on the forest floor. In southern Alberta, where poplar forests form golden galleries along prairie rivers, the wind blows harder than farther north. Leaves dance along river floodplains until many of them light in the water. Good timing: autumn rivers flow slowly. Instead of washing away, the leaves accumulate in increasingly sodden drifts in back eddies and shallows until, eventually, they sink.

What a lucky coincidence. Autumn's short days barely warm those prairie rivers. Where summer's heat and sunshine yielded a bounteous harvest of algae and other aquatic plants to sustain the bacteria, fungi and invertebrates that fish need for food, sun-starved autumn rivers no longer produce much food. That annual subsidy from fallen leaves arrives just in time. Through the long winter, the decomposing leaves feed micro-organisms, insects and fishes until the days grow long and warm again in spring.

Fortunate timing. It's no less fortunate for the poplars that Alberta's climate produces spring floods in late May and early June. When melting snows and spring rains send brown floodwaters churning down our river valleys, the same poplars whose fallen leaves helped deer escape hunters and fed the river ecosystem all winter are green again. Seed buds burst on female poplars in early June, setting billions of cotton-like seeds adrift on the wind. Just like the falling leaves a few months earlier, many of those fluffy seeds light on the surface of the river.

Perfect timing; natural river flows subside through June. The ebbing floodwaters reveal fresh new deposits of silt, sand and gravel on every point bar. The poplar seeds lodge on the wet, new material and take root. Those new deposits lack competing vegetation to shade the baby poplars or compete with them for water. And the next generation of poplar forest is born – even as old trees pile up in logjams on the outside curves of eroding river banks. It's like a perfect conspiracy between river and forest.

If poplars released their seeds a month earlier or a month later, river valley forests would have little hope of renewing them-selves because they would miss that perfect moment when new, wet seed beds glisten in the spring sun beside an ebbing river. And there would be no leaves to warn the deer or feed the winter fishes. In fact, on rivers like the St. Mary, where irrigation dams have changed the timing of floods, forests are gradually disappearing.

We tend to think of natural selection as being how individual species evolve, but in fact it contains countless feedback loops that link organisms and processes together. River ecosystems need poplars; poplars need river ecosystems. Through millennia, they have become synchronized with one another. Nature's timing has nothing to do with random luck.

Late each April the first poplar buds burst and new leaves poke out. Instantly, triggered by scent cues released by the new leaves, insects appear in the canopy. Perfect timing; earlier insects would starve. And virtually the same week, orange-crowned warblers appear, having timed their migration home from the tropics just in time to feed on the first canopy insects of the year. The river flows by; but all are linked.

Timing is everything. Robins and kingbirds nest in those poplars as insect populations peak. They fledge their insect-fed young in late July, just in time for nearby saskatoons and raspberries to appear: perfect food to fatten their young for the fall migration. If berries should appear too soon or too late, fewer young birds survive the southward journey. But day length signals are the same each year; nature usually gets its timing right.

Usually.

Edmonton botanist Elisabeth Beaubien has monitored the phenology (seasonal timing) of common Alberta plants for several decades. She has found that as Alberta's climate warms, many species now flower and produce seeds or fruit days, or even weeks, earlier than they used to. Animals that rely on day-length cues for migration or breeding may have problems if bugs and berries that respond to temperature cues no longer appear when they need them.

The complexity, productivity and beauty of Alberta's wild ecosystems is a matter of timing – syncopated rhythms, harmonics and chords arising from the meshing of countless living instruments over thousands of years. Predictable seasonal signals tie nature together in a living symphony with near-perfect timing.

Climate change, river modification or misuse of land can change those signals. The consequences may prove discordant.

CHAPTER 4

The Hunt

Hunting with the Kids (1999)

Corey blinked groggily up at me in the near-darkness. I held a finger to my lips. "Don't wake your Mom," I whispered. "Hunting time."

His eyes widened and, suddenly awake, he sat up and stretched.

Katie didn't stir until I tickled the bottom of her foot. Then she glowered at me.

By the time my son and daughter arrived blinking at the kitchen table, I had fresh coffee in the thermos and the back door open as I loaded the van in the dark. The chill air outside was full of the smell of frost and fallen leaves. Lisa, our golden retriever, whined and wagged her tail. She knew what that smell meant. She and I were going hunting with the kids again.

L ike my own kids, I started hunting when I was about 8 or 9. I was the second-oldest of ten children. Most of us, at one time or another, accompanied Dad into the irrigation farming country where he grew up. Saturdays during hunting season were sacred; whoever was going along with Dad that day would be up well before daybreak and home – socks full of burrs and dried thistles, eyes burning from sun and wind – well after dark.

Back then, most families included a hunter or two. There were no firearms acquisition certificates, no training requirements before a kid could buy his or her first licence, and no real difficulties finding a place to hunt. I can't recall ever wondering if hunting was right or wrong; it was just part of how we lived.

Hunting trips soon became a passion for me; nothing else immersed me so thoroughly and intimately in wild nature. Only now, looking back from the perspective of middle age, do I know that those early hunting trips were moral training grounds too.

Afield, I learned about responsibility and the consequences of bad decisions. Each Saturday was a dawn-to-dusk series of small learnings as I tagged along with Dad or, later, hunted alone along the irrigation canals and coulees. Irresponsibly trying to scare it, I wounded a coyote once and have never forgotten the remorse and self loathing that followed me home that day. Although I didn't realize it then, I had learned an indelible lesson about the power of humans to impose pain or death arbitrarily. The memory of that animal's suffering has stopped me many times since from pulling the trigger frivolously. My ethical education was strengthened by repeatedly witnessing the respect my dad showed for other people's property, or his refusal to abandon the search for a downed pheasant until we had scoured every bit of possible hiding cover several times over.

Dad is gone now, and so too are the days when most kids grew up with hunting. Fewer than 7 per cent of all Canadians now take up guns or bows each fall in pursuit of game. Most of us live in cities and large towns, disconnected from the wild. Perhaps our isolation helps explain why concern for the environment is higher than ever before – certainly higher than when I was a kid. Part of that concern for the environment is expressed by a growing movement to ban hunting. Hunting, in many people's minds, is exploiting nature: killing wild animals for fun. When hunters try to explain the complex reasons why we really hunt, our efforts, too often, sound like little more than weak rationalization.

Looking at the bright faces of my two oldest children as they scrambled into the back seat, I felt grateful to know that they had chosen to come with me into the field this morning. They might never end up carrying a gun afield in years to come, but at least now, in their formative years, they would be out in the real and living world with a parent who hunts.

We drove east through the darkness. Katie sat forward, eagerly watching for animals in the headlights while Corey huddled into the warmth of his jacket, still waking up.

"Stop, Dad! Look!" Katie cried. Something small zigzagged crazily across the pavement, then stopped, frozen in the headlight glare at the edge of the shoulder. It was a deer mouse. I waited while the kids leaped out of the car and crouched over it. Katie reached out to touch the dazzled creature, but it scurried away into the grass.

Later we saw owls, a jackrabbit, a few deer. The eastern horizon paled and a rich orange glow began to pool along the skyline. At length we slowed, then turned off the pavement onto the crunch of gravel. I pulled over to the edge of the road, uncased my gun, and shook some shotshells into my pocket. The wind was sharp on my face as I stood beside the van, bemused; this was what my own dad used to do. In some ways I've never really stopped feeling like one of the bright-eyed crew now waiting for me to get back inside, but the years have flown; now I am become the father I remember.

We had barely pulled back out onto the grid road when a flock of Hungarian partridges erupted from the edge of the road and sailed into a nearby stubble field.

"I saw where they landed, Dad!"

A decade or so ago I would have skidded to a stop and piled out after those birds. The field wasn't posted and there were no nearby houses. But things change as one's values mature.

"I don't know whose field this is," I replied. "There'll be more."

"But I can see them, Dad. They're right there! They're looking at us."

"Well, see if you can spot some more after this next corner. We have permission to hunt there."

Katie sulked, but only until we saw an owl on a fencepost. It waited until we slowed to watch it, then spread its wings and dropped to fly along the fence line a few hundred metres, then veered up and settled on a power pole. Its head pivoted to watch us go by. The kids stared back.

Owls were scarce in pheasant country when I was the kid trying to persuade my father to ignore NO TRESPASSING signs. Those we did see were often dead, hanging with their wings tangled around the barbed wire of roadside fences. In those days many hunters considered hawks and owls competition and had no compunction about filling them with duck shot. Coyotes were little better off – all Dad had to do was to put his foot on the brake for a watching coyote to take off across the prairie like all the demons in hell were on its tail. Even then, Dad never killed predators; now, few other hunters do either.

The first time I ever saw my dad act excited was one morning when we saw three mule deer. He pulled over to the side of the road and we watched as the strange creatures pogo-sticked over a rise and out of sight. Dad had grown up in the country-side where he took us hunting, and had never seen a deer there before. I remember thinking it strange to see my own father jabbering like a kid; that wasn't any part of how I thought I knew him.

Years later, I realize that I would have never have known my father in the same way if we hadn't hunted together. Maybe I never would have really known him at all.

The sun was well up by the time we parked in front of the USE RESPECT sign and stepped out into the wind. Lisa bounded about excitedly, tail wagging. The creek valley stretched away to the south, tangles of rose and buckbrush alternating with dense thickets of willow. Overhead, geese were gabbling. I pointed out the long wavering lines to the kids, but they had already spotted them.

"Let's go," I said, parting the barbed wire. The dog was already in the bushes, still bouncing her first burst of energy out of her system. As I stepped over the top strand of the fence there was an explosion of noise and the startled cackle of a flushing cock pheasant. I sent a hopeless charge of shot after the bird, then saw Lisa bounding along the creek hot on another scent. I started to run, but it was too late; another cock and three hens lifted from the far corner and sailed up the valley and out of sight, with Lisa in full pursuit.

There was a time when I would have been furious. Instead, I shook my head and muttered, "Idiot dog." Corey laughed.

By the time Lisa returned, panting hard and covered with burrs, we were well away from the road. Tree sparrows lisped in the undergrowth. Katie had stopped to study some raccoon tracks in the mud. Corey was practising on leaves with his BB gun, dawdling along on a parallel course to his sister and me. I didn't bother scolding the dog; she wouldn't have understood. Instead, I waved her into a long oxbow crowded with willow and hawthorn.

Shortly later I heard an indignant cackle, then nothing, then the explosion of a rising pheasant. Gaudy and sleek, a big cock pheasant towered out above the willows and arced away toward the far side of the creek. My shotgun boomed, and the bird crumpled into the brush.

"Fetch!"

"He got it! You got it, Dad!"

That was my daughter, who only last year had told me hunters were cruel. She joined me to watch Lisa deliver the bird to my hand, and asked if she could carry it. I knew I'd have it back soon. I well remember how quickly a pheasant grows heavy in an 11-year-old's hand and how the hardened spurs on its legs dig into soft flesh.

There was a time when I couldn't imagine taking kids hunting with me. I was too full of hunting urge. I wanted to cover the kilometres, to hunt from dawn to dusk and come home with a limit of whatever I was after. Our kids were babies then. Hunting was something I did away from the responsibilities of home.

But it didn't take long before I began to realize that those hunting trips were incomplete. However rich the day might have been, there was a hollow in its heart. My own dad had only hunted alone when there were no kids available; that was seldom indeed. My children had become older during the seasons when I went off on my own – not able to keep up with me but old enough to like exploring nature and to keep themselves entertained during long drives.

I started taking them along on sharp-tailed grouse hunts in the open bunchgrass country of the foothills. Parking them in a clump of bushes with strict orders not to stray, I hunted a wide circle across country, keeping an eye on them from afar. Alone together in what must have felt like wilderness, they discovered chickadees, made hiding places for their stuffed animals and invented elaborate stories with which they then regaled me during the drive to our next hunting spot.

As the kids became older, they sometimes tagged along for part of each day before finding some interesting place to explore until the dog and I came wandering back. Sometimes they flushed their own grouse or pheasants by mistake. Once the kids cornered a cottontail rabbit in an old outhouse and tried to pet it. Another time they managed to surround two raccoons. Fortunately, they had enough sense not to try petting them.

Back home, each day's adventures spill out breathlessly on the kitchen table along with whatever birds their father has been lucky enough to hit that day. Their mom listens with patient amusement, just as my mother listened to other children a few decades ago.

Years from now, I suspect, each of my children will know themselves, in part, by the memories they gathered, the lessons they learned, and the landscapes to which they bonded while hunting with their dad. That, after all, is how he has come to know himself.

I think now that if I didn't have my own kids, I'd have to borrow some.

The other day our family sat down to a Sunday dinner of fried pheasant and garden potatoes. Hunting season was over for another year. Lisa lay in her corner of the kitchen, twitching in her sleep. I could see some burdock burrs I had missed tangled behind one ear. The kids were talking about Corey's Canyon, as they have come to call one of our secret pheasant coulees.

"So," I said, "should I be thinking about getting you shotguns for next year? Corey and Katie will both be old enough to hunt."

Katie stared at me, startled by the immensity of the thought. Then she said, "No way! I would never shoot things."

Corey shook his head too, but his eyes were pensive.

I said, "So you don't want to go hunting after all?"

"Of course we want to go hunting," Katie corrected me. "It's fun."

That's good enough for me. Taking kids afield doesn't require making hunters out of them. What's more important is to make people out of them. I can't think of a better way than to take them hunting – helping them form their own lasting bonds with wild nature, develop a sense of freedom and independence, and learn the ethics of restraint and responsibility. Even if none of my kids ever chooses to shoot a gun, I suspect that they already are hunters in the most important ways.

Even so, I'm watching out for a good used 20-gauge. If history is any guide, I have a feeling there could be an argument over who gets to use it first, come next fall.

༃

Facebook Post

October 21, 2012. Lac des Arcs.

Returning from another unproductive sheep scouting expedition today I noticed lots of waterfowl rafted up on Lac des Arcs – flotillas of coots, huddles of scoters, drifts of geese and, along the far side, the white puffs of swans. One of the coot mobs suddenly exploded into foam as a big, immature bald eagle took a swing at them. I pulled off to watch as the eagle wheeled and grabbed again and again until suddenly he just vanished: he'd gone into the water. I thought he was going to drown. But after a minute or so he got himself airborne and wheeled past me carrying a very sodden, dead coot. So: success for a fellow hunter, and a hard-earned one to boot. But just as the eagle made it to a safe perch at the edge of the lake, out of the sky tumbled an adult bald eagle who promptly stole the dead coot, leaving a sodden, disconsolate teenage eagle huddled on a broken snag beside the lake, listening to his stomach grumble.

Bullying. It's a problem everywhere.

Witnesses in the Wild (1993)

As we ate our lunch high above a headwater valley one day, Bill Tilleman told me about his first encounter with a wolf. He had been hunting elk on the upper Red Deer River, on a grassy mountaintop with sheltered gullies and isolated stands of timber. Bill and his partner had separated after a hard climb. Bill was just strolling over a rise when he came face to face with a big grey wolf trotting up the other side.

"I was so close I could see the shock in his eyes when he saw me, and the contraction of his leg muscles as he put on the brakes. I could almost feel his horror at blundering into me."

The wolf, barely ten metres away, recovered instantly. Flipping end for end, it streaked away across the alpine tundra.

His partner demanded to know afterwards why he had not shot it. "It never even occurred to me," he said. "I was too awestruck. And I wouldn't have shot him anyway."

If Bill had not been elk hunting that day, he would have had no story to tell. Nobody would ever hear the delight in his voice when he recalls the experience.

His story got me thinking of one of my own elk-hunting experiences on a mountain ridge in southern Alberta. I had set out by headlamp at four in the morning to reach the high country before daybreak. I arrived in a howling windstorm on the long summit ridge just as the sun began to show above the flat rim of the distant prairie.

I was working my way along the ridge, leaning against the wind and scanning the shadowed meadows for feeding elk, when I saw a small bird flying up the lee slope toward me. As it crested the ridge, the wind hit it head-on. It dropped near the ground, wings beating hard, barely making headway as it fought its way into the chinook.

It was the first of a long flock of rosy finches – small mountain birds that nest in cliff faces and forage in the alpine meadows. As they crossed the ridge, several passed within centimetres of me, working hard but progressing with painful slowness. Their bright little eyes watched me until they made it past and could dive away down the windward side of the ridge. The birds glowed a brilliant rose in the rays of the rising sun.

I stood, entranced, in the middle of a strange, slow-motion dance.

The image has stayed with me ever since – a strange and privileged experience that I earned by not being at home in a warm bed, where most people are at first light on an October day.

Later that fall I shot my first elk on that ridge. Nevertheless, the most vivid image that remains is of those tiny birds, glowing in the sunrise, fighting their way past me. I could have reached out and touched them.

When non-hunters challenge us about our pastime, their criticism usually focuses on the fact that we kill things. Indeed, when we plan our trips and head out in the morning, most hunters are focused on the hope of success. Still, as any real hunter knows, a dead thing does not a successful hunt make, any more than an empty freezer equals a wasted fall.

Bill and my brother Gordon are both serious hunters. I can recall each deciding, having finally found bighorn sheep after long days of scouting, not to stalk them. They had already got what they sought.

Out there in the hills and plains, strange and wonderful things happen every day. Eagles play in the updrafts. Martens hurry along fallen logs. Chickadees mine dead bark for moth eggs. Wild things mate and play and die. Sun and clouds paint an endlessly changing mosaic across the spectacular landscapes and wildlands of the West. The real and natural universe continues to unfold in all the glory and complexity of Creation.

Who is there to witness it?

We are.

We who participate in the wild are witnesses of it too, in ways few others are. Our passion drives us to rise early in the cold, dark hours of the dawn. We often travel long distances to lose ourselves in favourite landscapes that resonate in our souls. Although we may start with friends or family, at some point we find ourselves alone. We move quietly, totally involved with small breezes, undergrowth, the hidden places in the vegetation, and the vast, overarching sky.

Hunters become predators, and thus one with the ecosystem – no longer outsiders or interested observers, but full participants. We are there, wholly and completely, and open to what will come.

So it is that we sometimes come home at season's end with our tags unfilled but our hearts overflowing. A successful hunt does not require a kill, only the possibility of one. It is that possibility that places us out in the heart of the living wild, where wolves trot casually over alpine ridges, small birds drag the sunrise into the wind, and bighorn sheep survey the wilderness from hollowed-out beds on talus slopes.

Sometimes we ourselves forget what those who do not hunt cannot understand: that it is not merely the kill that makes us hunters. It is the witnessing, the being there, and those transcendental moments of belonging when the living world reveals itself to those who work so hard to become a part of it.

That is why we will be there again next fall in the cold and the rain and the snow, working hard to penetrate the most secret of wild places. We won't be there seeking death. We will be actively participating in, and celebrating, the endless dance of life.

Environmental Education (1995)

North of Calgary, where Fourth Street's pavement gave way at last to gravel, there used to be a quiet little creek valley full of cows, gophers and silver willows. A few cottonwoods grew by the creek. Sometimes a farm truck rattled by, but for the most part the valley was an empty sort of place in summer. Few people gave the little valley a second look. If they had, they might have seen a kid getting an environmental education.

I found the place because when hunting season ended my father found other things to do with his Saturdays. Much to my regret, I was on my own until fishing season began in the spring.

Dad introduced each of his kids to the outdoors as soon as we could walk fast enough to keep up with him. I could never get enough of those precious Saturdays. We hunted weedy irrigation ditches east of Strathmore for pheasants or hiked game trails and cutlines into hidden foothills creeks to fish for cutthroat trout.

By the time I was 10, my identity was already steeped in the smell of autumn stubble, the evening whistle of passing mallards, the possibility of moose or bear. I was addicted. I couldn't get enough of the world beyond the city that my father's hunting and fishing trips revealed to me.

However, kids have more spare time than dads. When hunting season ended I faced the prospect of weekends without the wilds. I stuffed my pockets with stones and went looking for pheasants down along the railway tracks. There weren't too many there, but I spotted some birds I didn't know. Mom got me a bird book. Next weekend I went looking for more birds, becoming increasingly amazed to discover how many other kinds of wild things lived out there in the real world.

Come summer, bird book and sandwich tucked in a haversack, I bicycled out of the city into new adventures. That was how I discovered Beddington Creek.

It was a valley like those where we hunted pheasants, but close enough to the city that I could get there on my own in an hour or two. On my first visit I found a marsh hawk nest in some buckbrush. Next time I found a pair of western kingbirds sharing a nest tree with a pair of ferruginous hawks. It was poor planning on both parts. Every time the hawks tried to return with another ground squirrel for their hungry chicks, the kingbirds would launch an aerial attack on the hawks. Both pairs of birds must have had a miserable summer. I watched, fascinated.

One thing led to another. I still hunt, fish and watch birds, and now I have kids myself.

But Beddington Creek valley is gone. Calgary overwhelmed it while I wasn't looking.

L ast year I agreed to give a talk on nature and writing to elementary students in three northeast Calgary schools. It was only when I arrived at the first school that I realized my quiet Beddington Creek valley had become city; the school stood right in the middle of it. I saw no hawks or kingbirds.

The students were eager and attentive. I asked how many went fishing or hunting with their parents. A couple hands showed. The rest did not. I asked them questions about nature. The answers were naive, hopeful and obviously based on television shows. Some slides in my talk included scenes from hunting trips. Some of the kids were clearly uneasy with them.

Beddington Creek – its hawks, kingbirds, silver willows and pheasants – is buried under a generic urban cityscape. So too are most of the kids in Calgary, Saskatoon, Edmonton, Vancouver and the other cities that now contain most western Canadians. A friend describes modern Canadians as growing up "orphaned from nature." In the Beddington Creek valley that day, his description seemed doubly apt.

The schools I visited, like many others, have environmental education programs. In spite of excellent learning resources, however, most are taught in artificial settings by teachers having little real knowledge of ecology. Few of the students in those classes have ever had the chance to develop personal bonds with the wild. They learn about ozone holes and atmospheric change and pesticides, as if the environment is simply a mess of problems. Few get to learn what a pheasant track looks like in the snow, or how the sun looks through a swarm of hatching mayflies, or what it feels like to sit on a mountainside glassing for bighorns, talking lazily with an adult who listens.

The most effective environmentalists I have known balanced depth of experience and breadth of knowledge with a deep emotional commitment to places they loved. That's why environmental education should never be just about knowledge. Children are creatures of experience. They need to bond not only to the people but to the places in their lives too. They need to find themselves part of a community of life, not just of human neighbours. Childhood should be about experiencing the dance of life and filling one's heart with that burning ache that comes from being in, and of, wild nature. Later, there will be time enough to learn about environmental problems.

Ultimately, I suspect, the most valuable environmental education comes from bonding to nature while bonding with an adult. Children given experiences that help them understand life, death and the value of wild places will grow into adults who care about nature. They will become the kind of people most likely to give nature, hunting, fishing and wild places a tomorrow.

I fear that there are too few of them.

Recently, Gail and I made a deal with our kids. For each kind of bird, mammal, amphibian or fish that they identified during the year, they would get a dollar to spend on a book. Then we took them hiking, fishing and hunting, and left the rest up to them. It cost a few bucks, but we wanted them to have lots of books anyway. Already they are learning, on their own, to find, recognize and delight in the vast diversity of living things that comprise the West's rich natural heritage.

L ast evening, Katie asked me to take her out to look for animals.

At dusk we stood above an autumn-gold marsh, listening to the clamour of Canada geese as a dozen or so elk, statue-still, stood clustered in the shallow water. A six-point bull splashed through the shallows, stretching out his neck to bugle. Then the whole herd turned suddenly and stampeded across the marsh, through the sedge fringe, into the aspens. The geese vanished into cloud-shadow, and the world stood still and breathless.

I looked at my 9-year-old daughter, standing spell-struck beside me.

I thought of those kids in Calgary.

I wondered why nobody had ever taken them hunting or fishing. I wondered too what it will mean to things like Canada geese, elk and autumn marshes if the next generation grows up without adults who will take them, often, as deep as they can go into the real world beyond the pavement's edge.

৵

Facebook Post

November 5, 2013. Whaleback.

Today while sheltering behind a Douglas fir from the chinook that was howling across my foothills ridge, waiting for the magic hour just before sunset, I noticed a rosy finch feeding in the grass. Just at the same moment, a little pointy-nosed red fox came flying out from behind a tree in a totally futile attempt to catch the finch. I was wearing snow camo, so I squeaked with my mouth and the little guy sneaked up to within a couple metres of me before realizing its mistake. It hung around spying on me for a few more minutes before leaving me to my hunt and getting on with its own. Here's hoping it was more successful.

The End of the Hunt?
Address to the Saskatchewan Wildlife Federation AGM (2006)

I am a hunter.

This is neither apology nor boast. It is simply a fact. I'm glad of it, immensely grateful, in fact – but constantly humbled by the burden of responsibility it imposes upon me.

Many of my most meaningful experiences happened while afield. Almost everything I like about myself goes back, one way or another, to hunting. On the other hand, my most shameful failures were during hunts too – so hunting has contributed to whatever moral maturity I might have attained. I could never have been so successful a biologist, so passionate an environmentalist or so thoughtful a writer had I never ventured into the wild as a predator.

Hunting, in short, permeates every aspect of my being.

I believe that – done well, with skill, ethical restraint and humble respect for the animals whom we hunt and for the nature of the predator-prey relationship – hunting is an honourable part of our culture. I hope I'm never forced to stop. Increasingly, however, I fear that day will come.

What will end hunting will be cold science, hot rhetoric and the continued failure of too many hunters to accept that ethics and ecology must be always central to our understanding of the hunt – not fine-sounding rhetoric applied decoratively to the edges.

Hunters and hunting groups often proclaim that the threats to hunting come from animal rights and anti-hunting groups. Paranoia, perhaps, is more palatable than staring into the mirror and confronting the real problem face to face. We hunters – too often – are our own worst enemies.

This point came home to me most forcibly in 1999, when I watched hunters react to the Ontario government's hasty political decision to stop licensing hunters to kill black bears over bait in spring. Hunters and outfitters indignantly – and correctly – argued that shooting bears over bait barrels causes no harm to bear populations. In fact, they argued, the spring hunt is a good management tool because baiting allows the shooter to examine his or her prey and ensure that it's a mature male.

Cold science was on their side. There was no shortage of hot rhetoric. But they failed to advance the cause of hunting just the opposite, in fact.

Perhaps that was because what they sought to defend was ethically indefensible.

Much of the debate was over orphaned cubs. Animal rights activists say spring hunting leaves newborn bears orphaned. Outfitters' and hunters' groups argue that the spring hunt actually selects for male bears. I was at a bear management workshop the week the decision came down, so I took advantage of the opportunity to consult with several of North

America's leading bear biologists. They told me both sides are right.

Bait shooters kill many more male bears than female – but females die too. Even experts can't consistently tell a male from a female. Mother bears who visit bait barrels frequently hide their newborn cubs first. They do it because baited bears are almost always fully aware of the nearby hunter but simply can't resist the food bait.

That orphans nursing cubs. How many? Nobody knows.

Cold science concerns itself with populations, not individuals. From that point of view, a few cubs matter little if the population continues to thrive. Human compassion would suggest, however, that even one, two or ten orphaned cubs are too many. No hunter would ever argue that leaving nursing bear cubs to starve to death is ethical or right. None would do it purposely – yet some vehemently defend spring bear baiting, which inevitably does just that.

When we hunt, we become predators. In nature, predation involves an implicit ecological compact between predator and prey that ensures that prey have a fair opportunity to escape and predators must exercise skill and craft. That is how predation makes both wolf and deer stronger, elk and cougar cannier, and peregrine and mallard swifter. Predation is nature's way of honing both predator and prey to their finest edge.

If hunting is predation – if at its heart it is an ecological interaction that helps perfect both predator and prey – then it becomes hard to honestly define spring bear baiting as hunting. Baiting doesn't select for woodsmanship, craft, stealth, alertness, fitness or courage in the hunter. Nor does it kill the most vulnerable, inattentive, naive or blundering bears. Bears emerging from their winter dens have a massive energy deficit to make up; they've just burned off a quarter of their body weight. No spring bear can turn down a free meal.

Killing a baited bear is, in fact, a sordid, ugly act that has nothing in common with hunting. It degrades both predator and prey. It looks like hunting, but is a pathetic and shameful facsimile.[2]

In the United States, electors in many states have delivered this message to hunters, hunting groups, and the cold-science agencies who serve those hunters. Spring killing of bears over bait is illegal in California, Colorado, New Mexico and Minnesota, to name only a few of the states where citizen-initiated ballot initiatives to ban unfair chase hunting practices have passed by resounding majorities.

Indignant hunting groups blame the loss of bear baiting on slick ad campaigns by anti-hunting groups, and mass hysteria by an uninformed and biologically naive public. Some suspect a conspiracy to ban all hunting. Their spokesmen fume and

---

2   The use of bait to attract and kill black bears and wolves is legal across most of Alberta. In northern Alberta, bait can be used until mid-June, virtually guaranteeing the starvation of orphaned wolf pups and bear cubs.

rage in front of the media. They forget that we are, after all, a very small minority in a democratic society – and that our tolerance of unethical practices helped produce the ugly images those ad campaigns exploit.

Tom Beck is a talented hunter who pursues deer, antelope and elk each fall with bow and arrow. He's also one of the world's leading experts on black bear biology. For more than 20 years he has worked for the Colorado Division of Wildlife.

"I've been in the business long enough to know that there's an awful lot that's legal that isn't moral, and isn't ethical, and isn't appropriate," he says. Beck's name evokes scorn and anger in some hunting circles because his understanding of bear biology and serious concern for hunting ethics has led him to speak publicly against spring bear hunting.

"You know," he says, "we keep getting mad because we don't like management by citizen initiative or management by the legislature. But when you're unresponsive to what the general public wants, that's what you're going to get. It's like education. What you hear over and over again from the hunters that are upset is: you guys in the division, you gotta go educate the poor stupid public as to what's right. Well, there's no right or wrong: it's all value system – and we happen to have one that's out of step with a whole bunch of folks. These groups don't want to educate; they want to propagandize."

Another American hunter – Aldo Leopold, widely hailed as the father of modern wildlife management – would not have been surprised. In 1949 he wrote: "I have the impression that the … sportsman is puzzled; he doesn't understand what is happening to him … Wildlife administrators are too busy producing something to shoot at than to worry much about the cultural value of the shooting …"

Things have become no simpler in the half century since Leopold published his famous *A Sand County Almanac*, with its eloquent plea for ecological wisdom and ethical restraint. Wild country has shrunk. Off-road vehicles have opened up the hinterland. New technologies enable hunters to find prey by their infrared signatures or by amplified sound. Global positioning systems, pheromone scents, animal calls, laser sights and night vision optics put space-age science into the woods. Bait barrels dot black bear country and "hunting" clubs buy truckloads of rotting vegetables to attract white-tailed deer into rifle range.

Prairie Canada even held a private lottery that paid out big money for trophy heads. The Ultimate Whitetail Challenge turned living animals into poker chips, and hunters into gamblers. Like other perversions of our hunting tradition, it was legal. Legal, however, is not the same as right.

The same anti-nature, exploitative world view that dominates so much of consumer culture has come to permeate hunting culture too. It's only natural that it would, after all; we live in a commercial economy. But hunters used to team up to fight against the cheapening of our hunting heritage – to demand sportsmanship and fair chase in hunting. It was hunting groups, not animal rights groups, who fought successfully in the early 1900s to ban commercial trade in wildlife, outlaw baiting and end the spring hunting of waterfowl and other wildlife.

What a difference a century makes. Today, many hunting groups seem ready to tolerate – or embrace – almost anything a government will legalize. Governments, in turn, have shown a pathetic willingness to legalize almost any practice that a commercial interest – for example, bear hunt outfitters or game farm speculators – will lobby them for. So we drift, ethical anchors dragging, into a future where hunters and hunting look less and less acceptable to society as a whole.

Is there a solution?

I believe there is. It is, however, almost the exact opposite of what the most vocal hunting groups have done to date over issues like the Ontario ban on killing spring black bears. It has four elements:

1. Cease the verbal attacks on animal rights groups. We share with those groups a common love for wild nature. We need to admit that the hunting community has failed to attend to some serious ethical issues. Hunters cheapen and degrade both our prey and ourselves when we use technology or tactics that overpower or bypass the natural defences of our prey. We shouldn't leave it up to animal rights groups to expunge practices – legal or otherwise – that are intrinsically unfair, shallowly competitive or inherently cruel. That once was, and will always be, our duty.

2. Hunters need to set aside the elitist and offensive position that our woes are because of an ignorant, urban, non-hunting public. Instead, we should listen to non-hunters carefully and

with respect. Those animals we are privileged to hunt belong to everyone, if in fact they belong to anyone. Community standards change. Hunting's continued existence depends upon the tolerance of a much larger non-hunting majority. We'd better know what they consider honourable behaviour.

3. Hunters must exorcise the Ted Nugents of the hunting world who fill the media with hot rhetoric and angry images. Marshall McLuhan said, "The media is the message." Yelling into a camera, no matter how lucidly, is simply free advertising for the anti-hunting movement: "See, we told you all hunters are aggressive, hostile rednecks!" Hunters need humble, honest spokespeople who demonstrate that we care deeply about animal welfare, ethics and integrity – about what we can give back to nature, not just about what we can take from it.

4. Most importantly, perhaps, we need to rethink the nature of hunting and our role as hunters. As Tom Beck frequently points out, hunting – cold science's ruling myths notwith-standing – is not the engine that drives wildlife management. It is merely one possible output. Bears and wolves regulate their own numbers without any help from hunters. Pheasants don't need to be shot. Other predators could do as good or better a job on deer or elk numbers, if we were prepared to let them. Using wildlife management arguments to promote hunting simply doesn't stand up to critical scrutiny.

Yet hunting is profoundly important – as part of our culture, and part of our ecology. At its best – but only at its best – it produces insightful ecologists, fiercely dedicated conserva-tionists, deeply connected human beings.

At its best, hunting is ecologically grounded in the eternal compact between predator and prey – an ongoing partnership that brings out the best attributes of both hunter and hunted. At its best, hunting is built upon the fundamental principle of fair chase, whereby the prey always has an advantage over the hunter. And at its best, it is always, unfailingly, grounded in ethical restraint, humble respect and human decency.

At its best, hunting may survive.

At its worst, however, it is both damned, and doomed.

CHAPTER 5

In the Woods

Forgotten Rainbows (1987)

Not far from where I live, a small stream slips out of the forest, bubbles unnoticed through a culvert and slides back into the shadows of an old spruce forest. A few vehicles cross it each day. Few, if any, of the drivers even notice the furtive flicker of water beneath alder foliage.

It is not much of a creek. Even at its widest it is narrow enough to jump over. There's little risk of an unwary fisherman going in over the tops of his hip waders. In fact, there's no reason most fishermen would even give it a second look. There are plenty of rivers and lakes in the area that produce big fish.

All the same, I drop in for a visit now and then. I bring a dozen muddler minnows because I know I am going to leave a few stuck in the alders and spruce overhanging the stream. I flatten the barbs on the hooks with a pair of needle-nosed pliers because I know that I will be releasing quite a few trout. Then I crouch over and force my way into the underbrush to spend a few hours with Alberta's only native rainbow trout.

These rainbows are beautifully marked and scrappy, but rarely more than 14 centimetres long. It is not trophy fishing, by any means, but it is special. In catching those little forest trout, I am continuing an angling tradition that goes back almost a century and a half.

On June 14, 1863, Dr. Walter Cheadle wandered away from his party's camp somewhere near where Edson is now. He "soon captured a small trout of some 2 oz. but could not get another run; the fish was very like an English burn trout, but instead of red spots, it had a red line along each side about 1/8 inch broad; the black spots similar to English variety...."

Fisheries agencies have since introduced Cheadle's English burn trout – which we know as the brown trout – to most parts of western North America. It is now one of the most sought-after fish in the West. The little rainbows, however, live out their lives in muskeg streams and foothills riffles, ignored by all except a few local anglers who like the way the little guys taste when fried up with salt and pepper.

There's a sad irony in the fact that the native Athabasca rainbow trout is both unique and threatened but receives only neglect. Meanwhile, fishermen lavish admiration and management money on introduced exotics that infest the waters of five continents.

When Milton and Cheadle travelled through what is now western Alberta, none of the streams now famous for their rainbow fishing actually held rainbows. The Bow and Crowsnest had bull trout and cutthroats. The Brazeau and North Saskatchewan had only bull trout.

Famous western rainbow trout streams are, almost without exception, artificial creations of modern technology. The famous rainbow and brown trout of Alberta's lower Bow River, for instance, do not belong there naturally. A series of dams control the river's water levels. Its abundant insect life depends on the City of Calgary's continuous supply of treated sewage effluent. Fishing the lower Bow for trophy browns and rainbows is healthy outdoor exercise, but it's no more natural than hunting stocked pheasants in a cultivated grain field.

Through most of the 20th century, government agencies and local fish and game clubs released hatchery-raised trout into just about every accessible body of water in Alberta. Fishermen believed that a trout was a trout, and the more you stocked, the better the fishing would be. Fisheries biologists soon found that stocking trout actually reduces stream fishing quality. By the time they realized that native fish stocks are the ones that thrive best in most streams, the zeal of the early stockers had hopelessly confused any effort to figure out what belonged where.

There was no doubt, however, that the dark little rainbows in the headwaters of the Athabasca River were not the product of some misguided early trout stocker. Milton's journal, written in the days before hatcheries, proved that.

Still, who cares about a trout's pedigree, anyway? Especially considering that the Athabasca rainbow is usually a stunted little thing, barely reaching 20 centimetres in length before dying of old age. They are lively little fighters, admittedly, but hardly a sporting fish considering how easy they are to catch.

Carl Hunt, Alberta's fisheries biologist for the Edson district, disagrees with those sentiments on a couple of counts.

For one thing, he says, the idea that the Athabasca rainbows are a stunted race is just not true. "We took some out of one of the Tri-Creeks streams [a fisheries research area south of Hinton]," he says, "and put them into a little slough in the area where there was all kinds of food available but no hope of any fish surviving the winter."

Four-year-old trout – only 15 centimetres long when placed into the slough – grew to more than 25 centimetres long by the time the biologists netted them again that fall. Hunt concludes that Athabasca rainbows are small simply because the habitat where they naturally occur does not give them the chance to grow large. Most native rainbows live in small headwater streams where food supplies are scant and the growing season may be less than three months.

In any case, he says, "biologists and fishermen alike have come to see fishes as more than just so much aquatic protein."

Each native population of trout has evolved to fit the particular watershed and habitats in which it is found. The Athabasca rainbow is genetically distinct from the west coast rainbows stocked elsewhere in Alberta. It is the only rainbow trout that occurs naturally in waters flowing east from the Rockies, anywhere in North America. Uniquely suited to this place on the Earth, the native Athabasca rainbow has an intrinsic right to exist.

It also has a complex and fascinating ecology that allows it to thrive in small forest streams.

✤

hen I caught my first Athabasca rainbow, I was struck by
how different it looked from the silvery rainbows I was
used to catching in the Maligne River, only a few kilometres
away. The Maligne rainbows are stocked exotics originating
in waters that drain to the Pacific Ocean. The rainbows in my
little stream are dark and narrow, with slaty parr marks and an
intense rainbow stripe along their sides. Their gill plates are a
rich golden brown. Some show faint cutthroat-like markings
under their gills. They look like exactly the kind of trout that
should live in shadowed streams that slip through dark forests
of spruce and pine.

A species is much more than the physical expression of its chromosomes. The Athabasca rainbow is cold water, mossy stream
banks littered with alder leaves and pine needles, flickering
shade, the whine of mosquitos and the vast hush of Alberta's
boreal foothills. The Athabasca rainbow is tiny streams slipping
over clean gravel, losing themselves amid the roots of fallen
spruce, then bubbling out into sunlit pools where mayflies bob
and dance amid the splashy rises of hungry fish. The Athabasca
rainbow is stunted, no matter what Carl Hunt may say about
its potential to grow large, because habitat – at least as much
as genes – is what ultimately gives definition to real creatures.

Unfortunately, few fishermen take the time to reflect on what
a trout really is, or on what values fishermen truly derive from
fishing. Without reflection, it becomes too easy to reduce
angling to a matter of catching more, and bigger, fish than the

next person. By those standards, the Athabasca rainbow will never stack up very well.

Biologist George Sterling found that a female rainbow produces only about 300 eggs each year in streams he studied south of Hinton. Even with good survival, very few fish hatch each year to replace the ones lost to fishing. A major flood can wipe out an entire generation.

Nor does it take much fishing pressure to knock back the populations of so unproductive a fish. Fishing pressure comes with access, and the headwater streams of the McLeod, Athabasca, Wildhay and Berland have been opened up at an incredible rate during the last two decades. Coal exploration and development, oil and gas exploration and forestry operations have produced a maze of roads and cutlines. Few streams are free from fishing pressure.

"On unfished streams," says Carl Hunt, "we've found up to 1,200 native rainbows per kilometre of stream. On most of the angled streams around Edson there's only two to three hundred per kilometre."

Fortunately for the Athabasca rainbow, a female can mature and produce eggs when she is barely 14 centimetres long. Since few fishermen would keep a trout that small, even in the most heavily fished streams a few spawners usually make it through each season to deposit their sparse load of eggs the next spring. Provincial regulation changes in 1987 improved prospects for the little natives, since anglers now have to release all trout less than 17.75 centimetres in length. A native rainbow of that size is likely to be six years or older, and to have spawned three or four times.

The biggest threat to the native rainbows of the Athabasca River watershed, since the new regulations came into effect, is habitat loss. The small streams where the rainbows spawn are fragile environments. Old forests and undisturbed ground-cover capture snowmelt and rainwater and release them gradually to the streams. Spring floods shift and re-deposit the clean gravels at the tails of pools. In each stream there is an annual equilibrium to which the fish populations have adapted.

One new road can change that. In 1974 Champion Forest Products built a new logging road near Deerlick Creek, one of the Tri-Creeks research streams. Up to 18 times more silt and clay flushed into the stream during rainstorms after the company built the road.

All streams turn brown during the spring runoff, but spring floods flush most of the silt and clay on down the stream or out onto the floodplain. When road cuts enable each summer rainstorm to wash raw sediments into the stream, however, the reduced summer flow is not strong enough to wash them away. Instead, silt and clay clog the fine gravel where trout eggs or fry develop, smothering the young fish.

Resource development brings roads. In the small corner of the world where Athabasca rainbows live, this means coal mining, logging and petroleum exploration. Most of the land east of

Jasper National Park is committed to coal mining or wood pulp production.

Coal strip mines have operated in the headwaters of the McLeod River since the early 20th century. Sprawling open-pit mines have eradicated important rainbow trout streams and periodically dump catastrophic amounts of sediment into downstream reaches.

Logging companies occupy the rest of the landscape. In the late 1970s the Alberta government began actively promoting logging of the foothills around Hinton and Edson. A decade later, the government approved a huge pulp mill expansion. Logging requires a network of roads and landings, each feeding raw sediment into the once-clean streams where the native rainbows spawn. Each road also brings more fishermen to catch the adults.

The bad news does not stop there either. Logging removes forests that formerly released water gradually into the trout streams. As forest cover disappears, the total water yield increases, but it also comes more frequently as big floods.

After trout spawn in late spring, the big June or July floods spilling off the clearcut landscape can wash away the spawning gravels and destroy the whole year's trout production. Major floods flushed George Sterling's research streams in 1969 and 1980. Both times, an entire generation of trout was destroyed. As floods become more frequent in the wake of logging, successful spawning seasons become rarer and rarer.

ოჯ

I t's a grim picture. Logging and coal mining buy more groceries than choosing to leave the wilds alone. The little forest trout may be well on their way to becoming victims – with the caribou and the grizzly – of a resource-based economy that creates short-term wealth out of long-term, massive landscape degradation.

Hope, however, might come from the ecology of the fish themselves. "One of the unique things about these rainbows," explains Carl Hunt, "is that they seem to thrive in real head-water, marginal habitats. In some of the places where we've found them overwintering, the riffles freeze right to the stream bed each winter and the trout are surviving in the little bits of water at the bottoms of a few deep pools."

Sedimentation and flooding inevitably grow worse farther downstream. Perhaps a decade or two hence, if the streams that feed the upper Athabasca River become permanently disrupted by industrial forestry and mineral extraction, the dark little natives will still survive where headwater streams bubble out of muskegs before dropping to the gullied clearcuts below.

On the other hand, there may still be time to rein in the hasty industrialization of Alberta's boreal foothills. We could still choose to protect what healthy trout habitat remains, and to begin restoring that which we have damaged. If our remaining native fish populations are worth saving, then resource management should mean more than just dividing the spoils.

A few unlogged, unroaded watersheds seem a small sacrifice to make, to maintain the dark native trout of the northern foothill forests.

The stream where I visit the little rainbows each summer is in a national park. Perhaps the fact that a park protects this one native rainbow stream is enough cause for hope.[3] I don't think so. A national park, after all, is a kind of museum. What sort of society would insist that things of subtle value and beauty should only be found in museums?

The neglected rainbows of the northern foothills have thrived amid the forest shadows for millennia. They will continue to persist only if we – who came so recently and with such sudden impact – choose to protect the clear streams and ancient forests in which they dwell.

---

3 Being in a national park didn't help. Native Athabasca rainbow are now extirpated from this stream (Devona Creek). Non-native eastern brook trout have replaced them.

༈

Facebook Post

October 30, 2015. Ghost River.

There are times when you don't want a stranger around. Like when that phone call you've been dreading comes in from the diagnostic lab, or you see a police officer on your step with hat in hand and a stern, pale face. Loved ones, yes; strangers, no. These moments are too personal and too hard to share with someone you don't know.

So I felt awkward and off-balance today when Dave and I rode over the ridge into the little stream basin parallel to Lesueur Creek and he turned in his saddle to look up the hill, looking sucker-punched.

"They've already logged it," he said in a voice struggling with denial and shock. "I thought there was still time. I mean, they haven't even finished the road."

Lodgepole pines lay in stacked piles, waiting to be trimmed. White stumps showed through the October grasses. Somewhere up ahead, I could hear the straining sound of an engine; they were at work even now, carving Dave's quiet paradise into clearcuts.

"It's too late," he said. If I'd known him better, the pain in the voice might have made me put my arm around his shoulders. Instead, I wished I hadn't even gotten out of bed this morning. I shouldn't be here, witness to a stranger's trauma.

I had only met Dave that morning. A friend had suggested to him and his wife, Jacquie, that they might want to show me the areas near their ranch that Spray Lake Sawmills was planning to clearcut. They were at their wits' end; they had only learned of the cutting plans the Wednesday before. Jacquie called me up and said Dave would like to take me for a ride, show me around a bit. Maybe I could do something; I knew some people.

So I met them this morning. It was one of

those perfect, calm October days in the Alberta foothills when nothing can possibly go wrong in the world. Their horse ranch, a couple of kilometres from the Ghost River, was established by Dave's parents back in 1934. They have two teenaged kids; a third generation. They run trail rides and back-country trips and it's a good business; a sustainable one that leaves little mark on the land and has proven compatible with protecting wildlife, watershed values and vegetation.

But it may soon be over. Spray Lake Sawmills seems to have gone crazy; in a frenzied assault on the Ghost watershed, the company has taken a 20-year logging plan – one that was designed to spread out the logging over two decades so as to minimize damage to the watershed – and decided to implement it over two years. The Alberta Forest Service has signed off on it.

A pall of dust stirred up by passing logging trucks hangs over the valley all day long. This is liquidation logging – the polar opposite of the sustainable harvest the company's rhetoric insists it does. From the road, the forest looks intact. Pop over a hill, and clearcuts stretch for kilometres into the headwaters. Ribbons in the forest mark the cuts that are coming. Soon.

And now they have come for the trees that carpet the slopes where Dave takes his clients for full-day horse excursions. The company representative called him last Wednesday to say they were starting to build a new road back into Lesueur Creek. "But you don't operate up that way, right?"

Five days later the bulldozers arrived. Still, Dave and Jacquie thought there might be time to save their secret valley. It would take a while to build the road, right?

We found the slashed opening where the road will go; in fact, we watched a track-hoe carving its way across a sidehill as it extended the road up the valley, cutting into the water table; heading for the springs Dave had told me about. But the valley was already logged.

"I can't believe it," said Dave. "They sent the loggers out ahead."

I believe it. The company is doing what aggressive logging companies have done many times in the past. Get the equipment in as fast as you can and cut as many trees as possible before anyone can mobilize any opposition. It can't ever be saved once you've got it scarred up with roads and clearcuts. Better to apologize after than seek consent in advance.

The headwaters of the Bow and Oldman rivers, where Spray Lake Sawmills operates, produce barely 1.5 per cent of Alberta's annual allowable cut of timber. But they produce more than 90 per cent of Canada's prairie water supplies. And massive, aggressive clearcutting diminishes summer water supplies while increasing flooding. There are going to be some big floods coming out of the Ghost in the next few years.

Dave and Jacquie and their kids might have to come out of the Ghost too. Next winter, Spray Lake plans to cut the entire slope across from their ranch, taking out their scenery and their half-day riding trails. Tourists don't pay good money to ride through eroding clearcuts. Small, sustainable businesses don't seem to matter when big, watershed-wrecking companies are in a hurry.

We turned back. The logging road had torn through a barbed wire fence and tangled it across the horse trail as well as creating a

metre-tall cutbank the horses couldn't nego-
tiate. We couldn't have continued if we'd had
the heart to. Dave clearly didn't. It was less
personal for me; I just felt angry.

Two fully loaded logging trucks chugged by
as we loaded the horses back into the trailer.
Dave kept muttering, "I can't believe it."

I didn't hang around. There are times when
strangers aren't needed in the family home.
Times of loss and grieving.

The Smell of Jobs (1988)

The day is almost warm for mid-January, the temperature hovering near freezing, but everyone knows a blizzard is coming. Here in the Rocky Mountains community of Jasper, few people take weather forecasts seriously. When the wind brings a sour pulp mill stink into the national park town's streets and alleys, however, everyone knows that an Arctic storm is bellying up the Athabasca valley from the Berland country.

A hundred kilometres north of Jasper, the Athabasca River escapes the last of the Rocky Mountain Front Ranges to begin the second leg of its 3200-kilometre journey to the Arctic Ocean. In doing so, it leaves Jasper National Park and ceases to be a Heritage River. Once a river arrives in provincial lands, the Alberta government puts it to work. It is available for whatever industrial purposes the Alberta Ministry of Environment will permit. The ministry takes a pragmatic view of rivers: it calls them water resources, not ecosystems.

At Hinton, a few kilometres downstream from the national park boundary, a pulp mill belches out a double load of pollution. The bitter wind that drives the first snow pellets up-valley toward the mountain wall catches plumes of sulphurous steam from the mill's twin stacks. Below, tea-coloured effluent pours into the Athabasca, discolouring it and filling the air with a sewage odour.

The Champion Forest Products[4] kraft pulp mill is the largest single-point source of pollution on the Athabasca River. So much waste flushes into the river that cancer-causing chemicals contaminate river life for hundreds of kilometres downstream. The government's premise for licensing so much pollution is that several downstream tributaries swell the already large Athabasca and help dilute Champion's lignin compounds, chlorine, dioxins and other pollutants.

Ninety-six kilometres downstream, the Berland enters the Athabasca from the north. A Canoe Alberta reach report says: "On arrival at the Berland River confluence, the contrast between the clear Berland and the polluted Athabasca is evident. Along the whole tour, the river water is not considered drinkable...." Upstream from the confluence, however, the Berland is sweet and clear.

The Berland and its tributaries – the Wildhay River; Pinto and Hightower creeks – drain a vast area of rolling, forested foothills and muskeg plateaus north of the Athabasca River. Their gravelled runs and quiet meanders support populations of native Athabasca rainbow trout, some of Canada's most southerly Arctic grayling and huge bull trout.

Few who fish the Berland and its tributaries care to hike in from the road. In the Hinton area, motorized off-highway vehicles are generally considered more prestigious than walking boots. If you work at the Champion Forest Products mill or on a cutting crew, chances are that you can afford to

---

4 Now Hinton Forest Products, a division of West Fraser Mills.

buy an off-highway cycle or quad. Oil and gas exploration cutlines and new logging roads penetrate the muskegs and sidehills north of the Athabasca. There is always somebody who can give you a tip on how to get in a little farther back than you thought you could.

Nonetheless, the country is still pretty remote. Grizzlies roam the floodplains. Deer, moose and elk range the aspen sidehills and alluvial meadows. In winter small bands of woodland caribou – like the grayling, a northern species occurring only this far south in Alberta's foothills – forage in the old spruce and pine forests for lichens.

Perhaps the most unique animal population in the area is a herd of mountain goats. More than a hundred kilometres from the nearest mountain, a small band frequents the forest edges along steep-walled reaches of Pinto and Hightower creeks. If the country were less remote, those goats would probably have vanished long ago, easy victims of poachers.

The Champion pulp mill is only an occasional irritation, when the wind is from the south, to the goats bedded on the cutbanks overlooking Pinto Creek, or the caribou quietly foraging in the snow-muffled forest along the Berland. Life goes on pretty much as it always has in the Berland country.

For now. Change, as well as hydrogen sulphide, is in the wind.

I stop at a service station fronting on Highway 16 in Hinton. A woman runs my credit card through her machine and hands me the slip to sign. The pulp mill smell is on everything.

"Sure can smell Champion today," I say.

She sniffs and shrugs. "We call that the smell of jobs."

The line is not original, but I smile to be polite. It is true, after all. Champion employs several hundred people at its mill and in the bush. Hinton is typical of many Canadian towns. Its counterparts can be found from Tumbler Ridge to Kenora, and from Port Alberni to Baie Verte: resource industry towns dependent on the cyclical demand for their commodities and sullenly protective of the companies whose payrolls sustain them. In Hinton, the commodities are coal and timber.

The town council tries to promote tourism too. It hasn't caught on – tourists don't seem to like the smell of jobs.

Outside, the sun has disappeared into haze. The Rockies lie silhouetted against a yellow sky. Traffic is heavy on the Yellowhead. Truck drivers, impatient with the 60-kilometres-per-hour speed limit through town, use their engine retarder brakes to revenge themselves on the residents. Motel, restaurant, service station and equipment dealer signs glare along the highway strip. A pickup truck cuts me off and its young male occupant gives me the finger. I don't know why.

I'm in town to spend the evening at the Legion Hall. Champion Forest Products has organized a public meeting to release a draft environmental impact assessment (EIA) on its planned mill expansion. The company wants to double its mill capacity to take advantage of the growing demand for bleached kraft pulp. Paper companies use bleached kraft pulp to produce high-quality paper for printing books like this one.

More than 50 people in the Legion meeting room sit facing a table full of Champion representatives. The meeting is orderly and polite. Bill Gunning, the company's technical superintendent, explains the pulping process in great detail and describes the new pollution controls Champion will install.

The crowd, however, is restive. They ask a few questions about pollution almost as if they feel obliged to do so, but this is obviously not what they came for. Some seem irritated when they learn that the company's statistics – which imply pollution levels will drop once the new mill's modern technology is up and running – disguise the truth by focusing on relative levels in effluent rather than the absolute quantity released in the much greater flow of effluent. The expanded mill will actually produce more pollution. Despite some exasperated muttering, interest in the mill is clearly slack. These folks are used to the smell of jobs.

Only when the floor is opened to questions does it become apparent what is on people's minds. To feed the expanded mill, Champion has to cut more wood. The company is negotiating an expanded harvest area, and has surveyed two roads into the area they have in mind.

They already control 8000 square kilometres. They want 3000 more.

The map on the display panels shows the existing harvest area and the newly surveyed routes. One cuts through caribou winter range. The other bypasses the Pinto Creek goat herd. Both extend well north of the Berland.

The president of the Alberta Fish and Game Association has made the long trip out from Edmonton. A hunter in the crowd asks if Champion is willing to keep a gate on the new roads since only aggressive access control will protect caribou, goats and other game from over-hunting, poaching and legal harvest by indigenous people under their treaty rights. The company representatives say that the government will not allow them to gate the roads.

A representative of the Alberta Wilderness Association stands up and formally requests that the company enlarge the EIA to include the forestry operations, rather than just the mill expansion. He gets told no. Another member argues for total protection of caribou winter range from the chainsaws. He gets even less encouragement and merely succeeds in setting off a company forester on a long sermon about how cutting old forests guards against pine beetles. Most of the old forests are spruce.

Sitting quietly beside the wilderness advocates and fish and game contingent, several men look out of place in so formal a setting. One, a hawkish-looking individual with long black hair and a heavy wool jacket, stands and introduces himself as a fur trapper. He looks like he wishes he were somewhere else; most of us feel that way by now.

"The problem is," he says, "you're after mature timber, and we need mature timber. We try to manage our harvest just like you do: on a sustained yield basis. The seed areas we leave are the old timber, where the older martens live and breed. The animals we trap in the younger stuff are the surplus, the ones that get pushed out of the old forest. But you're telling us that you cut the old stuff first."

This time, the Champion representatives bend a little. They agree to meet separately, later, with members of the Alberta Trappers Association to discuss how to avoid conflict. However, one points out, "We have two fundamental principles we operate by. One is that you balance the haul distance from year to year. The other is that you cut the old growth first."

The meeting runs out of steam quickly. Outside it is nearly dark. Everyone wants to go home. An air of palpable cynicism has settled among the ranks of the wilderness contingent. They have been here before.

It has become apparent, in the course of the evening, that Champion is interested in efficient, industrial timber production. They are willing to discuss any wildlife species that can adapt to early-successional vegetation. Anyone concerned about old-growth forest, caribou, fur-bearers or other values unlikely to survive in a landscape dedicated to wood fibre production must talk to the government departments that regulate the forest industry. They won't listen either.

Driving home, it occurs to me that most of those present at the meeting had at least one piece of common ground no matter how divergent their views. All discussed the Berland in terms of its resources. The argument was over who would get how much of the pie. Nobody talked about what kind of pie they were divvying up, but everyone wanted as big a share as possible.

To the north of my little ribbon of a highway, in the dark beyond the hills, the Berland is chattering quietly to itself, just as it has always done. In its cold backwaters, schools of grayling are picking mayfly nymphs from the limestone cobbles. Perhaps wolves are howling at the edge of a floodplain meadow. If so, the elk and deer will be listening, stilled for a moment by the reminder that their deaths wait somewhere beyond the shadows.

Live hard, you guys. You're resources. Your time is going to come.

February 1988. Champion has already cut the new roads. The government has approved the pulp mill expansion. Now a Japanese firm has announced plans for a huge new pulp mill at Peace River, to the north. Everyone is excited. It all means more investment, more jobs; more timber commitments.

The pie has been divided. As usual, the largest piece went to those who created the most new jobs – especially smelly ones. Next year the new roads will bring rifles deeper into caribou winter range. Soon the trees will start to fall.

"There wasn't even a road to Grande Cache 20 years ago," the Metis trapper told me after last summer's public meeting. "Now those damn quads and dirt bikes are everywhere in there."

I guess he'll need one of those new jobs, soon.

Another winter storm is on its way; I can smell Hinton this morning from my Jasper backyard.

The smell takes me back to the first time I floated the Wildhay, one of the Berland's chief tributaries, by canoe. It was nine years ago. There were no trikes then. There were still a lot of native rainbows and grayling to be caught. I remember sitting up one evening to watch the water ripple quietly by in the shadows beyond the fire. A coyote shrilled in a meadow down the river. The smell of Hinton's pulp mill was in my nostrils again that night, as it no doubt was in his.

That was the smell of jobs. I didn't want to believe, at the time, that it might be the smell of the future. But we all belong to a culture where we grew up believing that wealth and abundance are honourable rewards for those who exploit the fruits of the frontier. New roads are a way of life in Alberta. Progress is a religion. Progress means new jobs.

There are still some wild and beautiful places in the Berland country. There are trout that have never fled from an angler, and caribou that have never dodged a bullet. There is still a bit of the original wilderness left.

Live hard you guys. We're creating jobs, and jobs vote. You don't. And while 50 people attended the public meeting where we argued over how to divvy you up, nobody even thought of asking where we got the right to do it.

The Flower of Fishes (1988)

The Smoky River drops from its sources in the glaciers of the Continental Divide, from one wild rapid to another. It emerges at length from its wilderness headwaters as a broad, grey waterway winding along the bottom of a deep valley incised into the agricultural plain of Alberta's Peace River country.

For the most part its tributaries are smaller versions of the Smoky. They are mountain-bred and volatile, turning brown and thunderous after each summer freshet, filling the valleys with the roar and crash of hurrying water. Their cold temperatures and silt-clouded water combine with dramatic flow fluctuations to keep their fisheries unproductive. Bull trout, whitefish and some Arctic grayling dwell there but few anglers pursue them.

The Little Smoky, however, is different. A humble stream, fed by muskeg springs, it meanders from one long pool to another through a wilderness of spruce and tamarack, caribou and wolves. Since it arises in a heavily forested watershed rather than the high mountains, it floods less frequently and violently than other tributaries. Its stream bed is more stable and its fishery far more productive than other nearby streams.

Even with four-wheel drive an angler can only drive to within five kilometres of its upper reaches. Its quiet chatter goes unheard by human ears most days. Its weed beds and gravel runs shelter grayling, bull trout and whitefish that have never tasted the sting of an angler's hook. It is a quiet river in a quiet valley, unnoticed and rarely visited.

It has only two real claims to fame: it is one of the last intact watersheds left in the Alberta foothills, and it is one of the finest Arctic grayling streams in Canada.

The province's regional fisheries biologist, Carl Hunt, has recorded a catch rate of six to ten grayling per angler hour on the Little Smoky. "We have a set of standards that we use to judge the productivity of different fisheries," he says. "For a stocked trout lake, for example, we expect about 0.5 trout per angler hour. For perch, it goes up to 0.7 per angler hour. Carson Lake, one of our best rainbow trout lakes, produces between one and two fish per angler hour. So you can see where the Little Smoky stands."

Darryl Smith, a Valleyview, Alberta, angler, is a zone director for the Alberta Fish and Game Association. Smith says that the river "contains the finest Arctic Grayling fishing in Alberta, and it would be difficult to find finer fishing anywhere in North America."

Smith recently submitted a management proposal to Alberta's Department of Forestry, Lands and Wildlife. It contained recommendations aimed at perpetuating this threatened wilderness fishery.

"The western Athabasca River watershed is the most southerly distribution of Arctic Grayling in Canada," he points out. "The watershed had good access developed in the 1960s and 1970s and grayling populations are a fraction of their former levels. Many people recall the glory days of the '50s and '60s when catches of 100 fish or more were common. Lying immediately north of the Athabasca is the Little Smoky River watershed which remains the farthest south quality grayling fishery in North America."

In 1988 the Alberta government, caught up in the enthusiasm that attends each boom cycle in the pulp and paper industry, approved several new pulp mills in the western part of the province. To provide timber for the new mills, they have put the entire Little Smoky watershed on the block. As part of this heavily subsidized new forestry development, the government has already begun cutting new, high-quality roads into the area. Oil and gas exploration companies, meanwhile, continue to punch cutlines down to the river's edge. Many hunters and fishermen use the seismic lines to travel deeper into the wilds on off-highway vehicles.

For the first time in Alberta's history, however, fishery managers took steps to preserve a high-quality fishery before problems developed. Historically, the regulations remained generous until well after the fishery had begun to fall apart.

Effective in 1989, the upper Little Smoky River was designated a catch-and-release fishery – the first such designation aimed at conserving Arctic grayling in Canada. Darryl Smith's initiative may be paying off.

Early in 1988, Carl Hunt told me he and his technicians were planning a trip to the Little Smoky. They needed accurate population numbers so that Carl would be able to evaluate the success of the new regulations. He also needed to know how widely the grayling travel within the stream. When Carl told me that in order to tag the fish they had to angle for them with fly rods, I asked him if he needed any help. Who could resist helping the cause of science under those circumstances?

On August 9, 1988, I met Carl Hunt and Rudy Hawryluk at Edson, halfway between Edmonton and Jasper. Their four wheel drive truck, with a trailer containing two off-highway vehicles, was waiting in front of the Fish and Wildlife office when I arrived.

We headed north into the forested foothills that stretch along the northern flank of the Rockies and merge to the north and east with the vast forests of northern Canada. The forest was endless, the sky was endless, and great dark thunderstorms dragged grey sheets across the hills. The rainstorms occasionally intersected with our route, turning stretches of the gravel road into slime that threatened to swallow my little station wagon.

Three and a half hours out of Edson my car was caked with mud and I was growing a tad weary of oil development roads and rain. At the Berland Fire Tower Road, Carl and Rudy stopped and Carl walked back to me.

"The road gets bad from here in," he said. This was news to me. I thought the road had been bad for the last three hours. "You'd better leave your car here and come the rest of the way in the 4X4."

We ground and jolted our way along a summer seismic line for another 15 kilometres. Finally, we spotted a wall tent on the skyline. The rest of Carl's crew had started a day earlier and pitched camp where we would not miss it – right in the middle of the road. The camp was deserted.

It was six in the evening. At this latitude, that meant it wouldn't get dark for another four hours. We decided to head down to the river rather than wait for the others to get back.

The camp was right on the drainage divide between the Berland and Little Smoky rivers. As we set out for the river, I looked out on a sight that has become rare in most of Canada and the United States: an unbroken sea of old-growth timber. Huge spruce and balsam fir grow on the better-drained slopes, with understories of alder, cow parsnip and horsetail. On more gentle slopes the big timber gives way to muskeg – sphagnum bogs with lichen-draped tamaracks and black spruce. Moose and caribou feed and shelter in the muskeg and share the floodplain meadows with grizzly bears, elk and mule deer.

We trundled down a grown-over gas well road on the OHVs

and wound our way through a kilometre of muskeg. As we drew near the river, the muskeg gave way to willow tangles and meadows of tall grass. At length we emerged in a clearing among several huge spruce. The gentle chatter of running water rose to meet us.

The Little Smoky was quieter than I had imagined. We stopped beside a long pool. It was shallow and weedy, punctuated with strips of clear water the colour of weak tea. Rising fish dimpled the surface.

The others had tagging gear to prepare, so I rigged my rod and tied on a black ant. At my second cast, a fish jumped clear out of the water and intersected solidly with the hook.

It jumped twice and fought with short, powerful runs. As I recovered line, I caught my first sight of the fish. Its huge dorsal fin was rimmed with a band of turquoise and covered with a scattering of red spots. Its body had a purple tinge and its pectoral fins were tiger-striped in black and white. Fins erect, quivering with vivid life, it dashed for the bottom in brief flurries, then jumped again at my feet. I lifted it gently from the water and shook it off the hook into Carl's holding net.

For 15 minutes we caught one grayling after another. I had never seen fishing like it before; the fish ranged in size up to 35 centimetres and took dry flies with gusto. No matter how many we caught in a pool, the others seemed no less willing to rise. At one point, a fish took Rudy's lure as it trailed in the water right beside him.

Once the net was full, Rudy and Carl measured and tagged the occupants. Each tag was a short fluorescent orange tube with a number on it. As the biologists released each fish, it would ease down to the river bed to sulk briefly, sometimes right beside our feet.

"The fish of the future," I said.

Carl looked puzzled.

I pointed at two grayling resting beside him, orange tags trailing behind their dorsal fin. "Built-in strike indicators," I said. He grimaced.

It felt wrong to be attaching plastic tags to wild fish in so remote and wild a setting. We all knew, however, that little of value survives untouched for long in 20th-century North America. The road crews were already at work. The future was on its way to the Little Smoky. I hoped that the efforts of Carl and his crew – and of committed individuals like Darryl Smith – would shape a different future for this river than what has already befallen so many other grayling fisheries.

The Arctic grayling represents a strange dichotomy of values among the angling fraternity. We both revere and squander it.

Linnaeus, who made his life's work the naming of every living thing he could get his hands on dead examples of, called the grayling *Thymallus thymallus*. The Latin name refers to the suggestion of thyme in a freshly caught grayling's characteristic odour. Many great angling writers have spoken of the fish with respect. In fact, the first reference to the artificial fly in writing was by the Roman rhetorician Aelian, concerning the grayling. St. Ambrose, the bishop of Milan in fourth-century Italy, described the grayling as "the flower of fishes." Roderick Haig-Brown called it "Poisson Bleu" for its translucent mix of purples, blues and reds. He also called it the standard-bearer, or *Thymallus signifer*, preferring this scientific name for a fish whose huge, elegantly shaped dorsal fin is so much a part of its beauty.

In spite of its renown and respect as a creature of subtle beauty that rises readily to the dry fly, fights nobly and occupies the finest of wilderness streams, humans have nonetheless exploited and abused the grayling during the last two centuries. Over much of its original range, the grayling is now extirpated.

The famous Au Sable River was only one of several Michigan streams that supported large grayling populations during the frontier era. In a privately published book on Michigan's fish, Harold Smedley described how fishermen would mine the spawning runs, filling "the box of a common lumber wagon full of fish, not just one load but half a dozen each spring for several successive years. All sizes were taken; the larger were kept, the fingerlings thrown on the bank to rot."

The Michigan grayling Smedley described is extinct. Those that survived the fish hogs of the frontier died out when lumberjacks and their great log drives ruined their rivers.

Grayling were also native to the headwaters of the Missouri River. Montana grayling now persist only in the headwaters of the Big Hole River.

In Canada, many grayling fisheries declined over the past century because of a combination of too much access and too little restraint among anglers. Grayling are fish of the fron-tier, and meat-hunting is a time-honoured frontier tradition. Grayling take flies, spinners and bait enthusiastically; as a result they are quickly fished out.

Carl explained that grayling reach sexual maturity only after reaching 26 centimetres in length. Consequently, many see the bottom of a frying pan before they see their first spawning season. Many anglers keep and kill fish as small as 15 or 20 centimetres long. In the first real attempt to conserve gray-ling populations in increasingly accessible Alberta streams, the provincial government imposed a 30-centimetre minimum size restriction in 1986. Catch-and-release for the Little Smoky represents a further step, aimed not only at maintaining the fishery but at protecting its trophy quality.

Darryl Smith feels that the government should take another step to show the Little Smoky the respect so rare a river deserves. The Alberta Wilderness Association recently took up his proposal to set aside the entire upper watershed of the river as a protected wilderness. Alberta has set aside no large wilderness areas in the foothills or boreal regions. Protecting the Little Smoky from roads and machinery would do more than preserve grayling habitat. It would assure future anglers of the opportunity to rediscover the stillness and wildness of the original north.

Darryl Smith considers the Little Smoky to be unique because of both "the high density and record size of the fish in the population. Fish exceeding 50 centimetres (19 inches) are taken each year and it is probable that some of these would be new provincial records if they were officially registered."

Of the 60 or 70 grayling I released, none was more than 40 centimetres long. The following day we fished for several hours, wandering upstream from pool to pool, catching, tagging and releasing fish after fish. Besides grayling we caught mountain whitefish and bull trout, both native species. No one has ever introduced exotics into the Little Smoky watershed – yet another feature that makes this river a rarity among North American watersheds.

At one pool I stopped to study the tracks of deer, elk and wolf on a point bar. The cries of an osprey caught my attention, and I looked up to see it diving repeatedly at a bald eagle. Both species are common along the river, as are mergansers, kingfishers, river otters and other fish-eaters. The high density of grayling sustains an ecosystem more similar to what one might expect to find along a coastal salmon stream than a boreal river.

The grayling fed all day, although the fishing occasionally tapered off after we had taken several fish from a pool. They rested on the bottom of the pools rather than hanging in the water column like feeding trout. Rising for a dry fly, they had to race to the surface before the fly drifted away. The result was quick rolling rises that often carried the grayling right out of the water – spectacular fishing. Immediately upon being hooked, they would make a downstream run; upstream fishing was an exercise in frantic stripping and missed strikes.

The two crews tagged well more than 150 Arctic grayling during my brief stay. After chugging back up the cutline to camp on the second day, it was time for me to leave. When I arrived at my station wagon, I felt like I was awakening from a dream. I shook hands with Carl, got into the car and drove off, re-entering the 20th century from a valley that time seems to have forgotten.

Behind me, night was pooling beneath the ancient forests of the Little Smoky watershed. In shallow pools where bats flickered overhead and water crowfoot flowers winked back, the grayling were no doubt dimpling the surface and sipping mayfly nymphs from the gravel. Perhaps a wolf was lapping from the river or standing on a gravel bar, testing the wind for the rumour of caribou or moose in the nearby muskeg.

I was leaving the Little Smoky's hidden wilderness and schools of delicate grayling behind. I had glimpsed, too briefly, the kind of wilderness fishing that, in far too many places, resides only in the past.

I will be back. When I return, I hope sincerely to find the Little Smoky unchanged, its tea-coloured water still slipping over clear gravel riffles to pause in weedy eddies or darken in deep, clear pools where schools of grayling eye the surface, waiting for a passing fly. I hope I will be able again to stand beside the river and hear only water-chatter and wind, and the long slow silence of the living wild. I believe I will.

Grey Ghosts (1991)

In June 1938, Henry Stelfox saw his first woodland caribou near the headwaters of western Alberta's Clearwater River.

"I approached to within sixty yards of them," he wrote later. "They were not afraid, they stood facing me, as if to enquire, 'Well, what do you want?' Two of these caribou were magnificent specimens."

Caribou no longer live in the high country where Stelfox saw them. The Alberta government built the Forestry Trunk Road (now Highway 40) in the 1950s to make it easier for resource companies to exploit the timber, gas and other resources of Alberta's foothills region. The caribou soon succumbed to over-hunting and habitat loss.

Stelfox, a volunteer Alberta game warden during the early 20th century, reported that caribou also ranged the Bighorn Mountains north of the Blackstone River, the headwaters of Brown and Chungo creeks, and the Coalspur area.

Like the caribou of the upper Clearwater River watershed, all those herds are gone.

Today only a few small bands survive, all north of the

Athabasca River. Alberta's woodland caribou population has dropped from as many as 8,000 in 1966 to fewer than 2,000 today. In fact, says Dianne Pachal, a conservation biologist with the Alberta Wilderness Association, the province's once-abundant woodland caribou may soon vanish altogether.

Caribou are wilderness animals. In a continent that passed from wilderness to post-industrial civilization in barely a century, caribou have consistently come out the losers. Woodland caribou no longer occupy their former ranges in Maine, New Hampshire, Vermont, Michigan, Minnesota, New Brunswick, Nova Scotia, Prince Edward Island and southern Ontario.

"The range of the woodland caribou has decreased considerably since the 1800s," says biologist Frank Miller of the Canadian Wildlife Service, "probably due to the destruction of climax forests and over-hunting." Parasites carried by white-tailed deer in some areas can be lethal to caribou, too. Deer invade caribou range as logging companies convert mature forests to second-growth.

So severely did caribou numbers drop in Alberta in the 1970s that the Alberta Fish and Game Association – a hunters' and anglers' club – asked the provincial government to cancel caribou hunting seasons north and east of Jasper National Park.

In 1981, the government closed the season. The decline continued. The following year, the provincial government officially designated caribou a "threatened species" – the first such designation in Alberta.

Closing the hunting season did little to halt the decline of caribou numbers, because hunting was not the major problem. Just like everywhere else that caribou have vanished, habitat loss was – and still is – the biggest problem facing the grey ghosts of the north woods.

North and east of Jasper National Park, industrial activity has increased dramatically since the 1950s. A major railroad and highway transect caribou migration routes and wintering areas. Oil and gas exploration cutlines crisscross the landscape, like jackstraws scattered through the forested foothills. Logging roads and clearcuts are now spreading across the last forested wildlands.

Jan Edmonds has spent most of the past decade following radio-collared caribou through the area's muskegs and mountains, sampling feeding sites. She has measured lichen growth rates, autopsied dead caribou and interviewed hunters, trappers and others who share the forested wilds with the elusive creatures. Her studies paint a bleak picture.

Edmonds found that caribou need old, unbroken forest. Slow-growing lichens typically festoon the branches of the ancient spruce and pine trees; other lichens cover the forest floor. These lichens are vital to caribou survival. Loggers, however, cut old trees by choice; in so doing they eliminate the lichens.

When logging opens the forest canopy, the openings create habitat for moose, deer and other animals that feed on deciduous shrubs and young vegetation. Higher densities of moose and deer support higher densities of wolves. Caribou – being easy prey – fall into a sort of "predator pit." Predators like wolves – their numbers supported by other, less vulnerable, prey species – kill more caribou than are born to replace the losses.

Clearing old-growth forests has other impacts on caribou too. If the clearcuts are large enough, they can interrupt the annual movements of caribou, isolating them from important parts of their range. New roads associated with forestry and mineral exploration are irresistible to hunters, who can quickly deplete newly accessible areas. While Alberta's caribou are no longer legal targets for hunters, some inevitably fall prey to poachers or eager novices who mistake them for elk or other species.

Jan and her co-workers found one caribou that snowmobilers had evidently run down and killed for entertainment. Off-road vehicles rarely penetrate pristine forest, but where cutlines and forest development open new access into caribou habitat, snowmobiles, motor quads and dirt bikes soon follow.

Jan co-authored a caribou recovery plan for the Alberta government. Based on several years' study, it identified habitat loss as the biggest long-term threat facing caribou, while predators, poaching and road kills were the chief short-term problems. Alberta Fish and Wildlife released the draft plan for public comment in 1986.

The plan called for no-hunting zones along several key roads; public education to reduce road kills and accidental killings by hunters who confuse caribou with elk or moose; long-term protection of key habitat areas from logging and motor vehicles; and a three-year program to reduce the number of wolves in key caribou areas. It might have worked.

Wolf control was the stumbling block. Fish and Wildlife's proposed wolf kill undermined the recovery plan's acceptance by the public.

"I guess I was a bit naive," Jan confesses now, reflecting on the uproar that resulted from her proposal for a three-year reduction in wolf numbers. "But if you look at the data, there was no other conclusion you could make. Predators are taking up to 19 per cent of the adults each year. Calf recruitment is only 15 per cent. If we are going to buy time for those caribou, there has to be wolf control."

Some environmentalists were willing to consider a one-time wolf kill if it came with a firm commitment to habitat protection. The public outcry, however, was sufficient to give Alberta politicians cold feet; the recovery plan remains "under study."

In 1986 Jan and her colleagues in the Alberta Fish and Wildlife Division's Edson office released a follow-up report identifying five critically important caribou wintering areas east of Jasper National Park. The report called for the Alberta government to protect two of these vital areas from any industrial activity. For the remaining three areas, it recommended special logging guidelines that would ensure a continuous supply of old forest and reduce access by motor vehicles.

That report too remains under study by the provincial government.

༚ཞ

O ne thing that did not require so much study, however, was the decision to turn all five caribou ranges over to logging companies. In 1988 and 1989, a veritable blitz of new forestry projects was launched in northern Alberta: within one year, over a quarter of the entire province was handed over to forest companies. The cut-rate forest giveaway was to supply wood to seven new or expanded pulp mills and some smaller lumber and particle-board plants.

Public uproar over wolf control paled in comparison to Albertans' reaction to the big forestry projects. A subsequent environmental review of one of these projects – the Alberta-Pacific bleached kraft pulp mill north of Edmonton – showed that the government lacked even the most basic inventories of fish and wildlife populations. Reviewers found that the government had no baseline data on forest ecology and had barely consulted the public. First Nations people, as usual, were utterly ignored. In fact, most of the area so suddenly dedicated to wood fibre production was virtually unknown to government planners.

Where caribou are concerned, Jan Edmonds admits that nobody knows what shape most of the province's northern herds are in. "We've only really studied the populations in the Hinton and Grande Cache area," she says.

"Woodland caribou," warned a widely distributed Alberta Wilderness Association tabloid, "may be extinct in Alberta within the lifetime of our children. They will be the first big game mammal extirpated in Canada in this century."

Jan Edmonds tries to remain optimistic. Nonetheless, she says, "All five primary winter ranges are scheduled for logging within the next 20 to 30 years." While the political debate over the future of Alberta's forests continues, Edmonds has turned to working with the forest companies who received cutting rights to the areas. She continues her research and correspondence with other caribou biologists across the continent, in hopes of finding ways to reduce the impact of huge forestry operations on an animal that needs old forest.

"Five years ago," she confesses, "I had a lot of confidence that we could do this, that we could manage for the long-term survival of caribou. Now, I just don't know."

The special management guidelines recommended by Edmonds and her colleagues for three of the caribou winter ranges call for long forest rotations. Loggers would have to wait 80 to 150 years between clearcuts and limit the width of cutblocks to 150 metres or less. They would also leave unlogged buffers along streams and muskegs. The recommendations are based on an experimental logging strategy that Grande Cache Forest Products pioneered in the late 1970s.

Rocky Notnes, a Hinton-based outfitter and director of the Alberta Wilderness Association, feels the proposed guidelines should not apply to such a large area. "These are just experimental guidelines," he says. "What if they don't work, and they ruin the habitat? We will never get those caribou back."

Rick Bonar is a biologist who works for Weldwood of Canada, a pulp company whose kraft mill at Hinton controls an immense cutting area that includes primary caribou winter range. He disagrees with Jan Edmonds too, but he argues for bigger clearcuts, not forest protection.

"Fragmenting the habitat and keeping a third of it uncut may not be the best option," he says. "There are differences of opinions among biologists. It may be better to cut whole areas – big, progressive clearcuts – and then allow them to recover over a long period. That way you can ensure that there are always big, unbroken blocks of mature forest available to caribou."

Edmonds concedes he may be right. "Our recommendations may even be the worst case possible," she says, pointing out that understanding of woodland caribou ecology is still in its infancy. "We could save the lichen-producing habitat but mess up the predator-prey system."

Bonar feels that small cutblocks may create too patchy an environment. He points out that natural fires burn large areas in Alberta's foothills. Caribou have always had to adjust to changing forest-cover patterns on a large scale.

Non-industry biologists point out, however, that logging has vastly different effects on caribou forage than natural fire. Lichens take several decades to grow back after a fire, even though fires usually leave patches of living trees and spars scattered across the landscape, providing a supply of lichen to recolonize the rest of the area. Clearcut logging, on the other hand, leaves a barren landscape and damaged soil – a much more drastic form of disturbance. Researchers only recently started looking into how well lichens regenerate after logging. By the time their results come in, the landscape of northern Alberta will have been changed forever.

The logging companies aren't prepared to wait for answers. Rick Bonar argues pragmatically for designing clearcuts at least to look like burned areas, at least to humans. "If you cut on a whole-landscape basis, it actually looks more natural," he says, "apart from the roads."

The roads, however, are one of the thorniest dimensions of the caribou conservation issue. Traditionally, government resource agencies saw logging roads as a public benefit of forest development. New roads meant new access to fishing and hunting. Forest companies were loath to close roads, and government, in fact, demanded that they leave most roads open. However, once the trees were cleared, road hunters usually quickly depleted the newly accessible areas of wild-life. Remote road networks are also irresistible to poachers – a more insidious threat for scarce animals notionally protected by closed seasons.

Alberta's pulp and lumber companies are aware of the growing level of public concern about caribou and other wildlife. Since the late 1970s one company – Grande Cache Forest Products – has experimented with an extended rotation system. Their approach ensures that forest more than 80 years old always covers at least a third of their timber lease. Weldwood is developing a logging strategy that tries to take into account the habitat needs of a variety of wildlife species, including wilderness-dependent caribou and grizzly. If their plan works, it might offer hope for species like caribou whose ecology is totally incompatible with traditional timber management.

Conservationists remain skeptical, however. They point out that a corporation's first responsibility is to its shareholders. Deferring clearcuts on caribou range may be good for public relations, but it does nothing for the bottom line. The Alberta Forest Service's forestry standards still require timber companies to liquidate old-growth natural forests and replace them with single-aged plantations that have little wildlife value.

Perhaps the greatest cause for concern, however, is continued government failure to protect any unexploited habitat for wilderness-dependent wildlife. As early as 1979 government biologists identified key wildlife areas east of Jasper National Park. With the caribou recovery plan, and subsequent habitat plan, they refined these recommendations and gave them greater urgency.

To date, however, not one hectare has been set aside for the protection of Alberta's first large mammal to be listed as a threatened species. Loggers are clearcutting the Redrock caribou winter range. The A la Peche winter range has been partially logged under the Grande Cache Forest Products experimental system. Weldwood plans to log the South

Berland winter range within the next decade. The Prairie Creek winter range, recommended for long-term protection by the Alberta Fish and Wildlife Division, has been "under study" for two years.

The Alberta Forest Service handed over the Little Smoky River winter range – recommended for long-term protection by Fish and Wildlife and all major Alberta conservation groups – to Alberta Newsprint and Canfor Industries in 1988. The Forest Service belatedly agreed to consider a 30-year deferral of industrial activity in the Little Smoky, but Alberta Newsprint refused. Ironically, all used newsprint in Alberta ends up in landfills, since neither Alberta Newsprint nor any other Canadian pulp companies have recycling mills. Newsprint made from caribou habitat is cheaper than newsprint made from newsprint.

Oil and gas companies continue to explore all five winter ranges in hopes of a big find, which would lead, inevitably, to more roads and fragmented caribou habitat. During the exploration phase, however, new government guidelines oblige the companies to rely on helicopter-assisted, hand-cut seismic lines, and to refrain from activity during the caribou calving season.

Jan Edmonds continues to struggle with the increasingly daunting task of sustaining caribou in a landscape given over to the forest industry. Meanwhile, conservation groups futilely lobby government and industry to put the long-term security of caribou on at least an equal footing with the profits of logging company shareholders.

History, however, suggests that Canada's woodland caribou will be doomed by human greed. A future of massive forestry developments in Alberta's boreal wilds stacks stiff odds against the beleaguered animals. Rocky Notnes says, "If there were a real commitment to protecting the caribou, we'd have seen at least one major boreal wilderness area established. We would have at least that much insurance against the possibility of all these experiments failing. But there's nothing."

Henry Stelfox promoted the idea of a protected wildlife area in the upper Clearwater. His idea did not catch on with the government of the day. The caribou he saw there are gone.

John Stelfox followed his father's footsteps, devoting his life to conservation. Recently retired from a career as an ungulate biologist with the Canadian Wildlife Service, John was a member of a panel appointed by Alberta's minister of forestry, lands and wildlife. The minister instructed the panel to review forest management concerns in the wake of public uproar over the recent Alberta forestry announcements.

The panel called for a large boreal wilderness area, echoing recommendations of public advisory panels, government biologists and conservationists over the past decade and a half. The government again dodged the issue. The official line is that wilderness-dependent wildlife can survive in a "multiple-use" landscape managed primarily for wood fibre production.[5]

Across northern Alberta, small bands of woodland caribou – unaware of distant arguments over their fate – continue to browse lichens and travel the quiet trails that stitch together their northern forest mosaic. From time to time they pause to sniff the strange odour of distant pulp mills. That smell is here to stay. The caribou, however, may not be.

Alberta's Wolf Failures (2015)

Alberta might have been made for wolves. Thousands of elk and deer thrive on the windswept bunchgrass slopes of the foothills. Farther north, deer and moose thrive on abundant second-growth where industrial activity has broken up the boreal forest.

Alberta might look like wolf heaven, but it is easier for a wolf to die than to live here.

Wolves were virtually eradicated from most of western Canada by a 1950s rabies-control campaign. Thousands of poison-laced meat baits were scattered across the landscape during a

---

5 A caribou recovery plan released in 2016 by the Alberta government now proposes several large protected wilderness areas in the very northern part of the province and a fenced caribou rearing area in the Little Smoky, where habitat is so badly damaged that caribou can no longer avoid predators. The plan proposes to continue killing wolves.

two-year program that killed off most of the wolves south of the Athabasca River watershed.

But, so long as food is available, wolves will turn up again eventually. They've been coming back for years now.

I encountered my first wolf pack in 1975 in Banff National Park. It wasn't long before my work as a biologist brought me into frequent contact with wolves. Later, I had an active role in managing them in southwestern Alberta.

My growing affinity for wolves, however, soon led me to realize that most of the wolves returning to the wildlife-rich southern foothills and mountains were simply coming there to die. Alberta's wolf management policies are designed so that those who fear or distrust wolves can kill them. Alberta's regulatory regime makes it seem that the frontier war on wolves never ended.

The Alberta chapter of the Wild Sheep Foundation is the most aggressive sponsor of Alberta's wolf kill. It subsidizes trappers who target wolves. In the winter of 2013–14 alone, the sheep hunting group paid out $32,500 to trappers in bounties for 115 wolves.

In a recent email, the sheep-hunting group's president asserted that, "predator growth is out of control," although he offered no evidence to support the statement. "Is the ungulate enhancement program working and effective? Based on these numbers, no, but the government is doing very little about predator management in this province, and this is where the WSFA ... has stepped up and will continue to offer this program to the trappers of Alberta in the future."

It's hard to take seriously that oft-repeated complaint that predator numbers are out of control and the government is failing to protect game herds. Alberta's elk, deer and moose populations have never been higher. Alberta Environment and Sustainable Resource Development (AESRD) is unable to sell all the big-game licences available.

And, in any case, the government does, in fact, kill wolves to protect game herds. It does so both indirectly by looking the other way when special interest groups pay out bounties – which several municipal governments and hunting clubs continue to do – and directly by conducting aggressive wolf kills where caribou populations are in decline.

The most notorious example of the latter has been going on for almost a decade. The headwaters of the Little Smoky River, northeast of Jasper National Park, were a pristine boreal wilderness when I first saw the area in the 1980s. The river itself teemed with Arctic grayling and bull trout, as well as otters, mink and bald eagles. Its lichen-draped forests harboured a healthy population of woodland caribou as well as a few moose, and a very few wolves.

In the intervening years, ignoring a popular campaign to have the area protected as a boreal wilderness park, the Alberta government issued timber-cutting rights to a pulp company and sold oil and gas leases to energy companies that carved roads into the formerly intact watershed. As clearcuts expanded, so did the lush second growth of willows and poplar that moose and deer thrive on. Ungulate populations grew. Predictably, so did the number of bears and wolves. The new roads and cutlines offered easy travel for the predators. Caribou numbers began to decline.

Rather than put the brakes on habitat fragmentation – the actual problem – Alberta's aggressive resource development culture required a different solution. Having declared the caribou a threatened species, the government decided to kill wolves to save them.

The province used trapper subsidies, aerial gunning and a widely banned poison, strychnine, in an effort to save the Little Smoky caribou herd from wolves. In its first seven years the program killed 841 wolves (154 by poisoning) as well as accidentally poisoning 6 lynx, 31 foxes, 91 ravens, 36 coyotes, 4 fishers, 8 martens and 4 weasels.

Unfortunately, the government spent the same seven years allowing further habitat fragmentation by the forest and energy industry. There is less caribou habitat than ever. The Little Smoky – pristine only 25 years ago – is now classified as 95 per cent disturbed.

Even if the Alberta government were not mass-killing wolves for caribou, or looking the other way while trophy-hunting organizations and rural governments pay bounties for dead wolves, Alberta's wolf policy would still resemble full-scale war. Anyone, without a licence, can kill as many wolves as they want, almost year-round. In parts of northern Alberta it is even legal to kill lactating mother wolves over bait in late spring, dooming newborn pups to starvation. This sort of officially sanctioned sadism would never be permitted for other species, but ethical considerations are consistently set aside where wolves are concerned.

But Parks Canada is the only government agency regularly criticized for wolf deaths – ironic, since it actually strives to keep wolves alive. The federal agency spent more than $10 million over two decades to stop wildlife deaths on the Trans-Canada Highway through Banff National Park. Wildlife-proof fencing along both sides of the highway, seven massive forested overpass structures and several dozen underpasses have reduced wildlife deaths by over 80 per cent. Wide-ranging animals like wolves no longer find their travels blocked by fast-moving traffic.

Unfortunately, wolves occasionally learn to tippy toe across the cattle guards at intersections. When one becomes roadkill, Parks Canada gets bad press for failing to save a wolf. I retired as Banff's park superintendent in 2011 – the same year I was shown a pile of decomposing carcasses near the park boundary. A trapper had snared eight wolves to collect bounty money. The skinned carcasses were left as bait for any survivors. The irony was a bit galling to me: Parks Canada had just endured another week of public pillory for a road kill while far more wolves were dying unseen and unreported just outside the park, because of deliberate choices by Alberta's government.

The province is quick to defend its liberal killing of wolves and third-party bounties. Kyle Fawcett, the minister of AESRD, says, "There is no evidence that wolf bounties are causing a decline in Alberta's wolf population." His staff insist that wolves have increased from an estimated 4,000 in the early 1990s to 7,000 today – population estimates they admit are based on guesstimates by trappers and wildlife officers.

AESRD is almost certainly right, however, that the wolf population is not threatened by the constant killing. But focusing on wolf numbers is just a way of deflecting the discussion from the real questions. Those questions are, or should be: What exactly is Alberta trying to achieve with wolves, and does the current regulatory regime achieve it?

If the management objective is simply to appease those who hate or fear wolves, then all is good. Regulations allow anyone to kill any wolf pretty much anywhere, anytime. Trappers have no quotas and are encouraged to use choking snares. The use of strychnine by government wolf control teams ups the ante further. If the goal is to kill and maim lots of wolves, the current system works.

If the goal is to limit wolf numbers, that's not happening. All the death and suffering doesn't stop wolves from quickly repopulating prey-rich habitat. Wolves compensate for mortality with increased reproduction, pup survival and dispersal. Even Alberta's own biologists concede that more than 70 per cent of the province's wolves would have to die every year before all that killing reduced the population.

The ultimate goal, in any case, should be to minimize wolf problems, not wolf numbers. Nobody wants wolves attacking humans or livestock, or to see critically threatened prey species wiped out. So how does Alberta's approach address these problems?

Human safety is a non-issue: abundant or scarce, wolves prefer to avoid us. One can't really blame them. Livestock safety, on the other hand, is a real issue. But Alberta's "kill any wolf, anytime, by almost any method" management regime doesn't reduce livestock losses. In fact, it probably increases them. I know at least one rancher in the Oldman River headwaters who works hard to keep "his" wolves alive. His regular presence among the herds he manages have conditioned the Willow Creek pack to leave cattle alone; other wolves might not. His efforts to sustain a wolf pack he has grown to like and respect are hindered by a regulatory regime that promotes random wolf killing, which destabilizes packs and creates more inefficient hunting units and disperser wolves. Research in Montana shows that those are the wolves most likely to start killing cattle.

For critically threatened caribou herds, predation can also be a real issue. But trying to save caribou by killing wolves is treating the symptom while leaving the disease untouched. Caribou decline is a symptom of ecosystem collapse. Declaring war on the rest of the ecosystem is a perverse solution. Alberta can afford to leave large tracts of boreal wilderness intact and to restore impaired habitats. That's the only real hope for caribou – not strychnine, aerial gunning and snares. Without habitat protection, caribou are doomed regardless of how many wolves die too.

Wolf Matters, an Alberta group promoting ethical wolf

management, wants the Province to ban third-party bounties, prohibit inhumane killing practices like snares and strychnine, and classify the wolf as a species subject to special management. Special management might mean protecting wolves until problems develop, and then targeting specific problem packs rather than all wolves. It would likely require radio-collaring wolves so that individual packs can be monitored. While costly, that would almost certainly be more cost-effective than the current approach – and far more ethical.

Basing 21st-century wolf management on biology and ethics, rather than frontier tradition and prejudice, would make more sense than today's counterproductive and often cruel war on Alberta's wolves.

Santa's Pickup (2014)

Jolly Old St. Nick was not feeling jolly.

It was early December. Santa and his head elves had gathered for the last planning meeting of the year. Things had been going well until the head logistics elf broke some news she'd clearly saved for the last.

"Alberta is going to be a problem this year," she said. "On the one hand, we'll need 10 per cent more presents, because it seems like everyone in Canada, and a lot of temporary foreign workers, are moving there to try and cash in. But on the other hand, we can't get a fresh team there like in the past."

"Fresh team?"

"You know. Fresh reindeer to pull the sleigh. Of course, Alberta's never had any reindeer, so we've always used caribou. Almost the same thing."

Santa tried not to roll his eyes. Still, he couldn't help saying, "I know that. I kind of hold the reins every year."

The logistics elf had had the grace to look embarrassed.

"The thing is," she explained, "the Alberta government is wiping out their caribou. We're not sure why."

"Wiping them out? You mean letting hunters shoot them?"

"No, there's no hunting of caribou allowed in Alberta. They're protected. The government declared them a threatened species."

"You're not making sense. If they're protected, how can the government be wiping them out?"

"Indirectly. They've got logging companies cutting down the old forests that caribou need for survival, and energy companies putting roads and gas wells everywhere so that wolves find it easier to hunt them. Poachers too. And then there's all the mess in the oil sands region ..."

Santa stared at her, clearly puzzled. "So they've classified caribou as protected but won't leave them anywhere decent to live?"

The elf nodded.

"Well, what about Christmas future? Surely they plan to keep some around? Other than on coins, I mean."

The elf brightened and leaned forward, "Actually, in the Little Smoky River area they're spreading strychnine poison baits to kill the wolves. If wolves don't kill them, then some caribou might survive until the forest habitat recovers."

"So they're sadists too," Santa said slowly, scratching his head. "Well, then, how long until the forest recovers?"

The elf sat back again, looking depressed. "Actually, they're still logging it and selling new oil and gas leases. The country-side's getting more chopped up every year. Too bad. Alberta used to be pretty nice."

"Then why poison wolves?"

The elf opened her mouth, closed it, then shrugged helplessly. "Not sure. And, truth is, it's not just wolves. That poison kills wolverines, chickadees, foxes and ravens too. The Little Smoky's actually kind of a mess."

Santa was silent for a while, frowning as he nursed his eggnog. The elves glanced at one another uneasily; Santa wasn't often grumpy.

"Well," the less-jolly-than-usual old elf said, at length, "I suppose they need the jobs. Alberta's a have-not province, right?"

"Uh, no," the logistics elf said. "Their economy is actually superheated. Everyone's rich but in debt, contractors charge whatever they want, the schools are crammed, cities bulging at the seams ... they're kind of a have-too-much province these days. Boom times."

Santa thumped the table. Everyone jumped. "Then why in blazes can't they afford to leave some intact forests for caribou?"

"They can. They just don't. They seem to be in an awful hurry to cash in. On everything. Right away."

"They expect more presents but they're too greedy to leave the caribou anything?"

The logistics elf shrugged helplessly and nodded.

"So how am I supposed to pull a sleigh without caribou?"

The logistics elf looked like she desperately wished she'd called in sick for the meeting. "Well, one possibility had occurred to us. The planning team that is, not just me ..."

Santa cocked a questioning eye at her. "Well, go ahead. What?"

"A pickup truck. There are fewer caribou every year, but lots more pickups. Trucks are sort of the opposite of endangered."

"Those big, gas-guzzling ..."

The elf nodded, avoiding his eyes. "It's sort of an Alberta thing."

Santa's rosy cheeks looked redder than usual. He patted his pockets until he found a candy cane and sucked on it for a few moments. Finally he leaned back.

"Okay," he said. "We'll use a pickup."

The logistics elf heaved a sigh of relief. "I'll get one lined up right away. Easy. We can lease. And we'll have the big sled waiting for you too."

"No big sled."

"No big sled?"

"The little sled will do. I'm delivering lumps of coal in Alberta this year. Presents are for people who care for more than just themselves."

He stood to leave. "This is why I prefer children," he muttered. "Grownups can be such utter dolts."

Our Next Forests (2016)

The prairie grizzly bears that once haunted the spruce forests along the river valley near Red Deer had to make do each fall with a diet of saskatoon berries, chokecherries and other native berries. Should the big bears ever return, they would find a richer bounty. The forests along the Red Deer River now have a sub-canopy layer of *Sorbus aucuparia* – the European mountain ash. Where the tree grows naturally, its showy red berry clusters are a valued bear food. Near Red Deer, however, the tree was never native. It's there now because flocks of Bohemian waxwings spend each winter feeding on the berries of ornamental trees along nearby city streets and roosting at night in the shelter of the spruce woods just outside town. Their droppings have seeded a whole new kind of forest.

Birds have changed other Alberta forests too. Cottonwood forests along prairie rivers near Lethbridge and Medicine Hat now have Russian olive and buckthorn trees in their understories – exotic ornamentals whose fruits have turned other birds into agents of change. Last fall while hiking in the Canmore area I noticed an unusual red-foliaged shrub amid the conifers. It was a cotoneaster, a hedge plant native to Europe. Native birds such as waxwings and robins also eat cotoneaster fruit, excreting the seeds in faraway places. Cotoneaster is now a minor but permanent addition to the Bow valley's montane woodlands.

All over Alberta, urban horticulturalists and native birds are collaborating, unknowingly, in the enterprise of redesigning our forests. Climate change is doing its part too.

Years ago in university I studied Clementsian ecology. Its basic premise is that each climatic region has a typical "climax" vegetation type. Leave things undisturbed and plant succession – progressive changes from simple plant communities to more complex ones – will inevitably yield that climax type. According to Dr. Frederic Clements, landscape diversity is mostly a product of disturbance – fires, flooding, logging or other temporary disruptions to a region's climax vegetation. Forest succession, in Clements' theoretical universe, yields few surprises.

It turns out things aren't that simple. For one thing, climate is far from stable. One can't really expect a map of climate zones to hold true for more than a few decades, especially now, during an era of rapid climate change. For another thing, new plants keep on arriving. European settlers brought familiar trees and shrubs from home to re-create the "civilized" landscapes they had left behind. Non-native weed seeds hitchhiked here in bags of grain and vegetable seeds – those crops themselves being new to North America. My fellow students and I faithfully mapped out bioregions that were already in flux, while studying about plant communities that – in the real world – were already changing as new plants invaded.

On weekends, my friends and I went hiking in search of wilderness forests. Sometimes we bemoaned the fact that everything was already mapped and described. We were wrong on that too. There will always be undiscovered forests – as long as there is a tomorrow.

Foresters base their industry on the Clementsian certainty that tomorrow's forests will be like yesterday's and that natural disturbances like fire and insect outbreaks are undesirable. They design mills for pine or spruce timber because that's the kind of forest they found nearby. When they finish logging, they plant the same trees they just cut. Their long-term plans are based on the unquestioned assumption that forests won't change.

But their so-called "working forests" are indeed changing, just as forests along prairie rivers are. Silviculture itself changes forests by renewing them in new, unnatural ways. Where natural forest fires fertilize the ground with ash, and standing trunks remain to shelter the next generation of trees and shrubs, logging removes all the trunks, leaving only unburned debris behind. Neither the compacted soil under logging roads nor the scarified soil in clearcuts is natural. The damaged soils attract weed plants such as ox-eye daisy and bluegrass, and suppress natives such as fireweed, blueberry and orchids. Replanted pine and spruce forests have the same trees as before, but different, simpler understories.

Meantime, the changing climate is also altering those forests. Milder winters and more frequent summer droughts mean that forests face more frequent soil moisture deficits than before. Competition for water is too intense to allow trees to grow as densely as they used to. Crowded, drought-stressed forests become vulnerable to outbreaks of insects like mountain pine beetles. The insects kill the weakest trees and leave the most robust specimens behind, while changing dense, crowded forests into open stands better matched to the climate of the future. Beetles help forests evolve in response to climate stress. Expecting 20th-century forests to persist in our emerging 21st-century climate makes no sense.

Tomorrow's forests are *terra incognita*. We still have surprises to discover. And where forestry is concerned, all bets are off.

CHAPTER 6

Grass and Sky

Whoopers: Fiction (1988)

I avoided Mr. VanderWaal as much as I could that fall. It wasn't easy, since he helped at our place a lot after Dad caught pneumonia. But if facing Dad was hard for me, talking to Mr. VanderWaal was almost impossible.

When I shot Mr. VanderWaal's cow, he didn't act all that upset. It was Dad who wouldn't let go of it. He took away my gun. "You get it back when you can convince me you deserve it," he said. "A gun is not a toy. You don't make mistakes with a gun."

I still don't know how I hit that stupid cow. I was shooting gophers along the edge of the coulee, down past the correction line. They would stand up at the edges of their burrows, squeaking at me. At the shot they collapsed, kicking, in the dust or dropped down the hole.

I had 12 gopher tails and was just heading back for the road when I spotted two gophers. They were chasing each other about at the edge of the big field Dad had just finished seeding to winter wheat. Both ducked into a pile of rocks. One came out and stood up.

I sat, settled the sight on the base of his little rodent head, and squeezed. He dropped, twitching, and at the same moment there came a horrible bawling from the coulee. I stood up. Sweet Jesus, one of Mr. Vanderwaal's cows was thrashing about in the buckbrush a quarter mile down the coulee!

Her calf ran to her and nudged at her side. She tried to stand

and collapsed again. I felt sick to my stomach. My bullet had put her down; I hadn't checked behind my target. I also knew that only an idiot shoots a cow by mistake.

I thought of running away from home, pretending to be sick so nobody would find out who shot her; even – for a moment – of shooting myself. In the end, though, I could find no way out of facing Dad. I jogged for home along the fence line.

We drove over and picked up Mr. VanderWaal. Dad was too mad even to talk to me. Mr. VanderWaal gave me one long look and then ignored me. I sat between them and felt like a piece of crud.

The cow had stopped struggling when we got to her. Her belly was wet with dark blood and covered with flies. I hung back as the men leaned over her.

"She's a goner," Mr. VanderWaal said.

"Shit." Dad flashed a look at me.

Mr. VanderWaal took his rifle from the truck. He fed one brass shell into the chamber, and closed it. He held the end of the barrel a couple inches from the back of her head. The cow's eyes rolled, bulging with mindless cow-fear as she tried to watch all of us at once. The calf pleaded hungrily from the coulee-bottom. The rest of the herd watched solemnly.

At the blast, the cow went rigid. One eye bulged half out of her skull and stayed there, horror fading to blankness. Her whole body stretched. One hind leg flexed, kicking. The leg reached, stretched, tense as if it were trying to resist what had already happened, then dropped limply. Blood dripped from her shattered mouth.

I threw up. Neither of the grownups even looked at me. I had never seen something die like that before; not the dozens of gophers I had murdered for a dime a tail, nor the chickens whose heads Mom so matter-of-factly hacked off, nor the partridges and prairie chickens Dad and Mr. VanderWaal shot each fall down along the coulee.

Later, after we had hauled the quartered carcass back to Mr. VanderWaal's place, Dad gave me his lecture about guns.

By then I had begun to feel persecuted. It had been an accident, after all. It hadn't been like the guys from town. They came out every now and then and shot up signs and mailboxes and things deliberately. It wasn't as if Dad had never made mistakes.

Like the time he and Mr. VanderWaal shot the whooping cranes. He had been a lot older than me when they did it. He had known it was against the law too.

We had a picture of the dead cranes in one of the family albums. Dad was holding one at arm's length by the neck. Its feet scraped the ground. Mr. VanderWaal was grinning. Dad had a moustache and his face was rounder and smoother than now. I couldn't help thinking he looked like somebody I wouldn't like if I met him today.

I studied that picture a lot after they told me about shooting the cranes. It was like a cipher. If I examined it long enough, maybe I would find some clues about what Dad had been like when he was younger – who he had been.

We had been hunting prairie chickens the day they told me about the whooping cranes. It was an Indian summer day, the coulee slopes red and gold with the fall colours of saskatoon, chokecherry and buckbrush. We already had seven or eight chickens when we stopped for lunch.

They were talking about how they used to hunt ducks in the stooks, before the days of the big combines. "They used to just pile in," Mr. VanderWaal said. "All you had to do was throw out a couple dozen tarpaper decoys, burrow down in the stooks and wait."

"Remember the whoopers we shot that one time?"

They had been sitting huddled into a stook in light drizzle. It was after sunset and the light was nearly gone. The only way to see the ducks was to look for dark shapes moving fast against the clouds as they arrived, wings whistling in the wet, gabbling quietly to one another as they set their wings and dropped toward the tarpaper outlines below.

Dad shot and saw a duck fold. It fell with a thud among the stooks a dozen yards away. He was standing to retrieve it when Mr. VanderWaal grabbed his arm and pulled him back.

"What?"

"Look."

Ponderous and heavy, wings lifting and falling in great slow-motion beats, seven huge birds materialized from the rain mist.

They were flying so low that they had to lift, one by one, to cross the fence line.

One croaked, and then the others began to call, a resonant, two-noted trumpeting.

They flew in staggered single-file, each riding the turbulent wash of another's wingtips. They were so white they could have been mirages, ghosts out of the Pleistocene past. Their wings hissed and creaked, up, down, up, down, as they passed within a dozen yards of the watching hunters.

At the last, without a word being spoken – probably without a thought being thought – Dad and Mr. VanderWaal stood up. The cranes were so close, Dad said, that even in the poor light he could see their heads turn, the primitive little eyes suddenly aware of the men.

Both men shot. Three birds fell. Two were dead when they hit the ground but one jumped to its feet and ran with long, awkward steps into the dusk, dragging one huge, snowy wing.

There were only two cranes in the photo. "You never found it?"

Mr. VanderWaal shook his head. "Coyotes must've got it or something. I never even saw a feather when I went back the next day."

"Never seen a whooper crane since then either," said Dad. "They were even pretty rare then. Most of them were further east."

"Geez they were pretty things," said Mr. VanderWaal.

It was something about the prehistoric look of those two huge birds, something in the way they seemed to represent a time already past, when grain was stooked rather than swathed, when ducks darkened the fall skies, when Dad had a moustache and went hunting on horseback with his school buddies. I kept going back to study that picture. Dad had an old leather wallet full of brightly coloured wet flies his own dad had left him; they gave me the same feeling. There was something important back there that I had missed.

I don't know what I wanted. Lots of those little sandhill cranes were still around. Sometimes I would stop and watch them, turning them into whooping cranes, putting unbroken prairie and undrained sloughs into the big grain fields. But they were not much bigger than geese, and I usually saw them on the winter wheat, the same as the big honkers that came up off the river each fall. It just didn't work.

I would look at Dad, his lined face, whiskers like steel filings on his cheeks, the bald spot on his head, and try to picture him young and unmarried. It was impossible. He was my dad; he had always been. I don't even know why it mattered. For some reason I just really wanted to know how it had felt to be young at a time when there were whooping cranes to shoot.

We had no shortage of sandhill cranes around, the fall he caught pneumonia. It was a wet one. The grain was sprouting in the swaths and it was mid-September before a chinook blew the fields dry enough to combine. Meanwhile, the ducks, geese and cranes got fat and happy on the swathed grain and the sprouting winter wheat.

Mr. VanderWaal lost time on his own land because of the time he spent on ours. Dad lay in the hospital in town and watched the sky outside the window, or paced the halls coughing. He was not used to being sick. The germs seemed to take advantage of his inexperience. After the first week and a half he rarely got out of bed at all, but just lay there and tried to sleep.

I didn't like visiting him at the hospital, although Mom insisted. I still felt rotten about the cow. So did he, especially since he had to sit there feeling useless while the man whose cow I had shot did his work for him. That's how I figured he felt, anyway. He hardly ever mentioned the work he couldn't do. Mostly he either slept, coughed or talked about the early days when he had been starting on the farm.

I wish I hadn't shot that goddam cow. I would have spent more time with him.

The rain had ended. The skies were clear, everything fresh-washed and golden in the late-afternoon sun, when I looked out the school bus window and saw the big white birds way out in the winter wheat. I could see three, and one smaller reddish one. Sweet Jesus: whooping cranes!

The bus turned the corner at the correction line. They were gone from sight. "Damn!" I said.

Mom was on the phone when I busted into the house. She didn't look up, just motioned for me to be quiet. I found Dad's binoculars, dumped my books on the couch, and headed back out. Mom put her pale hand over the phone receiver.

"Don't go taking off," she said. "I need you here."

"I'm just going up the coulee a little way." The door had slammed before I had finished the sentence.

Thinking about it now I'm almost embarrassed with how worked up I got over those things. It was like I was not even myself, I was so charged with adrenaline or whatever it was that swelled my face and sent my feet flying effortlessly across the ground. The excitement was almost sexual. For four birds. I can't remember having ever felt like that before, or since.

A big pasture of unbroken prairie stretched down from the bluff behind our house to the coulee. It was easier running than the field that stretched from the house to the big field, and shorter than going around by road. I flew across the close-cropped prairie grasses, dropping to roll under fences and skipping over badger and gopher holes. Rose prickles and thistle leaves filled my socks. I barely noticed them.

A quarter mile down the coulee I figured I must be just about even with the birds. I slowed to a walk and began to climb the slope, heart pounding in my head. I could barely breathe, more from suspense than exertion.

Over the rim. Nothing there. The field was empty.

Sweet Jesus: too late.

I felt sick with the letdown. I did not even know for sure that they had been whooping cranes. Maybe they had just been swans or waveys.

Then I heard a resonant trumpeting unlike anything I had ever heard before. It was like someone blowing over a bottle top, but higher, louder and more rolling, a sound that made the sky vast and the distance empty. I shaded my eyes with my hand, staring desperately ... and there they were.

They were in flight, already half a mile off, flying straight away. All I could see was the white flash of wings as they caught the sunlight on each upstroke. With each downstroke they disappeared into sky glare.

I watched them going, sick with regret. I willed them to come back, and I knew that they wouldn't. It was out of my hands. They were gone. White over gold, flicker, vanish, flicker, vanish; until at the last moment they veered to bypass our buildings and disappear for good behind the poplar windbreak. Even then, their great rolling cries drifted back to me out of the empty sky.

If I had stayed at home, they would have gone right over me.

I stood still. Nothing stirred. The whole prairie was gold and black, utterly still. The sky was barren. The whoopers no longer called.

My stomach felt sick. It was like when Mr. VanderWaal had finished off the cow and I had watched it trying not to die when it was already too late and nobody could change what had happened.

How could I have missed so narrowly something I wanted so badly? How could they have gone just then, when I was so near – when it was that important to me?

You can't call things back. You can't turn time back. You can't ever have the things you missed. And when I saw our pickup pull out into the road and accelerate down to the correction line, then turn and disappear behind the swell of land that hid town from view, I ran again, back down the coulee side and through the wet grass toward the house. Only now my feet no longer flew. What I ran toward was gone.

Quality (1994)

The old farmstead is one of the last remaining patches of pheasant cover in a countryside that teemed with ringnecks not too many years ago.

I never knew the people whose failed hopes the weathered old buildings represent. They had moved away well before my time. Large piles of stones, buried now in spreading caragana bushes, suggest that they did not fail for want of industry. A lot of labour went into making their fields safe for cultivator blades.

212 | KEVIN VAN TIGHEM

Whatever their story might have been, they are gone. Only decaying buildings remain amid a wilderness of caragana run wild. It is the caragana that makes the old place attractive to the few wild pheasants that remain in the area. When winter snows carpet the surrounding fields and Arctic winds sweep down across the plains, few places remain where pheasants can find shelter. The farmstead's abandoned caragana windbreaks are among the last surviving winter refuges in a barrens of grain stubble and snow.

Caragana is a tough shrub, native to the Old World. It arrived in prairie Canada during the late 1800s. The spiny shrub is so well adapted to drought that it thrives long after those who planted it move on. So hardy is this introduced legume, and so good at sheltering pheasants, that conservationists often plant caragana to restore some habitat diversity to the monotonous farmscapes we have allowed too much of the West to become.

Farmland without pheasants is a drearier place than farmland with pheasants. What could be more laudable than to plant a few caraganas? Reflection suggests, however, that caragana is barely the shortest of steps on the road to revitalizing the prairie landscape.

Less than a mile from the old farmstead, I know of another place that still holds a few pheasants: a steep, broken hillside covered with chokecherry, saskatoon, rose, hawthorn and buckbrush. Like the old farmstead, its shrubby tangles stand against the winter winds, offering shelter for poorly adapted Chinese ringnecks during the toughest time of the year. Unlike the old farmstead, this tangle of shrubs consists of native species that belong with the landscape: Canadian prairie plants. Elsewhere, such vegetation has given way to wheat, barley and canola. Here it survives in a place too steep and poor to cultivate.

From a pheasant's point of view, I suspect, the brushy old hillside and the brushy old farmstead are about equal; both serve just as well when the north wind blows. From a pheasant hunter's point of view, perhaps the old farmstead comes out a bit ahead. It is on flat ground, and hunting between the planted rows of caragana is easier. Nonetheless, this pheasant hunter finds himself drawn more strongly to the rough terrain and impenetrable tangles of the old hillside. When a hunting partner asked me why, I concluded that it was a question of quality.

Recently, trying to find a way to define that quality in my own mind, I drew up two lists. One was a list of the plants, birds and mammals that I know to use the old farmstead. The other is a list of those that use the hillside. Regarding woody things, the hillside is ahead five to one. It does even better in other categories.

The old farmstead has a heavy cover of brome grass and dense patches of Canada thistle, Russian thistle, goosefoot and sweet clover. All, like the caragana, are introduced plants gone weedy. In summer it offers shelter to the endangered logger-head shrike, perhaps because those shrikes hunt the introduced house sparrows that nest in the old granaries. Robins, gold-finches and vesper sparrows breed in the farmstead too.

The hillside, on the other hand, has a mosaic of plant communities containing, in total, more than a hundred species of native plants and many introduced plants that agriculture has added to our prairie flora. Twenty-six species of birds, at a minimum, nest on the hillside. One reason for this diversity is that native birds are adapted to native habitats. Another reason is that habitat diversity offers more ways of making a living. Mule deer live year-round on the hillside; they appear only rarely in the old farmyard. There is, as best as I can figure, at least 20 times as much biological diversity on the natural hillside as down at the abandoned farm.

Come hunting season, the wind has an empty sound as it hisses through the monotony of brome grass around the old farmstead. Sometimes a magpie or a sullen grey owl goes rattling out of the leafless caraganas. For the most part the old place is forlornly still.

Up on the hillside, however, waxwings and late robins feed on dried saskatoons and chokecherries. Migrating tree sparrows and white-crowns lisp shyly in the undergrowth. Chickadees forage among the hawthorn branches. Rough-legged hawks hang overhead, searching for meadow voles and deer mice. While the dog wears herself out trying to decode the trails of pheasants in the tangled shrubbery, I lose myself again, and find myself, amid the ecological richness of prairie Canada's natural heritage.

On balancing the books, then, it seems that the attraction of that hillside pheasant cover is obvious. The old farmstead is a richer place than the surrounding grainfields, but the natural hillside is several orders of magnitude richer yet.

The family that farmed that old place does not farm there anymore. Having done their part in turning the native prairie into a cultivated monoculture, they were long ago swept away by one of the 20th century's waves of social and economic change. They left behind a pile of rocks, several rows of caragana gone wild, some pheasants, and far too little of the natural wealth that was there when they arrived.

Today, some of us work to rebuild pheasant populations by restoring shrubby habitat. The return on our efforts, I suspect, will relate to how we define that work. If the work is merely to plant pheasant cover, then caragana will do. However, if we redefine our work as the restoration of natural wealth to wounded landscapes, then pheasant recovery becomes only one of many dividends. This latter is likely to prove a complicated, fascinating and far more rewarding enterprise.

Ducks Unlimited used to employ water engineers to restore ducks. Their reasoning was that ducks needed water. It helped some ducks. Eventually, DU changed its program focus to nesting cover, working with tame hay, alfalfa and other exotics. That helped some ducks too.

In the 1990s, DU started planting native grasses and restoring small, natural wetlands. They adopted more of an ecosystem, rather than a duck–factory, focus. The ducks benefit at least as much, if not more, from this latest approach. So too, however, do godwits, longspurs, pipits, buntings and the many other native species left out of earlier duck habitat projects.

There is a subtle difference between habitat development and ecosystem restoration. Both produce ducks, or pheasants, or whatever the targeted game species might be. Only one, however, offers any hope of restoring landscape quality, natural diversity, and the richness that was, and could again be, prairie Canada.

Save the Gopher! (1996)

As a young birdwatcher, I used to ride my bicycle out into the world of wheat, grainfields and scattered sloughs that lay beyond the Calgary city limits. Black terns and avocets shrieked as I hunted for their nests or waded through the cattails looking for bitterns and sora rails. Horned larks sang overhead and burrowing owls studied me from fenceposts.

My bird books told me that some prairie birds were rare. Those were the ones I was most eager to find. Most of those birds needed natural habitats, however, and little native prairie survived near Calgary even then. Most of the birds I found were weedy species that could live on the leavings of prairie agriculture or around the wetlands that still survived.

One day, as I explored the sandstone outcrops lining Beddington Creek's prairie valley, I heard a hawk screaming near a small grove of poplars. At my approach it flapped away from a large stick nest and wheeled overhead. It was a large, pale hawk with a reddish-brown V where its legs crossed its abdomen.

My field guide told me it was a rare ferruginous hawk – a species now on Canada's endangered species list. I returned often to watch from a distance where I would not disturb the hawk and its mate. They hunted the heavily grazed native prairie along the creek bottom, bringing back one gopher after another to feed their hungry little babies.

Watching them, I wondered why this overgrazed valley was the only place for miles around where ferruginous hawks nested. I didn't know then that the abundance of gophers in the native grassland pastures lining Beddington Creek accounted for those hawks' success that year. Ground squirrels like heavily grazed prairie; they also make up more than 80 per cent of the ferruginous hawk's diet in Alberta.

It turns out that it's difficult to discuss any endangered prairie wildlife without bringing gophers into the conversation – okay, Richardson's ground squirrels, if you want to be fussy about names. Real gophers are the creatures some people call moles and few ever see, since they live virtually their entire lives underground.

Most prairie Canadians use "gopher" as the colloquial name for Richardson's ground squirrels. The stubby little rodents seem ubiquitous, running around the edges of fields, standing erect at the mouths of their burrows or making bad decisions that leave them flattened on rural roads. At a distance, watchful gophers look like tent pegs or picket pins. Try to picket your horse to one of these pins, however, and it will squeak and vanish into a hidden maze of underground runways. Generations of gophers have learned that there is little profit in standing still for a human being.

Humans, for the most part, don't like gophers. That first gopher squinting into the March sunlight each year, of course, is in a different category from your ordinary gopher. That first one is a sign of spring. The problem is that they keep on coming until it seems like the prairie sprouts gophers faster than it does wheat or barley. By early May, gophers can seem to be everywhere.

Gophers are more than happy to eat wheat and barley. They are rodents, after all. They also eat garden vegetables and other green things. They dig burrows and throw the dirt up into conspicuous mounds, often in the middle of golf course fairways or newly planted lawns. Gophers breed prolifically: up to a dozen babies each year, year after year. All those babies dig holes and eat crops too.

It doesn't take much exposure to gophers before the average prairie-dwelling human develops a serious interest in finding ways to be rid of them.

There are many ways to kill gophers. If the Richardson's ground squirrel were not such a prolific breeder and so proficient at colonizing new terrain, it's a safe bet the species would be on Canada's endangered species list along with the ferruginous hawks that eat them. In fact, humans have already succeeded at eradicating ground squirrels from some parts of the prairies.

Flooded out of their burrows and snared with binder twine,

gassed in their dens, shot with .22 rifles and killed with strychnine-laced grain dropped down their holes, ground squirrels face endless persecution at the hand of man. One entrepreneur even invented a device that injects propane into gopher burrows and then blows them up; early testing resulted in the demolition of a pickup truck. Gophers would probably call that karma.

And it's not like life wasn't already rough for the Richardson's ground squirrel before modern agriculture turned it from a native rodent into a pest. Many animals like to dine on the plump and abundant little creatures.

Badgers snuffle about at night, sniffing out the fresh scent of sleeping ground squirrels, and then digging them out. Coyotes sometimes tag along and wait nearby in case the badger's quarry tries to make a dash for it out the back door. Even without the unwilling assistance of a badger, coyotes catch many ground squirrels. Long-tailed weasels specialize in hunting ground squirrels, as did the now-extirpated black-footed ferret.

Bull snakes hunt ground squirrels and kill them by squeezing them in their coils, like boa constrictors. Overhead, hawks circle patiently, watching for unwary survivors. Ground squirrels are larger than the more numerous mice and voles – making them a heartier snack – and they are active during the day. Most other prairie animals come out at night, when hawks cannot find them.

Bald eagles appear to time their spring migration to coincide with the emergence of the first ground squirrels from their winter dens. What could be better, after a long flight north, than a refreshing snack of small, furry hors d'oeuvres? The little animated treats must be easy to find as they stand squinting into the spring sunshine, silhouetted against melting snowdrifts.

No wonder ground squirrels spend so much time squeaking nervously. They are under perpetual siege.

&

G eoff Holroyd is an endangered species biologist with the Canadian Wildlife Service. He says that few people realize the importance of the humble gopher. "Not only are ground squirrels a critical link in the web of life that sustains endangered and threatened species such as the ferruginous hawk," he says, "but ground squirrels play a vital role in keeping many other predators off the endangered list."

Biologist Laurie Hunt agrees. She and Robyn Usher conducted a satellite-imagery study of an area along Alberta's lower Red Deer River to try and figure out the relationships between ground squirrels and their predators. The researchers found that ground squirrel colonies occupy less than 3 per cent of the landscape, mostly native prairie that has not been ploughed up for cropland. Ground squirrels from that tiny portion of the whole landscape provide up to 94 per cent of the food supply for the area's prairie falcons. The ongoing human war against ground squirrels, combined with continuing conversion of native prairie to cultivated cropland, may help account for the fact that barely half as many prairie falcons survive in Alberta as did 35 years ago.

The prairie falcon, one of the most spectacular wild hunters of the plains, is a dusty-brown raptor nearly the same size as the better-known, and endangered, peregrine. Prairie falcons nest on ledges on the cliffs that line prairie rivers and coulees, and range widely in search of their favourite prey: Richardson's ground squirrel.

Holroyd notes that federal and provincial governments have spent hundreds of thousands of dollars to bring the peregrine falcon back from the brink of extinction, with mixed results. Meanwhile, conservation agencies virtually ignore the prairie falcon, though acting now to protect a mere 3 per cent of the prairie landscape could go a long way to ensuring its continued survival. "It's far easier," he says, "to keep species from becoming endangered in the first place than it is to bring back a species once it's become endangered."

Will we only begin to worry about the prairie falcon after the last pockets of ground squirrel habitat are gone?

That's what happened with the burrowing owl, a species on the fast track to extinction in Alberta. Like the ferruginous hawk, the burrowing owl is another endangered species I first met during childhood bicycle excursions beyond the outskirts of Calgary.

One afternoon, while I was idly counting ground squirrels on an overgrazed pasture in what has since become a housing subdivision, I spotted two strange-looking creatures standing on a ground squirrel mound. My binoculars revealed two long-legged little owls, staring at me through fierce yellow eyes. One bobbed up and down, then flew a short distance to land on a fence post. The other vanished suddenly into the ground.

Two pairs of burrowing owls nested in that heavily grazed native pasture. Scarcely bigger than ground squirrels themselves, burrowing owls nest underground in abandoned ground squirrel burrows. They eat grasshoppers and insects that thrive in the same shortgrass habitats that ground squirrels prefer.

Since ground squirrels prefer low-growing vegetation, they benefit from grazing. Before Europeans arrived in prairie Canada, ground squirrels relied on plains bison to keep the grass down. Burrowing owls line their nests with bits of dry cow dung – evidence that bison, ground squirrels and the animals that depend on ground squirrels probably evolved as a single community of life.

Burrowing owls need ground squirrels, but that is not all they need. The burrowing owl may be doomed in Alberta for other reasons: the extensive use of toxic pesticides for grasshopper control, and the continuing proliferation of roads and highways. Cars and trucks kill grasshoppers, and then kill the little owls when they flutter across the path of passing vehicles to scavenge the insect remains. Irrigation expansion in southern Alberta continues to plough up native prairie essential to this unique little owl. Burrowing owl numbers, as a result, have declined by more than 70 per cent in less than a decade.[6]

❧

Unlike the burrowing owl, the swift fox may be on its way back from extirpation. The little native fox's hopeful future is the result of reintroduction programs supported by the Canadian Wildlife Service, the Calgary Zoo, and provincial wildlife agencies. Like the burrowing owl, swift foxes benefit from abundant ground squirrels. Swift foxes hunt mostly at night, so ground squirrels do not form an important part of their diet. Ground squirrel burrows, however, give the little predators a place to live. Swift foxes take over the burrows and enlarge them for their own use.

Mice, bull snakes, rattlesnakes and weasels all make their homes in ground squirrel dens too.

Many prairie Canadians think of gophers as vermin. Ecologists, however, describe Richardson's ground squirrel as a keystone species in what survives of the Great Plains ecosystem. Cleve Wershler, a noted prairie ecologist, goes so far as to describe the much-maligned ground squirrel as the "wildebeest of the prairies" – a dramatic comparison at first glance, but close to the truth.

Wildebeest, on the eastern African plains, feed lions, hyenas,

---

6   Biologists now consider burrowing owls functionally extirpated in Alberta. Almost none survive.

vultures and a host of other species. Their grazing maintains the natural mix of vegetation. They fertilize the land with their dung and shape it with their hooves. Without the wildebeest, the great pageant of life many of us picture when we imagine Africa would not exist. The wildebeest ties that ecosystem together. Remove it, and the whole thing falls apart.

We have already lost an important force in the prairie ecosystem – the bison – and with it the prairie wolves and grizzly bears that relied upon the bison herds. In much of what remains of the prairie west, ground squirrels play every bit as important a role as wildebeest still do in the Serengeti, and bison once did here. Take away the lowly gopher, and a whole suite of other species that depend upon it for vital elements of their ecology would follow the ghosts of the bison, wolf and grizzly down the silent halls of nostalgia and regret.

Yet, for the past century, government policies and rural culture have conspired together to eradicate ground squirrels by whatever means possible, even including the widespread use of inhumane poisons like strychnine.

What if we had succeeded?

Keeping It Together (2015)

When our son headed off to the South American rainforest, one of the items on his checklist was a water purifying system. He didn't want to pick up the wrong hitchhikers. The helpful sales agent at his outdoors store warned him not to rely on iodine tablets except in emergencies.

"You don't want to kill your gut flora," he said. "Then you'd really have a problem."

Few of us spend much time thinking about what lives inside of us. Maybe it's because our reductionist Western science tradition makes us isolate human beings from the rest of nature. But we are not alone. Far from it.

Each of us hosts an estimated 100 trillion micro-organisms on and in our bodies. We are not individuals; we are ecosystems. Our gut contains ten times as many microbial cells as body cells. Those little organisms help us digest efficiently, influence our moods, keep us from getting too fat and protect our bodies against colonization by harmful bacteria. We, in turn, provide all those microbes with a temperature-controlled, food-rich and warm environment in which to thrive.

Little creatures that live in our eyelids graze the vast plains of our skin each night, cleaning up harmful bacteria and getting rid of dead body cells. Other creatures only visit, like the mosquitos who sip our blood and the cold germs that propagate in our bodies and then migrate to others in handshakes and sneezes.

We're all in this together. If the recent medical concept of fecal matter transplants seems horrifying, it's only because we tend to think of germs as enemies, rather than community members. Once we understand our bodies as complex communities of life, it makes sense to wonder if any are missing and whether it might be helpful to get them back where they belong.

In school we're taught about symbiotic relationships between organisms as something unusual. Lichens, for example, are plants comprised of an alga and a fungus. Isn't that weird? Bark beetles carry fungus spores that attack the wood of the trees where beetles lay their eggs; when the eggs hatch, the baby beetles survive because the fungi made the wood edible. Neat.

But there is nothing unusual or exotic about that at all. It is the way the world works. And when we fail to acknowledge the complex webs of interconnections that make things what they are, we tend to make mistakes we don't recognize and get results we never intended.

My wife and I moved our family to Okotoks for a couple years in the 1990s. Suburban and acreage development was rampant. To my ecologist's sensibilities, it was heart-rending to see the rate at which bulldozers and scrapers were peeling the top off the fescue prairie and replacing it with roads, lawns and monster homes.

"It's okay," I recall being reassured. "Once the development is in, they'll plant the grass again."

I knew better. Prairie is not grass, any more than we are made solely of human cells. I decided to salvage some prairie and try to educate at least some of the neighbours so they would know better too. Weekends would see me wrestling matted lumps of spiky grass into the back of our van and hurrying home to wedge them against other salvaged clods in what the kids were soon calling our "front yard prairie." Passing neighbours looked askance or rolled their eyes as the patch of rough grass-land grew in front of our house. I put up a little sign explaining what it was and listing all the plants that actually lived in what looked, at first glance, like a bunch of unmowed grass.

In the first season, I found more than 70: from little drought-tolerant mosses hidden beneath the clumps of rough fescue to buffalo bean, prairie crocus, wood lily, needlegrass, oatgrass, shrubby cinquefoil and pasture sage. Every time I thought I had a complete list, another frond or flower would appear and another name went on the list.

Those native Alberta plants were dying all around Okotoks, to be replaced with seed mixes containing three or four commer-cial grass varieties. They still are. The people moving to the countryside to raise their kids close to nature didn't realize they were killing whole communities to do so, replacing them with a dumbed-down facsimile. They saw prairie as one thing – grass – rather than the real thing – a complex community of native plants, insects, microbes and fungi.

Health providers avoid prescribing too many antibiotics for the same reason the store clerk warned our son about iodine tablets. Kill the community that lives in your gut, and you lose that community's ability to keep you healthy and alive. The same thing happens when we sterilize Alberta's native grass-lands by blithely ripping them up in the misguided belief that we can always plant grass again.

We are not alone. But we could end up that way.

৩৫

Facebook Post

May 24, 2016. Canmore.

As Alberta moves to low-carbon energy sources, it's worth remembering that not all non-renewable energy is green. Damming rivers for hydropower is particularly destructive. But so is wind power, when wind farms are installed on native prairie. Native grassland ecosystems are among the most threatened in the world. They sustain rare species, store massive amounts of carbon in the root systems, and recharge groundwater aquifers. They are not the right places for wind turbines – those belong on already disturbed land, of which there is already too much. A responsible energy policy would protect rivers and prohibit surface disturbance of native grassland. It isn't just about carbon; biodiversity matters too.

A Prairie Proposal (2016)

Prairie is where the sky is big: almost impossibly big. Turn in a slow circle, watch endless cloudscapes spill down to the brim of the world and the idea of heaven – a vast, light-infused heaven – becomes tangible. If our ideas were as big as that sky, we would be giants indeed.

W.O. Mitchell's child protagonist in the classic novel *Who Has Seen the Wind* wandered out into the prairie while pondering the nature of God. He found gophers, grasshoppers, meadowlarks and his first sense of the divinity in Creation: "For one moment no wind stirred. A butterfly went pelting past. God, Brian decided, must like the boy's prairie."

Look down today, though, and heaven vanishes; the view at ground level is of paradise lost. There is little room for the divine here: sanctuary has been given over to exploitation.

Few Canadian ecosystems are as endangered as our prairies. From the time the first Europeans came searching for soil to plough, we have been killing the most fertile native grasslands and carving up the rest with roads, pipelines, wind farms and other intrusions. More than a third of Alberta's original prairie has been cultivated for crop agriculture, killing the dozens of native plant species and the soils and wildlife that depended on them. Much of the rest has given way to urban development, water reservoirs, feedlots and recreational property development. The remaining prairie is riddled with roads and pipelines servicing an estimated 150,000 oil and gas wells.

The upshot is that less than 35 per cent of our original fescue grasslands – the moist bunchgrass prairies of central and western Alberta – survive today. Only 29 per cent of the drier mixed grassland remains. The driest grasslands in southeastern Alberta have fared best, but even so most are gone. Little wonder, then, that more than 70 per cent of Alberta's at-risk wildlife are prairie species.

In ruining prairie ecosystems we squander not only a vibrant community of native life but an important part of our identity. We may not all seek God there, but until recently we could always find that part of ourselves defined by prairie – the smell of sage, the music of vesper sparrows and meadowlarks, the sudden flight of pronghorn antelope. Burrowing owls once bobbed their heads from the mouths of abandoned badger dens; both the owls and the badger are now at risk. Ferruginous hawks – pale raptors the size of eagles – once gathered in feeding swarms with the smaller Swainson's hawks to feast on small rodents left injured by prairie fires. Those fires are now virtually nonexistent; the hawks are threatened too.

W.O. Mitchell's wind still blows. We still cannot see it. But nor can we see the true Alberta prairie it once caressed.

Still, this is Alberta: a place noted for big ideas and brash implementation. And 21st-century Alberta needs a truly big environmental story for a skeptical world that thinks bitumen-soaked mallards tell it all it needs to know about the blue-eyed sheikhs of the northern plains. We have yet to prove otherwise.

Given that our prairies are one of the world's most threatened ecosystems, what if Alberta could boast that – unlike any other place in the world – we restored our grasslands to their former glory?

Early farmers ploughed up the prairie because its soil produced bumper grain crops. That soil fertility came from the immense amount of organic material that native grassland plants store underground. It was mostly carbon. Nowadays we're looking for ways to pull carbon out of the atmosphere and put it into storage. Restoring native prairie would do that, while also bringing back most of Alberta's endangered species and that part of our cultural heritage derived from the indigenous life-ways of First Nations and Metis people, the ranching way of life, early settlement history and great literary works such as *Who Has Seen the Wind*.

Most of our surviving prairie grasslands are public land. Our government could declare them conservation lands and restrict their use to sustainable cattle-grazing. We could go further than that: use carbon tax revenues to pay private landowners to replant native vegetation on their marginal cropland. That would enhance rural economies while at the same time storing carbon and restoring native prairie wildlife habitat. We could more strictly regulate the oil, gas and wind industries to shrink, rather than continually expand, their surface footprint.

Alberta need not regret the loss of our prairie heritage; we could simply choose to restore it.

It's a big, brash idea, but we could actually do this. And then we could tell the rest of the world: "We brought back the entire prairie ecosystem. Our endangered species aren't at risk any more. We store carbon in living soil. That's how we roll up here in Alberta. So what have you accomplished lately?

"Oh yeah, and we have some energy resources for sale too ..."

CHAPTER 7

Perhaps Protected

Have Our National Parks Failed Us? (1986)

Just east of Banff National Park, the Trans-Canada Highway bulges into a six-lane freeway. Entrances and exits spin off in all directions. Street lamps line the pavement, illuminating the surge and flow of tourists shuttling between Calgary and Banff.

South of the highway is Canmore, a sprawling community of old coal miners' homes and new condominiums, tourism employees and real estate speculators. Pervading the clear mountain air that whistles down the streets of Canmore, like a vision of wealth and fame, is the rumour of the 1988 Winter Olympics. Developers, with government money, are building a new ski resort on Mount Allan, a few kilometres away. Everyone's home has become an investment.

North of the highway, the mountains swell up and away. These are the Front Ranges of the Rockies: dry, windblown mountains whose grassy slopes alternate with gullies full of aspens and glacial terraces clothed in lodgepole pine and Douglas fir. Chinook winds wick away the winter snow that falls here even while the surrounding mountains remain deep in snow. It is an excellent place: a spectacular mosaic of vegetation, rock and wind, a haven for wildlife, and the scenic backdrop that draws visitors from around the world.

Mule deer and elk rely on these slopes for winter feed. Many animals come from Banff National Park, unaware of having crossed the park boundary. They come because the snow is shallow and feed is abundant. Bighorn sheep cluster on the higher slopes. Black bears den in the wooded gullies. Overhead, eagles soar.

The place is well-loved by people too. On any weekend day many people stroll, hike or lounge about, enjoying the scenery. Riders follow horse trails along the ridges. Children from town cross the highway and head up on the slopes in search of adventure. People scramble to the mountaintops.

Others calculate how much the view will be worth when the Olympic boom hits. They survey roads. They subdivide. They speculate.

One September day a couple of years ago, my wife and I took a walk in the aspens to watch autumn blaze across the valley. We saw an eagle, seven mule deer, a herd of bighorn sheep, two horseback riders, and a large bulldozed swath. Survey markers spread beyond into the forest; it was the beginning of a housing subdivision. The new subdivision's name, appropriate in its irony, is Elk Run.

The sight of a bulldozer scar on an unspoiled slope – of survey stakes next to piles of deer droppings – spoiled the pleasure of the day. There was something casually violent and amoral about the ease with which real estate developers could choose to strip off the soil and bury the crocuses, rose tangles, wildlife winter range and scenery, in order to build luxury second homes that will stand empty for much of each year. My disillusionment deepened, however, when I mentioned the destruction to a Canmore resident, a naturalist who has fought long and hard to limit development in Banff National Park. His response: "Well, I find it hard to get too upset about it. For one thing, it's not in the park. For another thing, it's zoned for municipal development."

His response struck a discordant note. On reflection, I realized the lesson buried in his response: our national parks, wilderness areas and other protected areas have failed us, in a very basic and vital way. They have not drawn us into a more thoughtful relationship with our habitat. They have not taught us that we should use land frugally, and with humility and respect. They have encouraged us to embrace an approach to conservation that consists mostly of trading a few protected areas in exchange for freedom to abuse all other land.

They have more than failed. They are now a symptom of the problem.

In 1949 the American conservationist Aldo Leopold published his famous argument for the development of a land ethic. He wrote that we are all members of a biotic community. As such, we should afford to the land the same ethical responsibility and restraint with which we strive to treat our fellow humans. He argued that if we saw our moral obligations extending to not just our neighbours but also the land that sustains us, then a sense of stewardship, or husbandry, would inform all our land use decisions.

In the four decades since, land use decisions have not become any simpler, nor have they come to be informed by Leopold's spirit of ethical restraint. Against the complex realities of a shrinking world, growing populations, increasing technology and spreading urbanization, the taste of despair became familiar to those who care about land. It's a bitter taste, and it led many to fall back into a siege mentality.

If we cannot treat all land responsibly, this point of view argues, then let's at least fight to defend some of the better patches from the despoilers.

As the destructive potential of man increased in the postwar years, so did the concern of those who saw that potential applied to land. The forces became increasingly polarized. "Conservation," which had once been seen as a hugely progressive leap forward from the "get it while it lasts" exploitation ethic of the colonial frontier, became replaced by "preservation" in the increasingly frequent confrontations between developers and environmentalists. Distrust on both sides fed a rhetorical war in which winning or losing were absolutes; creative dialogue became increasingly impossible. In the determination of both sides to establish and defend precedents, the most important questions went unasked. Rather than learning to live sustainably in the natural world, our debates contributed to its continuing fragmentation.

In a national park one is not allowed to pick a flower. One is discouraged from – and could be fined for – eating a berry. One must stay on the trail. The many shalt-nots are understandable because of the popularity of national parks. Parks staff speak of the danger of loving a park to death. Five hundred people a day can trample a mountain meadow to mud in a week.

But the unfortunate corollary of these restrictions is that they perpetuate the myth that humans and nature are not part of the same thing – that people are not full members of the biotic community. National parks do not bring people nearer to nature; on the contrary, their experiences there too often reinforce the idea that they are outsiders. By extension, park visitors are encouraged to believe that outside the parks, in those unfortunate places that do not enjoy protection from the inevitably destructive choices of us outsiders, nature must needs be – at least usually – written off.

Destructive development? Irresponsible land use? Well, it's got to be either people or nature, we've learned to assume. Thank God at least that we have our national parks.

The irony of this paradox becomes apparent when we examine trade-offs we have accepted in the seemingly sacred battle to save national parks from despoliation.

The Calgary Olympic Development Association (CODA) campaigned aggressively, and successfully, to have the International Olympic Commission (IOC) designate Calgary as the site of the 1988 Winter Olympics. A keystone of CODA's bid was Mount Sparrowhawk, in the Spray valley, south of Canmore. The Olympic promoters touted the windswept mountain as an ideal race site for the prestigious men's downhill skiing event.

No sooner had the IOC approved Calgary's bid than disturbing rumblings began to be heard in the press. Nancy Greene Raine stated that Sparrowhawk was the wrong choice. Others said its snow blows away too often in Alberta chinooks. Lobbyists suggested other choices.

Two years later the Alberta government announced its final site selection. Mount Allan, a few kilometres east, would be the Olympic ski area. The new choice differed from Mount Sparrowhawk in having less snow-holding ability, little suitable racing terrain, and one of the world's largest and healthiest herds of bighorn sheep.

Sixty kilometres west, in Banff National Park, is the sprawling downhill ski complex of Lake Louise. The area had been the subject of repeated controversy and a stormy series of public hearings in 1972 when Parks Canada and Imperial Oil jointly proposed a major expansion. Although public opinion saved the Lake Louise area from Imperial Oil (but not from Parks Canada, which incrementally developed the area anyway), environmental organizations remained on high alert, guarding the area jealously, if less than effectively.

With the first suggestion that Mount Sparrowhawk might be unacceptable, the watchdog organizations pricked up their ears. Could this be a new conspiracy to expand Lake Louise, they wondered? Perhaps CODA had intended to use Lake

Louise all along but had used the Sparrowhawk option, outside the national park, to win IOC approval. The government's subsequent selection of Mount Allan, an even more obviously unsuitable mountain, only served to deepen suspicions.

CODA denied all rumours. But the environmental groups eased into the firing line, just in case.

The ski resort at Lake Louise clearly doesn't belong in a national park, but it has been in existence for many years already. It has almost doubled in size since 1972. In spite of the National Parks Act, the area is far from unspoiled. It is in deep snow country in the central Rockies, too far west to sustain wintering populations of ungulates. It is within bus and train distance of Canmore and Banff, and already has parking facilities and other infrastructure.

It might have been argued that the men's downhill at Lake Louise would be unlikely to further degrade so heavily developed an area. It might have been argued that the undisturbed slopes of Mount Allan had higher and better uses than ski development. It certainly should have been argued that an ethical attitude to all land would favour the concentration of facilities, as much as possible, in areas already developed.

All those points might have been argued, but they were not. Lake Louise is in a national park. Mount Allan is not. National parks are sacrosanct. We can sacrifice Mount Allan.

Mount Allan's fate suggests that we have cheated ourselves with our willingness to settle for easy either-or decisions. We chose a simple, rational approach to land preservation that, in the end, works against conservation and an honest land ethic. We opted to draw lines on maps, zoning one area for preservation, another for development, another for exploitation. Somehow we convinced ourselves that this is a responsible approach to conservation.

We have chosen the easy road of trying to protect artificial units of land – making them somehow more valuable than other land, however similar. The more difficult road remains largely untravelled. It would require that we educate ourselves and others to see land as an extension of ourselves that we should use wisely and conservatively. All land.

It is the nature of policies and rules that they last only so long. Then they are changed or abandoned. Lake Louise will continue to develop and expand.[7] So will Canmore and – now – Mount Allan. People will flock to the national parks, where earnest staff will urge them to stay on trails and not pick berries because nature is fragile and we humans aren't part of it. Environmental groups will fight to preserve more land, and developers will rage about elitism and resource lockups.

And we will continue to wonder why, with so much seemingly sincere concern about our environment, we still manage to misuse it, abuse it, and put it to all the wrong kinds of uses.

Somewhere along the road we thought might lead to

---

7 In 2015 Parks Canada approved new ski area guidelines that will allow Lake Louise to almost double the capacity of its ski area and to expand into areas currently designated as protected wilderness in the Skoki hiking corridor.

sustainability, we took a wrong turn. It happened when we institutionalized and segregated both conservation and resource development. Rather than creatively bringing the two together under the imperative of a land ethic – in an environment of mutual education and a commitment to humble, shared stewardship – we chose to isolate them by drawing arbitrary lines on maps and laws on paper. Lines and laws can be – and are constantly – amended as either-or battles are won or lost. Only an ethic offers lasting hope, but our secular and selfish world is unable to look ethics in the eye without blinking and looking away.

If this were a perfect world and humans viewed themselves as citizens of their habitat, we would not need national parks. The very notion of national parks would be absurd.

However, this is not a perfect world. In too many cases we have chosen to make it a world where setting aside national parks and protected areas substitutes for ethical restraint and hard choices. We have traded our responsibility toward the land for a few small museum-pieces that too often become a symptom of our affliction, instead of the cure for our ills we had hoped they would be.

Through a Grizzly's Eyes: Ecosystem Thinking in a Fragmented World (1991)

It is late afternoon. The sound of meltwater is everywhere. The dull thunder of avalanches fills the valley as mountains release winter–long accumulations of snow.

In the alders at the base of an avalanche slope, a grizzly bear lies on his back, one paw poised above him and his head twisted to the side. He opens his eyes and focuses on the branches above him, then closes them again and heaves a phlegmy sigh. A fox sparrow bursts into song nearby.

Below, the rushing of Sage Creek mingles with the muted sound of wind in pines. The air is hazy with humidity and soft with spring.

The bear dozes. The long day fades.

As the first evening breeze comes sliding down the gullies, bringing a fresh chill from timberline snowfields, the bear stands and shakes himself. He tests the air, then follows his nose to a newly exposed patch of brown vegetation. Uprooting a clump of sweet vetch with one swipe of his claws, he munches on the stringy roots.

In the forest, thrushes are singing.

A bullet strikes the ground by his face. The grizzly sits back on his haunches, shocked. The rifle's crack echoes down the valley.

Another bullet strikes, this time behind the bear.

He lumbers for the timber, head weaving as he tries to find a scent that will tell him what is going on.

The third bullet creases the big bear's shoulder just as human scent hits his nostrils. Like a ball of silver–tipped fur, the grizzly races into the trees as one last bullet ricochets into the alders.

Behind him, the hunters are left with the dilemma of deciding what to do next. They have driven by four-wheel-drive truck to the end of a logging road, through vast clearcuts, to hunt grizzlies legally during British Columbia's spring bear season in hunting zone 4-1. They know how scarce grizzlies are, especially one as big as this. One hunter is sure his shot hit the bear. But it is growing dark. Neither of them wishes to surprise a wounded grizzly at close range.

❧

The grizzly, however, is half a kilometre away, moving steadily up the valley. The memory of the gunshots is fading as his powerful nose filters countless familiar odours from the mountain night – resin, snowmelt, mould, new buds.

By morning, the grizzly has crossed the Continental Divide, into the high country at the headwaters of the Waterton River. Wind roars through timberline firs as the bear descends to a small creek.

He forages half-heartedly along the stream meadow, but the ground is well frozen at this elevation. Wandering into a patch of old-growth spruce trees, he beds down against a log. He tries to lick the sore spot on his shoulder, but his head will not twist that far. Eventually he stretches out on his side, sighs and falls asleep.

It is unlikely that bears let worries disturb their sleep; in any case, he need not worry tonight. Although he is still in what humans have come to know as the Crown of the Continent ecosystem, well within his normal home range, he has crossed an invisible line in the darkness.

Two hours ago he could be legally shot and killed as a game animal. Now he sleeps in a national park, protected by law.

For three days the grizzly works his way downstream. The wind on this side of the Rockies seems to howl endlessly, sweeping its thawing breath down from spindrift-topped peaks into the brown foothills.

One night, as he digs roots along the edge of Blakiston Creek, still in Waterton Lakes National Park, the bear's hackles lift. He freezes, nose working, small eyes flickering. The wind has brought the scent of bear cubs.

He moves forward, pigeon-toed and stiff-legged. Something moves at the edge of the grassland. A low rumble rises in his throat.

A loud woof answers him.

The female charges from a clump of silverberry, snarling and swinging her paws. She stops a few steps short of the big male, moaning and drooling. Her ears are laid back. She clacks her jaws ominously.

Behind her, three cubs flee, hesitate, and dash back to cower behind their mother.

The male lowers his head as if to smell something in the grass, and walks a few paces to one side, his nostrils full of cub smell and his small brain full of blood. Still, the female's desperate rage makes him cautious. The female makes another rush and he braces for the attack, but again she turns aside. This time she herds her cubs away. The male does not follow.

Female grizzlies defend their cubs very aggressively, partly because some male grizzlies kill cubs. Since grizzlies, with their long digging claws, find it more difficult to climb trees than black bears do, grizzly mothers do not have the option of sending their cubs up a tree for safety. Instead, they sometimes find themselves forced to attack other bears to protect their young.

In Glacier and Waterton Lakes National Parks, grizzlies may not always be safe from one another, but they are safe from hunters. They are not, however, safe from the growing numbers of people who visit the parks to savour the scenery and tramp the trails. The aggressive instincts of female grizzlies are a constant hazard, because female grizzlies react to hikers very much like they do to other bears. As more people crowd into bear country, the potential for attacks by grizzlies on humans increases. Human injuries sometimes result in dead bears too.

The grizzly swims the Waterton River. The farther he travels east, the better the forage. The high passes are still locked in winter, but here at lower elevations, where chinook winds sweep away much of the winter snow, green grass and new spring flowers are everywhere. The bear lost almost a quarter of his body weight during his winter sleep, so the new vegetation on his spring range is like ambrosia.

Several days later he crosses another invisible boundary onto the Blood Timber Reserve, skirting a gas well. He leaves a string of huge, pigeon-toed tracks along the muddy well road. Then, completely unaware of it, he crosses back into the national park. One end of the glacier lily patch was under the jurisdiction of the Blood (Kainai) First Nation. By the time he ate the last lily bulb, he was in the park. They all tasted the same.

Late in June, the bear is in Poll Haven Community Pasture, well to the east of where he spent the winter. Rain mists the aspen forests and meadows. In the fogged treetops above Lee Creek, a robin sings steadily into the sodden dusk. This piece of the Crown of the Continent is owned – a human notion, alien to grizzlies and all other living things – by the Alberta government.

Green odours are everywhere. The bear steps silently over fallen logs and through rain-drenched buffaloberry shrubs, nearly oblivious to the wet as he follows his nose from one wet green smell to the next. He has been gaining weight steadily these past few weeks.

He is moving crosswinds when a delightful smell hits him square in the nostrils: the rich, strong odour of rotting flesh.

A cow, bloated and swollen, sprawls where lightning killed it a week ago. It is a windfall to the bear, who normally relies on more abundant but less nutritious vegetation for his meals.

Two days later, the cow carcass is nearly gone. The ravens who argue all day long in the treetops have splattered the remaining tatters of hide and broken bones with their droppings. Three coyotes have been working on the carcass too, carrying away bits and pieces whenever the bear's back was turned.

As he emerges from the timber for one last meal, the grizzly detects a new odour, that of engine oil and exhaust. New tire tracks mar the trampled ground near the carcass.

Poll Haven used to be part of Waterton Lakes National Park. The federal government surrendered it to Alberta in 1947 so that local ranchers could pasture their cattle there. Unfortunately, it is also an important spring range for grizzly bears. When range cattle die, bears scavenge on the carcasses. Rarely, a bear learns to kill cows. It isn't that difficult, really – it's a bit surprising that more don't.

When bears eat domestic cattle, provincial authorities remove the bears. Sometimes this means trapping the bear and removing it far from the Crown. In other cases it means killing it. Either way, the ecosystem loses a bear. In 1986 and 1987 alone, Alberta Fish and Wildlife removed ten grizzlies from Poll Haven to protect domestic cows.

When the Fish and Wildlife truck returns pulling a bear trap the following afternoon, however, the grizzly is already several kilometres away. He is bedded just below a ridge top in northern Montana, fast asleep.

He is safe now. In the United States of America the same bear that hunters can legally kill in BC, that dodges hikers and cameras in Waterton Lakes National Park and is considered an agricultural pest on Alberta grazing lands, receives the full protection of the US Endangered Species Act. It is a criminal offence for humans to disturb the bear on this side of yet another invisible line.

None of this would make sense to the bear, if he were aware of it. This is all his home range, all the same ecosystem. As the seasons change he will inevitably cross those invisible lines again and again. Each time he crosses another jurisdictional boundary, he encounters different hazards, land use patterns and human philosophies.

This October, when a poacher kills him beside a gas well road in Alberta's Bow-Crow Forest Reserve, the grizzly will have become another victim of ecosystem fragmentation.

The Crown of the Continent ecosystem – where the Rocky Mountains give way to the great central plains of North America – is a spectacular tapestry of bunchgrass prairie, aspen forest, evergreens, castellated mountains and wind. Viewed from outer space, it forms a pattern clearly distinct from the surrounding landscapes. Mountains fill the centre, prairie rims the edges, and forested valleys send their waters to three oceans.

To the west, headwater valleys feed the Columbia River system, flowing at length to the Pacific Ocean. To the north, streams drain to the Oldman River and thence by way of the Saskatchewan-Nelson River system to Hudson's Bay. To the east, other streams hasten to join the Missouri and, at length, the Gulf of Mexico.

The watersheds of the Crown may drain to different oceans, but they share geological origins, landscape patterns, weather systems and wildlife populations.

From outer space, large patterns are more visible than fine details. From an orbiting satellite, for example, one can easily see great Pacific weather systems rolling inland across the continent to squeeze up against the chilly heights of the Crown's 2000-metre-high mountains. As clouds form and thicken, those weather systems shed rain and snow along the western reaches of the Crown. To the east, where mountains give way to prairie, the descending winds – drier and warmer now – sweep across aspen thickets and fescue grassland.

Those sorts of patterns are visible from outer space, but the intricate details of bunchgrass prairie, with its dozens of species of native plants, are not. The gas well roads that trace a spiderweb pattern across the corners of the Crown barely show on satellite photographs. Cattle dotting the checkerboard grain and hay fields along the edge of the Crown are even more difficult to detect.

Other man-made changes, however, are clearly visible. On the British Columbia side, vast clearcuts look like mange on the Crown's green face. Highways slice into Crowsnest Pass and Waterton Lakes and Glacier National Parks. Irrigation reservoirs sparkle in the sun along the eastern edge.

Down on Earth, wholeness disappears into detail. It is hard to see a regional ecosystem from the perspective of the average human being, or bear. Mountains block the view. One literally cannot see the forest for the trees. Day-to-day detail proscribes the lives, and imaginations, of people who live in Pincher Creek, Polebridge, St. Mary, Montana's Blackfeet Reservation or any of the Crown's many ranches.

Our ground-level view of Earth may explain why, today, Waterton Lakes National Park seems more real than the Crown of the Continent ecosystem – though we invented the park and the ecosystem already existed. The Canada-US border slices blindly across drainage divides and wildlife winter ranges, yet most consider this artificial line more meaningful than the watersheds it severs.

ᴖᴖ

Humans invent boundaries, and then are forever confined by them. It seems ironic that some lines that often confound efforts to sustain the Crown of the Continent were originally drawn to protect it.

George Bird Grinnell, an American hunter and adventurer, visited the region in the late 1800s. Grinnell was impressed by the area's red-and-green mountains, crystal streams and abundant wildlife. Its unusual three-way continental watershed divide fascinated him. Grinnell ardently promoted the idea of a park that would protect this spectacular area from logging and development. Even in the late 1800s, he warned, frontier ambitions threatened its biological diversity.

"The game is almost all gone now from mountain and plain," he wrote. "Buffalo and bison are extinct everywhere, but in the dense forest a few moose, elk and deer still exist and, as of old, bears prowl through the timber."

Almost a century later, the threatened grizzly bear still prowls the timber. Thanks to Grinnell and Canadian rancher-conservationist Frederick Godsal, both the US and Canadian governments established parks early in this century to protect parts of the Crown. Glacier National Park, in northern

Montana, and Waterton Lakes National Park, in southwestern Alberta, together enclose more than 4625 square kilometres. of the Crown of the Continent ecosystem.

This is still too small by grizzly bear standards. An adult male's home range may cover more than a thousand square kilometres. Grizzlies survive today mostly because of the productive wildlife habitat outside the parks, in BC's Kishinena drainage, Alberta's Castle and Carbondale watersheds, some large private ranches and US Forest Service lands in Montana. All remained wild and remote for most of this century.

That is no longer the case. In Alberta, roads and pipelines invaded the wilderness as large petroleum companies developed the Crown's rich natural gas fields. The new access continues to open the area to hunting pressure and off-road vehicle abuse. Logging companies too created new access – and far more extensive habitat change – in both Alberta and BC. National parks concentrated roads and tourist facilities in the most productive valley-bottom areas. Developers continue to promote ski hills, golf courses and even waterslide parks in other valleys. Elk, bears and wolves are considered agricultural pests by many of the Crown's ranchers – often with good reason.

To animals, the Crown of the Continent is a whole – one great, interconnected living system. Wildlife continue to live according to their ancient patterns, but humans are changing their ecosystem at an accelerating rate. So far, we humans have had difficulty being sensitive to one another's needs, not to mention the needs of the ecosystem as a whole.

Is there a future for wide-ranging wildlife like the grizzly bear in southwestern Alberta? If there is not, then is there any real future for the ecosystem? And as the ecosystem comes apart, what kind of future is there for the human beings who now share this special place?

We are the latest comers to the Crown, but we risk changing it forever before we have really begun to understand it. As we change our environment, we change ourselves; just as the bear is ultimately defined by the ecosystem of which he is an element, so are we.

The past century has seen repeated battles over who will get what share of the Crown's jewels. Only now are we beginning to step outside those selfish arguments and ask how we can live together here without destroying the things that keep this ecosystem whole and – in the final analysis – make us whole too.

ॐ

Facebook Post

July 12, 2015. Wolf Willow.

*Evening on the Oldman – golden light on
clean riffles, a big cutthroat that escaped at
the last moment and then a silvery rainbow
that walked me a hundred metres downstream, stripping the reel well down into
the backing before I finally beached him on
a gravel bar. River talk and whiskey later
while nighthawks call overhead and a robin
sings quietly in the Douglas fir above me.
Cougar tracks in the sand. Mayflies dancing.
A young squirrel studying my foot. This
evening there is nobody on the planet richer
than me. Nobody.*

Unicorns in the Whaleback (*1995*)

You can always go back to the Whaleback and it will be there.

In a world where favourite places and secret retreats vanish almost overnight, that is reassuring.

It changes, of course. In spring you might arrive to find the slopes suddenly green, crowned with brilliant gold where giant, sunflower-like blooms of balsamroot have suddenly exploded from places where snowdrifts lay only a month ago. Later, in the brilliant glare of the midsummer sun the balsamroot may be faded, its time past. Instead, the hills glisten with a strange reflective gold where a billion rough fescue seed heads are ripening in the heat.

The gold of ripening bunchgrass lasts only a week or two, then fades to the familiar brown of foothills Alberta. The first howling chinooks of winter arrive soon after to try to bow down the Whaleback's stunted forests of limber pines and Douglas firs. But those trees have spent their whole lives bracing against the wind, their roots down in the cracks of the lichen-crusted sandstone outcrops that crown the long ridges. They are ancient trees, some of them, and the progeny of even more ancient trees that came before. They belong here, and so they dance and seethe untroubled in the wild winds that roar down off the Livingstone Range winter after winter.

Elk bed all day beneath those dancing branches, then feed by moonlight on wind-bared grasslands.

The Whaleback changes through the seasons, but doesn't change in the big ways to which my generation has grown accustomed. I went looking for a favourite deer-hunting forest one fall and it was gone completely: every trail, every chickadee, every remembered corner. Alfalfa, newly seeded, sprouted from the ground where it once had stood.

You can always go back to the Whaleback, even if you may never be able to go back to other places again.

This spring I returned, uncertain in my own mind why I was doing so; troubled by the spectre of impending loss. Sometimes, when you know you can always go back, you put off visiting until far too much time has passed. I did that with my father, and now he is gone. That had something to do with my decision to return.

This past spring, Amoco applied to the Alberta government for permission to drill for natural gas there. Suddenly the unimaginable had become possible: the Whaleback might soon fall prey to the 20th-century epidemic of roads, gas wells and industrial noise. I realized that even a place as sacred as the Whaleback might not survive forever – at least, not as the wild, secluded and inestimably rich place that it has always been.

Gail's and my children never knew their maternal grandmother and barely knew their paternal grandfather before he died. Our offspring might bear their genes and their names, but those people who formed a vital part of their heritage are gone. They are certain to be the poorer for having missed the chance to know them. At least we could make sure they knew the Whaleback before it too could be taken from them.

So Gail and I brought the kids with us.

Shooting stars were blooming in their millions, tucked down among matted tussocks of last year's bunchgrass. The sun was warm and the breeze gentle, rich with the green odours of new aspen leaves and melting snow banks. We turned our faces to the roadless north, and the kids raced ahead into the Whaleback.

Bluebirds flitted around us as we followed the brown swell of the main ridge up from the Oldman valley. Winter-weary legs struggled against gravity, and Katie and Brian started to make rebellious noises as their parents led them steadily uphill. At length we clambered out onto an outcropping of sandstone crusted with orange, black and grey lichens, like the ancient bones of the earth. Below lay a mosaic of aspen, willow, fescue grassland and fir forests – the rich ecological mosaic that typifies what remains of Alberta's tiny montane ecoregion.

The kids drank lemonade. We looked north and west into a landscape unmarred by roads, development or air pollution.

I once climbed the same ridge in the darkness of an early November morning. I will always remember the shadowed landscape going on and on into the north without a single light to break the darkness of the hills. Even so, the pale hills had reflected the glow of the blazing millions of stars that studded the blue-black band of sky that stretched below a chinook arch.

Today the anxious bellowing of a cow in the valley below

reminded us that the Whaleback country, though it has survived the industrial juggernaut of the 20th century, nonetheless sustains human economy. We could see no cows, however; only a small band of mule deer retreating into the dark forest two ridges over and a kilometre away.

I'm a father; I wanted to find some way to impress the kids with the significance of this hike and this place. Some dads feel obliged to pontificate about that sort of thing.

The kids, however, were too busy pretending to be lost in the wilderness. Their voices piped happily in the clear spring air as they clambered among the ancient rocks and tried to climb the gnarled old limber pines.

Once Katie ran to me and said, urgently, "Daddy, is this the kind of place where unicorns could live?"

"Yes," I said, "although I think they don't like to be around grownups."

"Good," she said, and hurried back to the others.

I was right too. Creatures of myth and exceptional beauty would be more likely to survive in the Whaleback than in the crowded roadscapes to which we have reduced so much of Alberta. But later that day, as we picked our windburned way out of the Whaleback wildland, the kids said nothing about having seen any.

Corey did, however, point out a golden eagle.

It traced long arcs as it rose on the spring breeze out of Bob

Creek valley. It knew, like us, that you can always come back to the Whaleback. No doubt it had been doing so for many years.

Its offspring, I pray, will still ride the air currents over the same montane mosaic when Gail's and my kids come back, years from now, with their own kids. There will still be mule deer, cattle and bluebirds. The chinook wind will still make pine trees dance, and the nights, if they should choose to wait and see, will still be dark with secrets and blanketed by stars.

My grandchildren will gaze into the distance – because in the Whaleback there will still be distance – hoping, perhaps, to spot a unicorn. What they see, in any case, will be every bit as rare and not one bit less worthy of wonder.[8]

Ghost Forests (1999)

It's usually late spring before you can hike up to Forum Lake. Tucked against the base of cliffs on the Continental Divide, the lake is often blanketed by ice well into late June. Its cirque faces northeast, sheltered from the high elevation sun. Snowdrifts linger in the shady timberline forests until July most years.

---

8 Shortly after the first publication of this essay, the Alberta government under the leadership of Premier Ralph Klein established the Bob Creek Wildland and the Black Creek Heritage Rangeland, effectively protecting the entire Whaleback area for posterity – a remarkable conservation achievement.

Morning mist tangles the treetops and drifts in shredded tatters along the walls of ancient rock that loom above the lake. Wraithlike and jagged, the whitened spars of dead pines rise high above the darker canopy of fir trees. Varied thrushes whistle eerily. A raven croaks. Later the sun will break through and burn a brave brightness into the mountain morning, but for now the timberline basin feels like a place of ghosts.

It is a place of ghosts. Bleached arms bent, dead whitebark pines stand mute and still, lifeless reminders of a time not long past when this basin echoed to the rasping cries of Clark's nutcrackers and the chatter of red squirrels. Most of the timberline giants have died over the past half century, starving the subalpine forest of its annual bounty of oil–rich pine seeds. A century ago, grizzly bears followed their noses from one squirrel midden to another in this part of the Canadian Rockies, raiding those treasure troves of whitebark seeds. Today's squirrel middens contain a more trivial bounty of fir, spruce and lodgepole cones; today's grizzlies make do with other foods. In Yellowstone and Jasper National Parks, where whitebark pine stands have yet to suffer the fate of Forum Lake's whitebarks, bears still rob squirrels.

Hike to timberline anywhere in the Rocky Mountains along the 49th parallel and the same picturesque ghost forests of whitebark pine snags will greet you. To those who don't know the story behind the dead trees, they seem to speak of little more than the difficulty of life up high near timberline. To those who know why the spectacular high mountain pine trees are dying out, however, the dead snags are mute testimony to a dark side of 20th-century conservation.

"Whitebark and limber pine forests are functionally extinct in the Waterton-Glacier International Peace Park," says American ecologist Kate Kendall. With biologists from Parks Canada, the US Forest Service and other agencies responsible for managing the pines' high country habitats, Kendall studied the ongoing die-off of one of the most spectacular – and ecologically important – of Rocky Mountain trees. Now, in what seems to some like a desperate race against time, she is working with those same colleagues to help the trees save themselves.

Unlike the better-known lodgepole, jack and ponderosa pines, the whitebark (Pinus albicaulis) and its lower-elevation relative the limber pine (P. flexilis) are members of the stone pine group. They bear their needles in bunches of five and produce large cones with nut-like seeds the size of a cherry pit. Stone pines are circumboreal, with several species in Europe and Asia. Most grow in semi-arid environments, often on rocky ridges and outcrops, where their deep roots and drought-resistant needles enable them to cope with limited water supplies. Although few other trees can compete with these specialized pines in their rugged habitats, the frequent fires that are a natural feature of dry landscapes help reduce competition further by burning the seedlings of upstart fir or spruce trees. Stone pines have fire-resistant bark and, by using up the available soil moisture near them, they minimize the grasses and other fine fuels next to their trunks.

Perhaps the most remarkable aspect of stone pine ecology is the interdependent relationship between the trees and nutcrackers – curved-billed members of the crow family. Whitebarks and limber pines are synonymous with Clark's nutcracker, a raucous and sociable black-and-grey bird somewhat smaller than a crow. Nutcrackers rely on energy-rich pine seeds to feed their offspring. Since cone crops vary in productivity from one year to the next, however, the birds need to hedge their bets by gathering pine seeds when they are abundant and hiding them for later retrieval when they may be scarce.

Nutcrackers use their stout beaks to pry seeds out of pine cones. Tilting its head up, a nutcracker will stash each seed in its gular pouch – a hollowed-out space beneath its tongue. Once it has five to ten seeds, it flies to a nearby open slope, lands on the ground, pokes a beak-length hole in the ground and empties its gular pouch into the hole. A couple of quick pokes and the hole is covered. Calling sociably as they flock back and forth between treetops and caching sites, flocks of nutcrackers work compulsively for hours on end.

Diana Tomback, an ecology professor at the University of Colorado, studied nutcracker food-caching behaviour as part of her PhD studies. She estimated that an individual nutcracker may gather and store up to 90,000 seeds in a single summer. Experimenting with captive birds, she found that their spatial memory is nothing short of astounding. Using sticks, rocks and other markers as reference points, her study nutcrackers were unfailingly able to retrieve every seed they had cached. Only if researchers moved one of the markers did the birds fail to find their hidden food supplies.

Nutcrackers, however, are overachievers. Their food-caching behaviour far exceeds the needs of the average nutcracker family. Of the 40,000 to 90,000 seeds each nutcracker hides, it usually retrieves less than a third. Some of the rest are lost but many are simply abandoned.

Pine seeds are critical food for nutcracker nestlings. The birds retrieve enough seeds to ensure the survival of the next nutcracker generation. The seeds that remain behind, however, ensure the next generation of pines. Each stash of seeds is at the ideal depth for germination. Because nutcrackers choose sunny, open slopes – they particularly favour recently burned sites – the sprouting seedlings enjoy abundant sun and little competition from other plants. The relationship between nutcracker and pine, in other words, works to the advantage of both parties: a classic symbiotic relationship.

It's a relationship that's in trouble, however, partly due to the misguided enthusiasm of North America's early forest conservationists.

During the early years of the 20th century, Americans became concerned about the rate at which timber barons were devastating that nation's forests. President Theodore

Roosevelt established national forests to protect what remained and hired Gifford Pinchot as the first head of the US Forest Service. Pinchot, a staunch believer in conservation – the philosophy of wise use of natural resources – set about to change the way American forestry was done. In Canada, prime minister Wilfrid Laurier organized several Forestry Congresses to promote a similar change in management philosophy for our forest estate. Gifford Pinchot was an honoured guest at Canada's first Forestry Congress, in 1906.

Among the changes to forest management that arose on both sides of the border with the establishment of public forests and forest management agencies, was a move to improve the quality of North American trees. Pinchot and others felt that North American forests were little better than raw materials, sorely in need of improvement through scientific management. They felt that selective breeding and progressive techniques of forest culture would improve our unsophisticated native forests. Since some of the best available silvicultural expertise of the day was in Germany, scientists in Pinchot's agency shipped seeds and seedlings of North American trees overseas to be improved by selective breeding in German plantations. Among the species that went to Europe were eastern and western white pines – five-needle pines that, unlike the related limber and whitebark pines, produce high-quality lumber.

When the "improved" trees came back to North America they brought a hitchhiker – white pine blister rust. Blister rust is widespread in Europe, where pine trees long ago developed resistance to its ravages. North America's five-needle pines, however, had never been exposed to the fungal disease. With no built-in resistance, our native trees were – and continue to be – extremely vulnerable to infection. Ironically, scientific forestry in the service of wise use proved more devastating to North America's five-needle pine forests than the ravages of the 19th century's unbridled commercial exploitation. Eastern white pine forests have yet to recover from the combined devastation of over-cutting and blister rust. Only an aggressive breeding program to select for rust-resistance has saved western white pine forests from vanishing too.

The commercial value of the white pines at least motivated foresters to try and undo the harm they had unleashed upon this continent. Lacking any economic value, however, wind-gnarled limber and whitebark pine forests were left to die. Death by blister rust is a slow, insidious process that begins with rust spores infecting a single branch, then gradually killing that branch as the fungus spreads down the tree's vascular system to the trunk. Blister-like swellings girdle the trunk at the base of the infected branch, gradually killing the top of the tree. After several years, the tree finally dies completely. Since slow-growing whitebark pines may be 100 years old before they produce their first cone, the disease often kills trees before they get a chance to reproduce.

Gnarled and scenic, the growing number of dead snags up near timberline went unremarked for many years because the attention of foresters was focused on economically productive forests farther downslope. A third of all the whitebark and limber pines in the Waterton-Glacier International Peace Park were already dead before Kate Kendall and her research associates began to investigate the problem in the late 1990s. More disturbing yet, from half to almost 95 per cent of trees in the surviving stands were infected with blister rust and, consequently, doomed.

Blister rust has been in western forests for almost a century. Its spread has been uneven. While the worst damage is concentrated along the 49th parallel in a fan-shaped area extending from near Vancouver to the Waterton-Glacier International Peace Park, whitebark pine forests farther north and south have yet to show much sign of damage. In Jasper National Park, flocks of nutcrackers greet tourists at the base of Mount Edith Cavell; on nearby slopes the rounded tops of healthy whitebark pines dominate a forest that shows no sign of infection. Yellowstone National Park is similarly healthy, although early signs of blister rust infestation have ecologists there worried. Whitebark pine nuts scavenged from squirrel middens are a critical summer food for the park's endangered grizzly bear population. If blister rust devastates Yellowstone's whitebark forests – likely, if global climate change brings a predicted increase in summer humidity – ecologists fear the ecosystem's capacity to support grizzly bears will be measurably reduced.

Nobody knows whether whitebark pines were once as important a bear food in the more badly infected regions along the 49th parallel. Two mid-century biologists reported signs of grizzlies feeding on pine nuts. During her 1997 field investigations in Waterton, Kate Kendall found bear scats full of limber pine seeds. For the most part, however, whitebark stands were already suffering heavy mortality before anyone started asking questions about their role in Rocky Mountain ecology.

The late 20th century brought a belated interest in non-commercial forest values among government agencies and conservation groups. A heavily attended 1987 conference in Missoula, Montana, drew forest experts from numerous agencies and universities together to plan strategies for saving the whitebark ecosystem.

What's needed, all agreed, is for whitebark pine populations to develop rust resistance. Some agencies, like the US Forest Service and the BC Ministry of Forests, have selective breeding facilities that they have used in the past to develop disease-resistant strains in other western trees. At least in the US, whitebark pine breeding programs are already underway. The problem with growing rust-resistant seedlings in nurseries, however, is that many die when planted back into natural habitats. Given the sheer geographical scale of the problem, selective breeding is unlikely to make a big impact.

Canadian and US national parks, unlike neighbouring multiple-use agencies, are mandated to work with natural ecological processes. Park vegetation specialists in both countries are now looking to prescribed fire as a way to kick-start natural selection for rust resistance. They point out that if it weren't for aggressive fire control programs, lightning strikes would have maintained a mosaic of various-aged forests at timberline through the 20th century, rather than the aging stands that dominate today. Without frequent fires, subalpine fir and other shade-tolerant trees eventually crowd out the sun-loving whitebarks and, ironically, expose them to the risk of death from much more intense fires fuelled by the dense foliage of the other trees.

The least rust-resistant whitebark pines in most stands are already dead. Although nutcrackers stash seeds from those that have survived the 20th century, mortality among pine seedlings is high in the timberline environment. Only on recently burned slopes, where conditions are ideal for regeneration, do high numbers of pine seedlings successfully sprout and grow. For vegetation ecologists like Kate Kendall and Kootenay National Park's Rob Walker, small burned patches offer the best hope of filling the mountain landscape with young whitebark pines. All of those, inevitably, will be exposed to blister rust spores. Most ultimately will die. Those whose genetic makeup keeps them immune to rust attack, however, will grow and, in a few decades, begin to produce new generations of pines with increasingly high rates of rust resistance.

The key is to get lots of young whitebarks growing while the dwindling supply of old whitebarks are still producing seed. And the challenge is getting the okay to set fires in scenic, high-elevation forests. Land use managers are understandably timid about letting their staff start forest fires that might upset a public brainwashed by Smokey the Bear. Even more worrisome is the thought that some fires could escape and burn neighbouring commercial forests, farmlands or other property.

Rob Walker feels there is little cause for nervousness with well-planned prescribed burns. He conducted Canada's only whitebark pine restoration burn to date. The 12-hectare prescribed fire near the Crowfoot Glacier in Banff National Park went off flawlessly in October 1998. "We know it was an intense fire," says Walker. "We got 100 per cent crown scorch and more than 70 per cent organic soil loss. Monitoring so far shows excellent herbaceous regeneration. We won't know how well we met our pine objectives until we get a good cone crop year, and that hasn't happened yet."

Farther south, forest managers in the Bitterroot National Forest near Missoula, Montana, have already found prolific whitebark pine restoration in experimental units they burned in the mid-1990s. Rob Walker is planning a larger fire in Yoho National Park's isolated Sodalite Creek valley, and his colleagues in other Rocky Mountain parks have similar plans on the books.

"One thing that works in our favour that I hadn't originally anticipated," says Walker, "is how dry the sites actually are. You think of them as cool and damp because they're at timber-line, but they're usually quite well-drained. The other thing is that we have our choice of many topographically isolated sites where talus and rock can be used to keep the fires from spreading."

Some British Columbia forestry companies have recently shown an interest in working with the BC Ministry of Forests to restore whitebark pine stands there. Most whitebarks grow above the operability line – the elevation contour where it is uneconomic to log. Even so, logging companies often use fire to get rid of logging slash in cutblocks just downslope from whitebark stands. Late-fall slash burns deliberately designed to burn upslope into whitebark pine stands could create patch-work openings full of young, regenerating pine trees. Given the role that commercial forestry considerations played in unleashing the blister rust problem, commercial forest compa-nies should certainly play a role in undoing some of the harm.

The silent snags reflected in Forum Lake's icy waters stand as a silent reproof to the smug hubris of early foresters, and a continuing challenge to the current generation. Twentieth-century forest management resulted in the slow, insidious devastation of an entire forest ecosystem. If 21st-century forest management fails to reverse that decline, the price of that failure will be measured in losses of Clark's nutcrackers, squirrels, grizzly bears, and the spreading silence of those high-mountain ghost forests. It is a haunting challenge.

Silence in the Park (2013)

Wading a cold river in the rain was not how I wanted to start day three of a nine-day wilderness trip in Banff National Park, but there was no alternative. Since my last visit, 35 years earlier, Parks Canada had demolished the bridge across the Panther River and rechristened the fire road as a trail.

When I first hiked the Cascade Trail in 1976, it was a good gravel road all the way from Bankhead, near Lake Minnewanka, to the Red Deer River. Park wardens and horse wranglers regularly drove its 80 kilometres between the town of Banff and the Ya Ha Tinda horse ranch east of the park. They still used the Spray and Brewster fire roads too. Years earlier, in fact, the road sometimes opened for public use; my grandfather used to drive in to fish lakes that are now a two-day hike from the trailhead.

Thirty-five years after my first visit, however, the road was grown in with willows, hairy wildrye and dryas. Mine were the first human footprints this year on what had become a seldom-used single-track trail. Yesterday I had waded Cuthead and Wigmore creeks several times, growing increasingly nostalgic for culverts, and today – June 26, 2011 – I had my first major river to ford.

Icy water tugged hungrily at my knees as I picked a down-stream route across a gravelly riffle. I emerged safely, feet aching, into a tangle of rain-dripping willows. Upslope from the willows the vegetation opened into a burned-off pine forest with lush tussocks of rough fescue – Alberta's provincial grass – and clumps of healthy young aspens.

Sitting on a fallen log to trade wet runners for dry socks and boots, I reflected on how much had changed since my last visit here. That first hike was at the start of my career with Parks Canada; this one was at the end. In the late 1970s I was a Canadian Wildlife Service (CWS) biologist working on the original wildlife inventories of the mountain national parks. A third of a century later I retired as superintendent of Banff, Canada's oldest, most revered and most controversial national park.

On that first solo foray along this route I saw no rough fescue and no young aspens. Heavy, sustained grazing by the elk that overpopulated the park through much of the 20th century had repeatedly killed young aspen sprouts and suppressed the most palatable grass species. But I had never known a Banff that wasn't defined by grazed-down meadows, aging aspens black with scars as high as an elk could reach and fire roads extending back into nearly every valley, so nothing about that trip had seemed unnatural to me. It was the Banff I knew.

Some years later, I helped biologist Geoff Holroyd compile final reports on what our CWS study teams had learned through many months of measuring and counting just about anything that moved anywhere in Banff and Jasper National Parks. Our inventory was part of the most exhaustive study of ecological conditions ever undertaken in the mountain parks. By its conclusion, I had learned that lovely scenery can conceal a lot of ecological problems.

And we hadn't even begun to think seriously about what climate change might mean to Banff.

The sad state to which the park's aspen groves, willow thickets and fescue grasslands had deteriorated by the early 1980s was partly the result of too many elk and partly the result of too little fire. The too-many-elk part of the problem resulted from too few predators, especially wolves. They were then only beginning to recolonize the southern Rockies after having been poisoned and shot out during the 1950s and 1960s. Bears too can be important predators on elk calves. Bear studies by Stephen Herrero, David Hamer and Mike Gibeau, however, showed that the park's many roads and poorly located trails were displacing grizzly and black bears from their most productive habitats and exposing them to increased risk of conflicts with people and collisions with vehicles and trains.

The too-little-fire part of the problem had a lot to do with the determination with which Parks Canada and neighbouring agencies fought back whenever fires flared up after lightning storms or human mishaps. Fire is among the most important agents of ecosystem renewal in western Canada. Lodgepole pine, aspen, rough fescue and countless other species rely on wildfires to put potassium back into the soil, open up the vegetation canopy, knock back competing plants and produce ideal conditions for regeneration. But by the 1980s fire had become almost a stranger to the forests and grasslands it had helped sustain for millennia.

The Cascade Trail I was following, in fact, was originally a fire road built so crews could quickly extinguish backcountry blazes.

As I set off up Snow Creek along the former fire road on this June morning, I was surrounded with the blackened spars of dead lodgepole pines. Parks Canada's fire crews had not fought these fires – on the contrary, they had ignited them. Since the late 1980s Banff's fire specialists have been recognized as international leaders in the science of using prescribed fire to restore ecosystem health.

As an ecologist, I was gratified to see the results – a patchwork of hillside grasslands, aspen woodland, patches of unburned pine forest and lush shrubbery where three and a half decades earlier I had hiked through a monotony of pine trees. As a hiker, however, it proved a bit disconcerting. A short way up the trail, I rounded a bend to see a grizzly bear eating sweet-vetch roots 60 metres away. A quick glance around confirmed that should events demand I climb a tree today, I'd be out of luck. They had all been burned through.

The bear, however, fled the moment he spotted me. I don't know how many human beings he had seen in his life, but I was almost certainly the first one he met in 2011.

During the first eight days of this wilderness pilgrimage, the only sign of humans that I saw was a single horse track. And yet I knew the park was crowded with people. More than three million visitors flock to Banff each year. Major special events were scheduled for the area near the town of Banff during the time of my hike, and the campgrounds were full. Yet mine were the only tracks amid this mountain beauty. It seemed strange.

A long walk in the lonely wilds is a good opportunity for contemplation. Reflection has a particular edge and poignancy when it comes at the end of one's career. What, if anything, had Parks Canada gotten right during my working years there? Several days later, when I finally arrived at Lake

Louise, I had concluded that we had managed to get a lot of things right.

Banff is in a wilder and more natural state today than back when I first discovered it. Wilder because fire roads like the Cascade have been closed to motor vehicles and turned back into trails, while at the same time unnecessary facilities and fences were pulled out of front-country valleys to remove obstacles to wildlife movement. More natural, in part, because fire and wolves are back. The ecosystem has responded with fewer elk, more aspens and fescue and greater vegetation diversity. More natural too, because bears no longer feed in garbage dumps, and in foraging for natural foods across the mountain landscape they are far less likely to die on the Trans-Canada Highway now that it has been fenced and fitted with crossing structures. Grizzlies die unnatural deaths today at less than half the rate they did in the early 1980s.

Clearly, the elements of Banff National Park's ecosystems that respond to park management decisions such as whether to close or fence roads, ignite prescribed fires, protect wolf dens or open up corridors of secure habitat for sensitive species had all improved. Challenges remain – like too-frequent deaths of bears from collisions with speeding CP Rail trains and the spread of invasive plants and fish – but on the whole, today's Banff is in better shape than it was when I joined the organization that manages it.

I should have felt good, but I didn't.

Banff and Canada's other national parks face bigger challenges than Parks Canada can solve by itself. Global changes, resulting from the thousands of decisions people make daily across the continent, threaten to overwhelm even the best cared-for of park ecosystems.

I was painfully aware that Banff had recently seen the loss of its last caribou – the first large species extirpated since park establishment. I also knew that Alberta glaciers have shrunk more than 25 per cent in the past 35 years – a worrisome omen of impending water challenges. But other changes I saw on my 2011 hike led me to suspect that global environmental change is causing less obvious, but more pervasive, ecological damage throughout the park.

From its earliest days, flower-strewn timberline meadows have been among Banff National Park's defining elements. Up where forests end and the alpine emerges, generations of artists have been enthralled and hikers inspired by the beauty of timberline. Clumps of subalpine fir with gnarled old larches and whitebark pines frame almost impossibly lush openings full of glacier lilies, windflower, paintbrush and valerian. The first time I broke out into Banff's timberline country, I felt like I had arrived in Middle-earth – it was hard to conceive of so much beauty set against such peaks.

Snow Creek summit was one such place. After 35 years I couldn't wait to see it again. To my dismay, however, its timberline meadows had almost vanished. Openings once full of greenery and wildflowers were now packed with dense young subalpine fir trees. Higher still, thousands of bushy saplings dotted what before had been open alpine meadows.

The late-lingering snows, frequent summer frosts and wet soils that used to keep the forest at bay can no longer be relied upon, in a time of rapid climate change.

Those high meadows, I soon realized, are filling with trees almost everywhere. A defining element of Banff National Park's unique mountain aesthetic – and a vital habitat for many kinds of wildlife – is shrinking as forests expand upslope. While these high-elevation meadows can be expected to migrate farther uphill, they need soil, and soil develops very slowly on high mountainsides. Meantime, the meadows are increasingly squeezed between advancing forests below and rocky, soilless ridges. A warming climate is quietly erasing Banff's timberline flower meadows.

Snow Creek summit also awakened me to another change I might have missed if I hadn't let so much time lapse between visits.

Many of Banff National Park's higher valleys have a sort of male-pattern baldness. The sides of the valleys are forested, but the valley floors are open. The valley bottoms are unfriendly to trees because of their high soil moisture and frequent frosts from the cold air that pools there at night. Streams in these valleys meander through mosaics of grassland, dwarf birch tangles and willow thickets.

Columbian ground squirrels live in the grassy areas and are an important food source for predators such as golden eagles and coyotes. Brewer's and white-crowned sparrows thrive in the patchy habitats. Moose, elk, grizzly bears and, until recently, caribou rely on the lush meadow forage.

Upper Snow Creek had those sorts of meadows a third of a century ago. Today, however, the grassy parts are hard to find. The dwarf birch and willows are taller and have filled in most of the open spaces. Charred stems show where park fire crews have tried to burn the shrubbery back, but to no avail.

Researchers recently learned that increased carbon dioxide levels in the air give some woody shrubs a growth advantage over grasses and forbs. If that's what is happening along Snow Creek and the other subalpine stream meadows in Banff National Park, or even if the causes are as simple as warming soils or changing snowpacks, then it would represent another loss of ecological diversity traceable back to pervasive atmospheric changes.

These sorts of changes may have contributed to the disappearance of Banff's woodland caribou. Never abundant after Alberta built forestry roads that fragmented their habitat outside the park and improved access for poachers, the Banff part of the herd dropped from 20 or so in the latter part of the 20th century to only 5 in 2009. All 5 died that winter in an avalanche. Biologists, however, suspect that wolf predation may have brought their numbers so critically low in the first place.

Caribou avoid predators by staying in remote areas where the snow is deep. Frequent hard winters used to kill off deer and force elk to migrate to low-elevation winter ranges east of the caribou. Today's gentle winters enable more deer and elk to survive, in turn supporting higher numbers of wolves than would have been normal in the past. That need not be a problem for caribou, which winter in high valleys whose deep snow used to discourage wolves. The increased frequency of mild winters, unfortunately, means that wolves can now travel much more widely thanks to a shallower, denser snowpack. Even before that final accident, climate change had probably already doomed Banff's caribou.

On my original 1976 hike I had hoped to see a caribou. This time I knew I wouldn't.

Perhaps most troubling, however, was the stillness. Mountain songbirds are at their most vocal in late June. But day after day I hiked through a sodden stillness broken only occasionally by the song of a kinglet, Brewer's sparrow, hermit thrush or robin. Olive-sided flycatchers were common in the recently burned forests, but some species were completely missing. The barn swallows that once nested under the eaves of every patrol cabin were gone. The businesslike chants of MacGillivray's warblers were nowhere to be heard.

I contacted Geoff Holroyd at the CWS when I got back. He confirmed that counts of many migratory songbird species are down across most of the continent. Even in protected places such as Banff National Park, their numbers have declined, but it's because of things happening elsewhere. Many die during their nighttime migrations when they get trapped in the lights with which cities, casinos and airports fill the skies. Many thousands are killed by pet cats or collisions with windows. Others can no longer find resting or feeding spots now eliminated by urban sprawl, agricultural intensification or development. Pollutants affect their health and reproductive success. Climate changes add to the stress of migration by exposing birds to unexpected weather and altered habitats.

For all the continuing improvements in Parks Canada's ecosystem management, Banff National Park's timberline meadows are shrinking, its subalpine grasslands are being overwhelmed with woody shrubs and the changing landscape is going increasingly silent. And nobody seems to be noticing.

That the causes lie almost entirely outside the park doesn't get Parks Canada off the hook. Canada's national parks are dedicated to the people of Canada for their benefit, enjoyment and education, subject to the requirement to keep them unimpaired for future generations.

The enjoyment part is no problem; millions of Canadians go home happy from the parks each year. But the education part requires that they also go home with new insights or understanding about how ecosystems work and how their daily choices affect the Earth's atmosphere and ecosystems – for better or worse. Without that, it's unclear how Canada, or Canadians, get lasting benefits from those visits. Nor, for that matter, how the parks themselves can benefit – since the global forces threatening to impair those parks are the cumulative effect of decisions made by those same visitors, and their neighbours, at home.

It's at home, not during our brief visits to national parks, that we Canadians leave lights on in high-rise buildings, putting more carbon dioxide into the air from the wasted energy while dooming migrating songbirds to death by exhaustion in urban light traps. It's at home where we choose whether to buy gas-guzzlers or fuel-efficient cars. It's between park visits that we decide between rapid and reckless development of tar sands or more frugal approaches to the exploitation of our boreal forests and the petroleum beneath them. Our most important decisions as consumers, and as voting citizens, are made during day-to-day life.

National parks exist at the will of Canadians – they give expression to our collective sense that nature matters, that our heritage gives us meaning, that some places are so special that they should be passed on like family heirlooms to those who come after us. But they also exist at the mercy of Canadians.

During my 35 years working in western Canada's national parks, the number of visitors to those parks more than doubled. Some environmental groups argue that's a bad thing; some tourism groups think it's great. It could be either. It all depends on what new insights, understanding and motivations those visitors take home with them. Parks Canada's core mandate says that visitors are to be educated. And if parks are threatened with impairment, then Parks Canada is mandated to avert it. Those two responsibilities are flip sides of the same coin, because the only hope for wise decisions about land use, energy consumption and climate policy is an educated, ecologically literate Canadian population.

I t is Canada Day, 2011, when I finally arrive at the Trans-Canada Highway near Lake Louise. Countless people are streaming through the scenery, many on their way to or from celebrations of this place we call Canada – a place whose nature we honour and purport to protect in places called national parks. None, I suspect, are aware of the silence in the woods, the shrinking meadows, the missing caribou. Most will go home feeling good about their national park. Far too few, I fear, will go home transformed or enlightened about the nature of their Canada, its ecosystems, its climate – and their choices as citizens.

It appears that, for the most part, Parks Canada got ecosystem management right by the end of its first century. The critical next challenge is ecological literacy. Our parks won't last their next century without it. We might not either.

☙

Facebook Post

September 4, 2015. Banff.

I spent much of today with a hungry grizzly bear at Hidden Lake. She caught and ate several ground squirrels and scarfed down a few hedysarum roots. There evidently weren't many berries to be had. She foraged her way around the lake until she was almost in our lap, then worked her way back. Food is an intense obsession for bears at this time of year.

The whole time we visited with her, she and we were on land designated as Wilderness under the Canada National Parks Act. Thanks to the single most irresponsible decision Parks Canada has made in decades, however, the whole area may soon have its Wilderness designation stripped away and be added to the Lake Louise Ski Area. I'm pretty sure this is not what Canadians had in mind when they overwhelmingly fought for amendments to the Canada National Parks Act – like designating Wilderness – to protect their national treasures from commercial exploitation and privatization.

They may need to fight again ... Who should own the land that was set aside more than a century ago to ensure that we could always visit wild grizzlies in wild places where the trappings of commercial culture don't dominate nature? And who is Parks Canada's ultimate boss? Hint: look in the mirror.

Renewing Our Vows (2015)

Before there were roads through the Rockies, there were old Indian trails. The indigenous people who dwelt here followed those trails along the larger valleys and through side passes to places where they could find pipe stone, hunt bighorn sheep and gather medicine plants. It all was sacred, but some places were particularly powerful. People resorted there for healing, inspiration and spiritual renewal.

Roads were still scarce in 1907, when the recently widowed Mary Schäffer decided to venture deep into the largely unmapped Rockies. With her friend Molly Adams and guides Billy Warren and Sid Unwin, she traveled by horse pack train to the still-remote North Saskatchewan River.

There she met Samson and Leah Beaver, Stoney Nakodas who lived among their sacred mountains. Samson Beaver drew her a rough map to a lake hidden deep in the mountains to the north.

Many days later, Mary Schäffer became the first white woman to see Maligne Lake. She was awed by its quiet majesty. Even today, long after a paved road invaded its stillness, its spiritual power seems little diminished from what Schäffer and her party found more than a century ago after many hard days of wilderness horse travel.

It helps that the motorized crowds retreat down the valley each evening. Parks Canada may have built a road, but it had the good sense to keep Maligne Lake a day-use destination. In the evenings, peace spreads across the valley like a benediction, golden light slanting in across the caribou meadows of the Maligne Range to set the green avalanche meadows aglow on Mount Leah. Thrush song haunts the shadowed woods; timelessness returns.

The national park ideal was something new in Mary Schäffer's day. Canada's version was born in the Bow valley as a result of squabbling speculators hoping to commercialize another sacred place for the indigenous people – one the speculators professed to have "discovered." Rather than let the Banff hot springs become a tacky commercial resort, the government reserved a national park for all Canadians and proclaimed it protected for all time.

The frontier era was a time of massive change. National parks came to be seen as antidotes to loss and conflict – places where world-weary souls could seek renewal. Here, the sacred would persist, undefiled, for all time.

But for Canadians to visit their parks, they needed services. The government was not in the lodging, food and guiding business. So even though the parks were reserved for the public, the government invited commercial interests back in on a limited basis. Long-term leases or renewable licences encouraged private businesses to provide services to the visiting public. It was a marriage of convenience – practical, but hard-wired for conflict.

Businesses like to grow. Parks are meant to be kept wild.

Those two imperatives came into conflict when some business operators failed fully to embrace Canada's national park ideal. Sometimes Parks Canada itself forgot its sacred duty to future generations.

Mary Schäffer ultimately married her guide, Billy Warren. Their marriage, in many ways, modelled the ideal relationship between national park idealism and private enterprise. They loved the mountain national parks for what those places were, not for what they could take from them.

Every marriage faces tests. In the mountain national parks, the awkward marriage between nature and enterprise has been tested repeatedly. In the 1960s, Parks Canada proposed master plans that would commercialize even the remotest valleys. Outraged Canadians said no. Ski hill expansion proposals became controversial in the 1970s; again, Canadians said no. In the late 1980s, Alberta oil money flooded the Rockies and even the smallest businesses were suddenly able to afford expansion proposals. Parks Canada, reacting again to public outrage, commissioned two expert panels, revised management plans, and brought in a series of new policies to control commercial growth.

Today, again, the arranged marriage between protected nature and private enterprise is going through rocky times. Commerce once more seems to be trying to get the upper hand. Parks Canada, again, is complicit and conflicted. Even Mary Schäffer's sacred lake is under threat by a proposal to replace public day use with private overnight resort facilities.[9]

We can wait for Canadians to remind us all of what national parks are meant to be. Or we can remind ourselves that parks must always be parks, and then renew our vows to cherish and protect these sacred places.

---

9   Parks Canada, in 2015, approved in principle a small number of canvas-walled luxury overnight units but rejected a proposal by Maligne Tours for a major resort hotel. In allowing overnight accommodation at Maligne Lakes, Parks Canada undermined its own protection policies.

CHAPTER 8

Choices and Values

✤

Facebook Post

December 13, 2012. Canmore.

Woke up to another beautiful day on a beautiful planet. Oxygen simply everywhere. Transformed starlight in thousands of forms. Family. Friends. This is so cool. No, there are no additives in my coffee – just noticing a few good things.

Violence at Mountain Park (1997)

I used to hike up through resin-scented forests south of Hinton to hunt bighorn sheep among the mountaintops.

I remember climbing out of predawn mist one day onto the open slopes of Prospect Mountain and seeing the world turn gold as the rising sun burned off the valley fog. Below lay a tapestry of green pine forest, golden shrub meadows where elk fed quietly, talus slopes and bogs. A thin grey ribbon marked the road from Cadomin to the Cardinal River Divide. As I had often before, I studied this wild Alberta landscape with the same aching pleasure I feel while watching the sleeping face of the wife I love. I felt rich beyond all hope.

As I sat by a streamside meadow to eat lunch, I was struck by the intricate weave of the vegetation around me. Wheatgrasses, pussytoes, louseworts and countless other native plants mingled in a dense, continuous mosaic of spruce forest, sedge meadow, alder thicket and aspen bluff.

Generations of weasels had hunted generations of mice amidst that living tapestry. Moose wandered from willow tangle to aspen bluff, wolves travelled the ridges, flocks of redpolls descended in enthusiastic chaos into the birches – sometimes the landscape teemed with life. Other times it seemed lifeless, as still as the cold cliffs above.

Picking my way along the sheep trails, I often felt like an outsider. I wanted to be part of all this; I studied to belong, but in the evenings I went home. That worked against me. Still, I persevered.

One day I finally got a sheep. Leaving the entrails for the ravens and eagles who watch over this country, I loaded the meat into my pack. Having been awake and working hard since before daybreak, I decided to rest awhile. I fell asleep watching ravens circle above the ridge. Later I woke, fought the pack onto my shoulders, stood up ... and there were grizzly tracks. I had slept, with a pack full of meat, beside his hours-old spoor. It was a reminder that in this sort of country, human beings are among the lesser creatures. Chastened, grateful for the reprieve, I headed home.

The road home cut through big strip mines where overfed bighorn sheep watched from the roadsides, complacent as cows. The coal companies really like those sheep feeding on the alfalfa they have planted on their slack heaps. See? Strip mining is green.

But there is no sense of history or place in those minescapes. The sheep are tame. There is no great bear. There is nothing to which a human being might ache to belong.

Now a new Cheviot mine is planned. It will strip coal from under the Mountain Park country, right to the edge of Jasper National Park.[10] They will sell it to the Japanese for electricity generation. When they are finished, there will be a few hundred square kilometres more of alfalfa, rubble, tame

10   The Cheviot open-pit strip mine was ultimately approved and built. It is operating today.

bighorns, and little else. Investors will pocket their profits and move on.

That humans can still seriously contemplate violence on this scale is, I believe, deeply frightening. It implies a fundamental moral deadness: a vast dysfunction.

Some argue that Hinton needs the strip-mining jobs so that young families will not have to move to find work. Mine jobs pay well. Good people work there. What else are we going to do in a tired frontier economy?

Swan Hills got its toxic waste treatment plant and Pincher Creek its mud-encrusted Oldman River Dam because of this sort of thinking. These are frightened arguments founded not on love of place or integrity of vision but on a collective inability to see beyond the near abyss. Just give me a few more good years until this mine runs out, the logic goes; somebody might come up with something sustainable in the meantime.

And if they do not, what are we left with? Ravaged landscapes, no pride, no jobs. It's not like we haven't lived that story before.

Stripping the life from that Mountain Park country, I would argue, should be an act of desperation. Surely a society that identifies itself with its land would consider this only as a last resort: like burning the furniture to keep warm.

Lately I have wondered if this time I should just go stand in front of the bulldozers. I will not, of course: we Albertans are a conservative bunch who tend to view that sort of thing as a radical act. Most of us, however, do not consider it radical for a transnational corporation to strip the life, history and meaning from an ancient, healthy landscape, in order to export a dirty fuel to an overpopulated nation on a warming planet.

Licence to Abuse (1999)

"Wild pigs!" my daughter said. "Look at all the babies!"

A neighbour had fenced off a few acres of coulee and stocked it with wild boars. I slowed so the kids could see the exotic animals. Large brown adults rooted beneath bushes. Striped piglets scurried about.

Each time we drove past that summer, the herd had grown by another litter or two. Soon the coulee was looking beat-up.

By late summer big barren patches were sprouting thistles. Saskatoon bushes were dying, roots exposed to the sun. The clear brook that watered the enclosure was algal scum by the time it oozed out. A patch of productive, healthy land had been abused into devastation.

The municipal government eventually shut down the wild hog farm. It wasn't because of land abuse, however; downstream neighbours had complained about water quality. Governments will usually step in to protect human health and property values. Rarely, however, do they intervene to protect land from abusive owners.

Ownership seems to mean something different when context

changes. We use the same possessive pronoun to speak of our land, homes, families and friends, but we mean something different by applying "our" to people than to land. Land – although in many ways as alive, responsive, generous and vulnerable as the people in our lives – is property. Ownership of land, consequently, can be the kind of exploitative relationship that would never be tolerated between people.

Abuse results from a perverted sense of one's rights and responsibilities. Were I to treat my family like some do their land, I'd soon be called to accounts. My spouse and kids may be "mine," but that imposes a duty of care on me; it doesn't grant me licence. I own my family not because I bought them, but because I love them and they, in turn, love me. That bond of love allows me to call them "mine" and them to call me "theirs." We earn those possessive pronouns by nurturing one another and restraining our selfish inclinations.

If I were to abuse my family, fail to care for them, degrade them into less than what they should be, I would lose them. I would no longer have the moral right nor, should the courts so rule, the legal right, to call them "mine."

So why should one kind of ownership be different from the other? Why, when we speak of "our" families do we concentrate on our responsibility to give, while when we speak of "our" land we concentrate on an assumed right to take? There was a time when the community kept its eyes averted from what went on behind a family's closed doors. Thankfully, few hesitate to speak up today against child or spousal abuse. Yet we still turn our eyes away from another form of betrayal –

abuse of land by those who don't see a duty of stewardship attached to the privilege of ownership.

There was a time, as Aldo Leopold pointed nearly a century ago in his famous "Land Ethic" essay, when it was perfectly acceptable to own, and kill, human slaves. Until well into the 20th century, a wife was considered property whose sole purpose was to honour and obey her husband. Those times are gone, and the world is a better place for it.

But little public shame attaches to those who abuse land, so long as they can prove that they own it in fee simple. Owner-ship of land, in the community's eyes, amounts to licence to do almost anything the owner wishes. As Leopold wrote: "There is as yet no social stigma in the possession of a gullied farm, a wrecked forest, or a polluted stream, provided the dividends suffice to send the youngsters to college."

Conservation groups rail against habitat loss, farming groups against soil erosion, environmental groups against water pollu-tion, and heritage groups against the loss of place. But for the most part, all ascribe to the view that a land title entitles its holder the right to take until the land is sick. This is why the view from the roadside is so often not a pleasant one.

A better approach would be to recognize land ownership not as a right but as the profound and awesome responsibility it is. Buying land is like a wedding – it's the easy part. The most difficult, but most important, part of the relationship comes after. It is not by signing papers and handing over money that we earn the right to own land. We earn that right in the same way that we earn the right to call spouses our own – through love, sacrifice and acceptance of an abiding obligation of service.

Abusive relationships – whether with people, animals or land – are always ugly and always wrong. Nurturing relationships are things of beauty. Thus far, we have failed to apply this simple truth to land ownership. The marks of that failure are everywhere.

Thanks for the Food (2014)

One of the lesser responsibilities of being a father is to help one's offspring perfect the eye roll. A father does this by instituting family rituals that he enjoys, and the rest of the clan merely endures.

My father's eye roll training ritual involved bringing out his slide projector after a family meal. Looks of subdued dread would be exchanged. Escapes would – too late – be considered. But then all of the kids would dutifully array themselves around the living room while Dad plugged in his instrument of torture and subjected us to a travelogue illustrated by far too many slides. As a product of the Great Depression, Dad didn't believe in throwing anything out. That extended to culling his slide collection.

In due time, I too became a father and inherited the responsibility of training offspring to roll their eyes hopelessly. Dad's technique was out of date in the digital era, so I came up with one of my own. It involves saying an extended grace before the family meal.

Some nutrition experts blame health problems like obesity, cardiovascular disease and cancer on the trend toward mindless eating. Fast food makes it possible to consume all kinds of calories, chemicals and fillers without even thinking about what is going down the hatch. Proponents of the 100-mile diet blame mindless eating for the increasing environmental footprint of the Canadian consumer. The solution to both the health and the environmental issues, then, would seem to be a more mindful approach to one's food intake.

The occasion for being mindful of the food we eat is at grace. Whether you thank the God I was raised with, a different deity you were raised with or, for the atheists who figure everything is just a very complicated accident, you simply thank fate, chance and the planet we occupy, the giving of thanks before a meal is both appropriate and an opportunity fully to consider what we eat and where it comes from.

Right kids? (Eye rolls all around)

Really, though: in this nation and province, at this time in history, our meals should certainly be occasions for thanksgiving. It seems no food is ever out of season. We are encouraged, and able, to enjoy a diverse diet previous generations couldn't even dream of. And the things we eat all come from such interesting places, by such intricate means. Sorry, kids, but if we're meant to be mindful, a simple grace or no grace at all simply won't do.

"Thank you for this elk meat, and for the fescue grasslands that fed this elk and the Douglas fir forests that sheltered it. Thank you for the generations of wolves and cougars who helped to perfect the wildness of these elk, and the system of conservation that has kept elk, grass, fir trees, wolves and cougars around for us to treasure and enjoy. And thanks for our rancher friends who let me hunt for this elk on their land. Thanks also for ibuprofen, that helped me recover from that weekend-warrior stuff involving very large, heavy animals ...

"Thank you for the potatoes and the farmers who grow them in Prince Edward Island. Thanks for the fertilizers and pesticides, although it's unfortunate they aren't better calibrated, and for the trucks that haul those potatoes so many kilometres to our community. And thanks to the Irish for not only perfecting the culture of potatoes but for providing us with grandparents and our genetic proclivity for storytelling. Thanks for the potato famine that sent them looking for new homes ...

"Thanks also for the lettuce and the garden soil we grew it in, and the thousands of years of rain and snow and root activity and decomposition and change that produced that soil, and for the rain that fell when it was needed so that the vegetables didn't get all withered like last year. And thanks for marmots, pocket gophers, voles, deer and bears, all of whom help to make this a wonderful place in which to live, especially since, for the first time in years, they stayed out of the garden so we didn't have to be thankful for store-bought vegetables from faraway soils ...

"And thanks for the milk and butter, and the cows that produced it, and for the farmers who raised the cows, and for the milking machines, even if they seem strange and a bit scary to us ...

"And thanks for the good fortune that placed us in this corner of this Earth at this time in its history, when conservation, good land husbandry and our admittedly unsustainable level of affluence enables us to enjoy so much of its bounty. We humbly acknowledge that this meal is just one reason why we owe an awful debt of gratitude and care.

"Oh yes, and thank you for the microwave, and the unfortunately coal-fired electricity that runs that microwave, so that we can reheat the food that has grown cold on our plates while we've been giving thanks for things we might otherwise take for granted."

Eye rolls all around. Dad's work is done for another day. The fledglings in this family are now even more motivated to leave the nest; that's important too.

Supper can begin.

༯

Facebook Post

May 18, 2014. Snake Trail (marathon training).

This being Sunday, I went to church. The service, which was essentially a meditation of thanksgiving, went on for 24 kilometres. The altar had taken about 15,000 years to prepare (that being about how long since it was brought out from under the ice) and I thought the flower arrangement to be particularly well done. It was understated but colourful – mostly prairie crocus and buffalo bean but with some eye-dazzling splashes of shooting star too. The hymns were sung, fittingly enough, by vesper sparrows – one every 15 or 20 fence posts. Occasionally a meadowlark would break in with a hallelujah. The swallows and bluebirds didn't seem to be paying attention to the sermon, which was the Gospel according to the West Wind, but I have to admit even I found the more insistent bits tiresome. Still, it was one of the better services I've attended.

I understand the robins will be doing evening prayers tonight. Can't wait.

The Sacred (2015)

Theologians often invoke a contrast between the sacred and the profane. Some religions distinguish between our earthly existence and the heavenly paradise to which we are told to aspire; earthly matters are considered profane and heavenly ones sacred. Through history, ascetics and hermits have rejected the profane attractions of earthly life in the effort to render themselves spiritually closer to God.

The Judeo-Christian tradition into which I was born sees this planet – this unique and utterly unlikely orb, its thin veneer simply throbbing with life and diversity, spinning around a burning star in a far corner of an immense and unfathomable universe – as a temporary stopping ground for fallen angels who must while away their threescore and ten years here, beset with profane temptations, while awaiting the death that will usher them, at last, into the realm of the spiritual and sublime.

This is a secular and cynical era, however. While many profess religious faith, fewer actually live it. Many treat their faith more as cultural identity than a source of moral guidance; others only haul it out to justify resentments. A growing number dismiss religion altogether, as if meaning has no meaning.

So the notion of sacredness on Earth gets scant attention from religious and non-religious alike. For most of us, talk of the sacred makes us a bit uneasy when others bring it up – kind of like opening the door to see two earnest young men in suits, holding small books full of sticky notes: uh-oh.

And yet ... stop by an evening river and watch its waters furl around stones; see the exposed roots of streamside poplars draped with spiderwebs that refract the slanting light of the setting sun. Listen to the quiet chatter of water spilling surely from its sources to the sea. Is there no possibility of the sacred here? Is the notion of baptism still strange, or the Hindu tradition of setting prayers afloat on sacred waters?

Up on a foothills ridge, surrounded with wildflowers, wind and wildness, watching a golden eagle trace shadows across the green slopes – can heaven remain a remote concept? Does it lie far beyond that chinook arch or might we have misunderstood the story of the Garden of Eden? Perhaps we left and stayed.

An irony of putting ourselves at the centre of creation and relegating the sacred to the afterlife is that soon our only remaining hope may be the unproven assumption that there is indeed a heaven outside this world. We are, after all, knocking the planet's very climate off kilter, triggering the extinctions of fellow travellers in time, and using up resources, lands and waters in a distinctly non-spiritual quest for more stuff, now.

Profligacy and greed, of course, are contrary to most of the world's spiritual traditions. Islamic teachings reject greed. In the Christian tradition Jesus says that it's easier to put a camel through the head of a pin than for a rich man to get into heaven. Hindu respect for all opposes the selfish exploitation of other species.

But actions speak louder than words; greed trumps spirituality nine times out of ten.

The Catholic catechism of my childhood started its lessons with a powerful creation myth in the Book of Genesis. In Genesis, God creates the world in six days. On the final day He creates humans. Finally, looking at all of His creation, He proclaims it "very good."

Not some of it; all of it. Not humans only; everything. There is no "Oops ... I didn't mean to make that" in Genesis. Nor, to my knowledge, in the core teachings of any other great world religion.

A convenient misreading of Genesis makes humankind the crown of creation – the ultimate purpose for which the Earth was created rather than a unique creature burdened with the responsibility of being its steward. Needless to say, this view is not shared by the grey whale, elephant, mayfly or kestrel. They are all part of the "very good" too, after all.

Even without Genesis, logic alone would argue that everything that exists is, by virtue of its existence, the purpose of creation. Each species is the pinnacle of evolution. Every species, every ecosystem – arrived here together after 4.5 billion years of change. A deer mouse could be forgiven for believing that the Big Bang's purpose was to set forces in motion that would lead, ultimately, to deer mice. The existence today of deer mice is as good a proof that they were its purpose as our existence is that we were.

If there is a purpose to existence and to time, then everything that exists today is intended. "He looked at all that He had made and He saw that it was very good." Even if there is no purpose, everything is part of the same miracle of existence.

The sacred, in short, is everywhere. Everything is sacred. To squander any part of what has been 4.5 billion years in the making should never be seen as some part of divine destiny. At best, it might be argued to be a necessary evil; at worst it is deep sacrilege founded in an unforgivable hubris.

Joni Mitchell wrote: "We've got to get ourselves back to the garden." Honouring the sacredness of this diverse, unique and natural world of which we are merely one part might be a good first step.

CHAPTER 9

Caring People

Toad's Legacy (1998)

"On the river, when you are
finally on the river and you are alone with a friend,
you can finally
let it go, all the rancour and the displacement
it does not matter here. They say I am a newcomer
and I say to them
get down to the river and say that, watch
the ducks fly up in laughter. This friend
knows the songs of all the birds by heart,
they are part of his heart
they are the reason he has a fighter's heart, he
stands up in the boat to see above the levees
and through the great black trees that
stand guard along the bank. We speak of
trees and mink and let it go.

"It goes by
and we drift through the world again like children,
after the first hour
we have settled in. An eagle hangs above us
like a man crucified to the sky.
There is a dead thing ahead, an elk
that crashed through the ice and turned instantly
to food for the ling, the suckered fish
following the canoe like shadows.
There is wind
there is the surface of the water rippled and stretched

by the wind. There is rot and the
smell of rot and there is finally a
blankness in the mind, it lets the eyes see again,
and the eyes look out from the dark heart itself
and they let in the timeless light of the wild.

"They see the banks of the river,
carved and broken and sometimes dropping down
like mud, pale faceless mud. They see
line of sand upon line of gravel and we wonder out loud
how long it took,
we want to know about
the writing between the lines. But we do not expect
an answer, that is not why we are here today.
We want to feel
small because then we will also feel
as large as the eagle and the white world of swans."

—an excerpt from Dale (David) Zieroth's
much longer poem "Columbia."
Originally published in Mid-River (House of Anansi, 1976).
Reprinted with permission.

O n the river, as you drift around the first bend and the
launch site vanishes behind cottonwoods, there is no
point in worrying about time or things left undone. This is
a different dimension now; the river will not be hurried. The

brown water seems not so much to carry the canoe along as to hold it back, obliging paddlers to surrender to the timeless peace of the Columbia River wetlands.

Beyond the river's natural levees, screened from sight by tangles of alder, red osier dogwood, willow and black cottonwood, the worried clamour of Canada geese and clucking of spotted frogs advertise unseen marshes and sloughs. Tracks of elk and deer pockmark muddy nicks in the levees; sometimes bear or otter tracks appear too. Warbling vireos and ruby-crowned kinglets sing. Brown water hisses quietly in the branches of sweepers. Time slows nearly to a standstill.

My first float trip into the upper Columbia River's riparian wilderness was in 1975. Recently graduated, I had come to the edge of the Columbia valley to work as a summer park naturalist. The green mosaic seemed to sprawl on forever, framed by mountains, humid, fecund, chaotic with birdsong. Ospreys, beavers, startled wood ducks and watchful herons: for a biology graduate trying to imagine his future, the long float among new friends was a heady experience.

At the centre of it all was my boss for the summer: a stocky man with a brush cut, a jean jacket and an impish grin. Ian Jack wore the air of unassuming competence that came naturally to foresters of his generation. He told us about a writer named Aldo Leopold, recounted humorous stories about old-time outfitters and modern-day hippies, and quietly made room for each of us in the circle of warmth around him. There seemed nothing he didn't know about birds, amphibians, bears and local history. In the evenings, while we camped on old steamboat landings, his stories held us captive. As robins sang in the cottonwoods and cicadas trilled amid shadowed alders, Ian's distinctive chuckle punctuated the quiet buzz of conversation again and again.

"Ian used to like to watch people's behaviour on the Toad Floats," says Larry Halverson, a noted naturalist and environmental educator who lives at the southernmost edge of the wetlands in Invermere, BC. He smiles at the memory of his close friend. "He always got a kick out of how some would start in paddling like they really had to get somewhere. Usually by the third day they'd have slowed down and be just drifting. Ian'd say to me, 'Looks like they finally found the toad.'"

The toad in question was a mythical beast Ian invented in the early 1970s. Spawned in the silty outwash of the Toby Glacier high in the Purcell Mountains west of Invermere, the great green toad had migrated downstream to the marshes and back-waters of the upper Columbia River. The Columbia wetlands – sprawling across the bottom of the Rocky Mountain Trench from Athalmer 160 kilometres north to the town of Donald – is the longest undisturbed riparian mosaic in North America today. The storied toad might be anywhere in there. Those who found him, Ian insisted, were certain to obtain wisdom and great blessings.

Beginning in 1973, Ian Jack and Larry Halverson organized annual expeditions to search for the great green Columbia River toad. Naturalists travelled from all over western Canada to join local conservationists for a three-day float down the river. In the middle of their motley flotilla, blinking like a mirror in the bright May sun, floated Ian Jack's aluminum rowboat. Over the years, Ian became known to his friends and admirers as Toad, and Toad Floats became less a whimsical quest for a mythical amphibian than a much-coveted opportunity to spend time with a man whose wisdom, humour and persistence will stand always as a model for those who want to make conservation work.

The river's sleepy rhythms may seem to slow time, but they cannot stop it. On November 9, 1996, Ian Jack collapsed and died of a heart attack while chopping wood at his home at Edgewater, just a few hundred metres from the wetlands he loved. He was only 60 years old. Unlike other great conservationists who died too young, however, Ian lived to see success after spending half his lifetime fighting for the Columbia wetlands. On April 30, 1996 – barely six months before his death – the BC government signed an order establishing the new Columbia Wetlands Wildlife Management Area.

Larry Halverson, who took over from Ian as chief park naturalist in Kootenay National Park after Ian's retirement, says that if there was any doubt about Ian's remarkable ability to unite diverse people around a common cause, his memorial service should have erased those. "Helicopter jockeys, loggers, hippies, trappers, hunters, politicians, coal miners – people of every kind were there." An overflow crowd of more than 250 people turned out to pay their last respects to the man who saved the Columbia River wetlands.

T he odds seemed hopeless when Ian Jack first began the battle to save the wetlands. In the early 1970s, BC Hydro was determined to put those wetlands to work generating electric power. Prevailing public sentiment was that what was good for Hydro was good for BC. The few who felt differently were resigned to the view that there was little point trying to stop the energy giant from implementing the river diversion provisions of the Columbia River Treaty.

The Columbia River Treaty, signed in 1961 between Canada and the USA, set the stage for a series of dams that destroyed nearly 600 kilometres of Canada's portion of the Columbia River. The Mica Dam, finished in 1973, backed the Columbia up into the Rocky Mountain Trench – a rift valley more than a thousand kilometres long. The reservoir flooded hundreds of square kilometres of the valley floor, adding to damage already caused by the massive W.A.C. Bennett Dam that – farther north – had plugged the Peace River in 1968 and. backed water up both the Finlay and Parsnip River valleys to flood more than 1600 square kilometres at the north end of the same Rocky Mountain Trench. At the south end of the Trench, the US Army Corps of Engineers erected the Libby Dam on the Kootenay River, backing water into BC under Koocanusa Reservoir.

With most of the Rocky Mountain Trench already flooded, there was no practical way to dam the headwaters reach of the Columbia River upstream from the Mica Reservoir. But the treaty threatened it anyway.

Most of the Columbia River Treaty's hydro power and

irrigation benefits went to the United States; the big reservoirs that flooded four-fifths of Canada's portion of the Columbia valley merely store water for American hydroelectric dams farther downstream. There was, however, one way that Canada could improve its returns: the treaty allowed BC Hydro to tip most of the Kootenay River's flow north into the Columbia at Canal Flats. There, instead of flowing south to turn turbines on the Libby Dam, it would flow through Canadian hydroelectric generating plants at the Mica and Revelstoke dams.

Ian Jack knew the upper Columbia River well. He hunted ducks, geese and deer among its lush backwater marshes and riparian thickets of willow and cottonwood. He volunteered his time to build nesting platforms for geese and erect nest boxes for wood ducks and goldeneyes. In spring, when willow catkins were yellow, song sparrows and redwings shouted about the return of another breeding season and winter-weary deer congregated on newly green sidehills, Ian often floated down one of the Columbia's many twisting channels with Larry, Dale Zieroth or some other friend, soaking up sunshine, counting migrants, and chuckling over his latest good story.

Most of his neighbours either didn't know about the proposed Kootenay-Columbia Diversion, or considered it pointless to resist BC Hydro. Ian Jack, however, considered it a simple question of values. It would be a failure of ethics, he believed, were he not to do all he could to protect the wetlands from a man-made flood. And so in the early 1970s he began a campaign that culminated more than a quarter century

later in the establishment of the Columbia River Wildlife
Management Area.

꿈

I an's strategy evolved as his network of contacts in the
Columbia Basin grew. The Toad Floats helped introduce
park naturalists and representatives of the outdoors media to the
place itself, building wider awareness of the ecological values
at stake and deeper commitment to the cause of protection.
Ian's sincere interest in and respect for people played no less
important a role, because it yielded an ever-widening coalition of concern among town councils, local fish and game
clubs, environmental groups and local businesses. Nobody, in
Ian Jack's world, was an outsider. Everybody, in his view, was
an environmentalist. His knack was in helping them realize it.

The diversion seemed a simple engineering issue to BC
Hydro's planners. Ian's understanding of biology and the inti
mate workings of the wetland ecosystem, however, helped
him frame the issue in terms engineers weren't comfortable
with.

"Ian just kept on asking them hard questions," says Larry
Halverson, "and forcing them to go back and find answers
rather than admit they hadn't really thought about what the
effects might be. For example, the Kootenay River is a lot
colder than the Columbia, so Ian asked how pouring all that
colder water into the Columbia River would affect warmer

water fish like the pike-minnow, and the swimming and waterskiing on Lake Windermere."

Ian's questions echoed through the Columbia valley, awakening people to the many ways the diversion could undermine their well-being. Questions about cold water, for example, got the attention of Invermere's Chamber of Commerce, which relies on summer tourism centred on Lake Windermere. No less canny was Ian's question about what would happen – with most of the Kootenay River's flow diverted north – to the pollution from a large pulp mill on the Kootenay River at Skookumchuk. In the 1970s dilution was still considered the solution to pollution – but with less dilution the pulp mill would be forced into costly technology upgrades to reduce its effluent levels. Ian's simple question produced another influential diversion opponent.

As his coalition continued to grow, their questions became more sophisticated and insistent and the costs – both in dollars and public goodwill – continued to mount. BC Hydro began to change its tune. By the 1980s water development projects no longer enjoyed the support they had two decades earlier. Energy conservation technology was emerging as a new way for electric utilities to make money. After waffling for several years, BC Hydro announced in 1990 that there would be no Kootenay-Columbia Diversion.

But the battle was far from over. Ironically, the diversion threat had actually protected the wetlands from other dangers. As long as BC Hydro held a flood reserve on the valley bottom, nobody seriously considered draining marshes for cropland, filling sloughs to create golf courses or developing recreational real estate. Now, with the threat of flooding gone, speculators began to look at the wildlife-rich wetlands and consider how to squeeze profits out of them.

The 1991 election of Mike Harcourt's NDP government, fortunately, came just in time. The new government, hoping to put an end to divisive land use battles, announced a new planning initiative for every square centimetre of BC's public land. Ian Jack retired from Parks Canada in 1992 and devoted himself full time to representing the interests of hunters, anglers and other conservationists when the Commission on Resources and Environment (CORE) turned its attention to the East Kootenay region.

Bob Jamieson, a biologist-rancher from Ta Ta Creek who coordinated the East Kootenay plan, says that Ian was in his element in the CORE process. "Ian was one of those rare people who crossed over the line between naturalist and hunter," he says. "He could go out and shoot ducks in the morning, then spend the afternoon finding some rubber boas and making notes on them. He was the antithesis of the modern computer biologist. He learned from talking to the people, and he could talk with anyone."

Ian's sheer enjoyment of people and consistent ability to steer conversations into the realm of shared values served him well in a process that demanded long hours of negotiation among people representing a diversity of conflicting interests – from logging and mining companies, government agencies, tourism operators and chambers of commerce to off-road vehicle groups, environmentalists and hunting outfitters.

"Ian and I both worked hard to get the wetlands protected," says Ellen Zimmerman, an eco-tourism operator from Golden, BC. She represented the East Kootenay Environmental Society during the CORE negotiations. "But we wanted a Class A provincial park and Ian wanted a Wildlife Management Area."

Under BC protected areas legislation, a Wildlife Management Area protects habitat from development while still providing for recreational uses such as hunting, fishing, nature study and eco-tourism where they don't conflict with wildlife needs. Ian preferred to keep the wetlands exactly as they were and not risk disenfranchising any of the traditional users who had, after all, played so important a role in the earlier battle against the diversion. He suspected a provincial park might result in new recreational development, more tourism, and less room for traditional users.

Ultimately, Ian's vision won the day – and, as usual, his wisdom proved itself when a controversy over motorized vehicles erupted only six months after his death. Participants in the 1997 Toad Float – which Larry Halverson had organized in memory of Ian and in honour of his widow, Joyce – encountered several aggressive stunters on motorized Jet Skis. The experience spurred several participants to start looking into the impacts of motorized boats and other vehicles on wildlife. A provincial park, with its recreational mandate, might not have supported their subsequent call for restrictions on motors. However, the Wildlife Management Area had to put wildlife needs first. The BC government quickly imposed a year-round ten-horsepower restriction on motorized traffic in the wetlands.

"The order includes all motorized conveyances, including snowmobiles, quads, dirt bikes jet boats and so on," says Dave Phelps, regional land management biologist responsible for the wetlands. "It was implemented to reduce disturbance and harassment of wintering wildlife, soil erosion and sedimentation on forage plants and invertebrates ... predation on waterfowl broods that scatter after being surprised by high speed craft, egg breakage from rapid flight off nests etc., and general habitat destruction."

It also restored the stillness.

One recent May evening, I picked my way down a narrow forest trail to Larry Halverson's rustic cabin on the edge of the Columbia River near Brisco. A kestrel harassed a bald eagle above the cottonwoods as I unloaded my gear and strolled down to the water's edge. A few hundred metres away, a massive stick nest dwarfed the poplar that held it. A white head showed above the rim; the eagle's mate was incubating eggs. A pike-minnow splashed in a nearby eddy.

It had been years since I had been down to the Columbia wetlands, but as I lowered myself into the grass and looked across the marshes at mountains hazed by the smoke of distant fires, I felt the old familiar quiet seeping into me. In a world with too much change, this was a place where almost nothing had changed. Geese still clamoured beyond the alders. Warbling vireos and ruby-crowned kinglets sang just as they had every other May morning for centuries. The green world enfolded me, welcoming me back.

Last time I was here, I had visited with Ian. He was putting up goose nesting platforms. It occurred to me now that Ian had been here on all my previous visits to this place. Suddenly conscious of a deep sense of loss, I listened for the rattle of an oar against the side of an aluminum rowboat or the sound of mirthful laughter. All I heard, however, was birdsong and the timeless whisper of passing water; and after a while I realized that was enough.

The Toad was there. And he always will be.

༄

Facebook Post

November 8, 2015. Calgary.

Fifty years ago I was a member of the Calgary Bird Club, along with a couple of other guys my age – Cleve Wershler and Wayne Smith. We used to sign up for every field trip and inflict our chaotic enthusiasms on the adult members with cars as we toured around with them from one birding hotspot to another near Calgary on Saturdays.

One of those grownups in particular stands out in my memory as a mentor and role model: Ian Halliday, a true gentleman and birder who had himself, years earlier, been part of a similar cadre of young birders in Ontario that included Robert Bateman. Last night I did a Heart Waters talk for Nature Calgary (the modern version of the old bird club) and Ian was there to introduce me. I felt like a kid all over again. We talked about where our roads had led from those good days back in the 1960s. I drove home feeling deeply grateful for old friends.

Take a kid birding. You never know where it will lead.

Hope on the Range (1999)

Another April chinook is spilling down across the Alberta foothills. Prairie crocuses dance in the wind as they've done here every spring for centuries.

The wind sweeping out of Waterton Lakes National Park chases rippling waves through brown fescue. Trumpeter swans and Canada geese dot the quiet wetland below the crocus covered ridge. A grizzly bear roots about beneath the nearby aspens, unearthing sweet glacier lily bulbs and pocket gophers. Two sandhill cranes strut and croak. The thin sweetness of a horned lark's song tinkles in the wind.

The grizzly emerges from the aspens and pauses to rub his heavy muzzle in the tangled bunchgrass. Unaware of him until now, several cows on the nearby ridge begin to bawl for their recently born calves. The bear watches with lazy interest as mothers gather calves and the herd crashes away into silver willow shrubbery along the base of the far hillside. Then he shakes himself and moseys down to the water's edge, investigating the odours to be found there.

Undisturbed by scent or sight of humans, he has spent all week here, in some of the most productive habitat occupied by grizzlies anywhere in Canada – a mosaic of rich wetlands, aspen forest and bunchgrass prairie. He cleaned up the remains of two stillborn calves earlier this month, but it's mostly the greenery that interests him today.

The same combination of productive natural habitat and lack of human activity that makes these foothills a haven good for bears benefits the cranes and swans too. Both will produce broods of offspring here later this spring. Amid the cow tracks down by the slough are the tracks of elk and deer. They too thrive in the solitude of the aspen parkland that stretches along the foot of the Rocky Mountains here beneath the chinook arch.

For those who visit the nearby Waterton Lakes National Park, this diversity of wildlife and habitat might seem unremarkable. The spectacular, but compact, park – designated an International Biosphere Reserve in 1977 and a World Heritage Site in 1995 – is famous for its abundant wildlife.

The grizzly, cranes and trumpeter swans, however, are on privately owned ranchland several kilometres northeast of the park. Much of Waterton's wildlife wealth is, in fact, less a product of park protection than of habitat that ranchers outside the park have protected for more than a century. Almost all the region's sandhill cranes and trumpeter swans nest on private ranchland – not in the park. Some rare plants like blue camas and blue flag iris are virtually unknown inside the park, but abundant on neighbouring cattle pastures. Even grizzly bears – although their opportunistic feeding habits sometimes bring them into conflict with ranchers – are more abundant on foothills ranches outside the park boundaries than inside the park.

Waterton is a paradox that confounds those who look for simple solutions to conservation challenges. Its wildlife abundance is at least as much the result of cattle ranching as it is of park protection. To many naturalists, the whole idea seems counterintuitive: aren't cows bad? Don't ranchers kill predators? How can a park not only coexist with, but depend upon, cattle ranching?

"Make no mistake about it," says the Nature Conservancy of Canada's western field director, Larry Simpson. "If the ranches vanish from the Waterton Front, there is no future for Waterton Lakes National Park."

Dave Glaister agrees, as might be expected of a man who's raised cattle for well over half a century. But the tall, lean rancher-naturalist is less concerned with proving that ranches help conserve biological diversity than simply ensuring that ranching will survive in a changing world. He isn't sure it can. Like the solitude-loving wildlife that lives on his family's Shoderee Ranch, north of Waterton, he's retreated before the tidal wave of development about as far as he can go. Glaister and many other ranchers are starting to know how it feels to be an endangered species.

Dave and Lucille Glaister raised their family west of Millarville, Alberta. Their ranch sprawled along the edge of the Bow-Crow Forest Reserve, in a foothills landscape rich in deer, elk, bear and moose. It was prime cattle-growing country, and a fine place to raise kids – perfect in all respects except one. It was only a half hour's drive from Calgary.

They don't live there any more. Their former ranch is now subdivided into small acreages, most of which house "rurban" commuters who work in the booming city, then retreat each night to million-dollar homes in the scenic foothills. Each acreage has its own roadway, lawn and buildings. Many feed horses on undersized, overgrazed pastures. Pet cats hunt in the underbrush and family dogs chase deer at night. Yard lights have banished the undisturbed darkness that used to greet the Glaisters when they rose before dawn.

Until recently, the Alberta foothills were among the last refuges for Canada's native prairie and the wildlife species that depend on natural grasslands. Elsewhere, most have been lost to cultivation and urban development. The earliest, and greatest, losses were in western Ontario and Manitoba, where much less than 1 per cent of the tall grass prairie survives uncultivated. The fescue grassland region – extending from western Manitoba in a fertile arch through Saskatoon and Edmonton south to Calgary – fared little better. The somewhat drier mixed grass region is Canada's wheat belt: thousands of square kilometres of rolling grain stubble stitched together with barbed wire fences. Ghost bison graze among granaries and grid roads.

Only those parts of the prairie too dry for cultivation or with too short a growing season survived the 20th century's epidemic of landscape change – and those are where ranchers now face the next wave of land conversion.

Ranching country is scenic, wildlife-rich and relatively inexpensive for those seeking a recreational hideaway or a scenic setting for a commuter home. Instead of cultivating the grassland, subdivisions and acreages carve it into weedy little bits. Grizzlies aren't welcome in acreage country – some human residents might appreciate them, but most don't. Wolves are a romantic idea until they run the family horse through the fence. Upland sandpipers, long-billed curlews and sharp-tailed grouse can't survive in patchwork prairie patrolled by pet dogs and cats.

The Glaisters sold their ranch when the trickle of new acreages around them became a flood. They liked some of the new neighbours, but trespassers, stray pets and other petty problems continued to increase. As land prices inflated, they could no longer afford to lease pasture or buy new land. Their taxes, based on development land values rather than agricultural ones, grew past the point where the economically marginal business of growing cattle could yield a reasonable income.

Larry Simpson puts the financial dilemma faced by development-besieged ranchers in perspective. "Land in the Alberta foothills was worth about $100 per acre in 1971," he says. "Today land sells for 10 to 18 times more. But cattle prices – well, back then you would have to sell maybe ten calves to buy a truck. Today it takes between 40 and 50. So beef prices have comparatively gone down while land prices have gone up."

Dave and Lucille, and their grown children, decided to get as far away as possible from Calgary's fevered real estate market when they sold the family ranch in 1991. Their search for a more remote refuge led them to the Shoderee, one of prairie Canada's last large ranches. The Shoderee sprawls along Pine Ridge, a long moraine carpeted with rough fescue grassland and aspen forest that connects westward with Waterton Lakes National Park's windy mountains.

At night, on the Shoderee, no lights show in any direction. By day, red-tailed hawks scream above the aspens, the sounds of geese and cranes carry from hidden sloughs, and the woods and willow tangles are a bedlam of birdsong. The family regularly see grizzly bears. From time to time they see wolves too.

"One morning I was having breakfast," says Glaister, who keeps a spotting scope mounted in the living room for watching wildlife, "and I saw 15 white-tail bucks go out across the hayfield. One after another. Fifteen of them."

The Glaisters love the wildness and diversity of their new home. They barely had time to settle in, however, before the juggernaut they had fled was at the door.

Quarter sections – normally the smallest un-subdivided unit of ranchland – adjacent to the Shoderee have recently sold for $1,200 an acre. Smaller acreages have sold for $40,000 an acre. No rancher can hope to pay the carrying costs on that kind of money simply by raising cattle. As land prices increase, in fact, even established ranchers who own their land outright find themselves caught in a tax squeeze; recently the Alberta government passed new legislation that forces municipalities to tax land based on its current market value. Some land-owners have seen their yearly tax bills triple or quadruple simply because of their location adjacent to one of the hottest recreational destinations anywhere: the Canadian Rockies.

Area ranchers are no longer surprised to return home after a long day to find a real estate broker's card tucked into their screen door. "Even the ones I've run off already do it," says one local rancher. "They just wait until they see me go out."

Larry Simpson says that the Nature Conservancy of Canada has begun to focus on the ranching country along the eastern slopes of the Alberta Rockies "because all the conservation values are there, including predators. Sure there are conflicts that occur from time to time, but the fact remains that those animals are there because the habitat exists. Landscapes can recover from most everything, but not from concrete."

Simpson represents an organization that calls itself the real estate arm of the conservation movement. His job is to invest donated money so as to get the greatest return in conservation of endangered nature. Spending other people's money is a big responsibility, so he does his homework. Real estate experts he has consulted predict that as many as 60 per cent of the ranches in western North American will be sold in the first 20 years of the 21st century. An entire generation of ranchers is nearing retirement age; many have complicated estates to settle. If current real estate trends continue, many of their ranches will end up in the hands of speculators and developers.

Like Dave Glaister, Larry Simpson is tall and lean, but the resemblance stops there. Simpson has an intense, focused personality. He seems driven by urgency – like time is running out. Indeed, he says, it is: "The western heritage and natural heritage of western North America could potentially undergo a transformation in the next 20 years that will be as profound and long-reaching as the loss of the buffalo. Different, yes: but no less significant."

Larry Simpson uses satellite images of Canada to make his case for what he calls Canada's 1 per cent challenge. For all Canada's vast size, he points out, only 1 per cent of the country is both arable and biologically intact. That 1 per cent – mostly in the dry southern prairies or in a thin arc along the Alberta foothills – contains almost half of all Canada's endangered species. And that 1 per cent continues to die the death of many cuts as gas pipelines slice through native prairie, towns and cities grow and – with increasing regularity – ranchers give up the struggle and cash in by selling their land to developers.

In the late 1990s the Nature Conservancy of Canada launched what Simpson calls the Waterton Front Project – an ambitious campaign to permanently protect at least eight major ranches adjacent to Waterton. Already the Nature Conservancy has placed conservation easements on several square kilometres of land and has other deals pending – but Larry Simpson points out that the same pressures that beset Waterton are at play in the Crowsnest Pass, the Porcupine Hills, and the foothills west of Calgary and Red Deer. The challenge is as immense as it is urgent.

"If Canada fails to meet our 1 per cent challenge – with our level of education and relative affluence compared to other nations – that suggests to me that the world must almost surely fail in conserving biological diversity."

Others share Simpson's sense of urgency. World Wildlife Fund Canada released its Prairie Conservation Action Plan in 1989, stating: "In only 100 years, the Canadian prairies – grasslands and parkland – have been so radically transformed by human activity that they have become one of the most endangered natural regions in Canada ... Canadians need to ensure that native prairie, with its wild plants and animals, survives in the west and is conserved for its intrinsic values, from which this and future generations can benefit."

All this is true – but why worry about ranching? Cattle, after all, are not bison. Cattle can overgraze prairie, helping weeds invade and reducing food and cover for native wildlife. Cows are notorious for spending too much time in riparian areas, where they trample and graze wildlife habitat and damage stream banks. Ranchers have rarely been noted for generous feelings toward large predators – in fact, it was agricultural "pest" control that erased grizzly bears and wolves from much of their North American range.

American conservation writer George Wuerthner goes so far as to argue that subdivisions are better than ranching. In the American west, private land is more limited in extent than in southern Canada. Once ranching is no longer viable there, he says, nearby public lands can start to recover from decades of cattle damage. His argument, however, has a fundamental flaw: the private lands are usually the most ecologically productive habitats – well-watered riparian areas that early homesteaders scooped up first.

Much of the range damage American conservationists complain about dates back to the late 1800s, when eastern speculators poured millions of cattle into the open range. Especially in the arid and semi-arid grasslands west of the Rockies, where native vegetation had evolved in the absence of large herds of grazing animals, the damage was massive.

Canada, according to historian Barry Potyondi, never suffered the massive overstocking of open range that took place farther south. Overgrazing was only a local problem that appeared in the 20th century as growing numbers of hopeful colonists fenced and cross-fenced the range, confining cattle into smaller and smaller tracts of grassland and reducing the economic margins within which ranchers had to operate.

Most of Canada's rangeland lies east of the Rockies, where vegetation evolved under the influence of large herds of bison. Spared frontier overgrazing and with enlightened range management practices, Canada's grasslands can actually benefit from cattle grazing, which promotes native vegetation diversity. The key is well-managed grazing – management that approximates what the native grassland was used to before the arrival of the domestic cow. After a century of ranching, most ranchers who are still in business have proven their ability to keep native ranges healthy.

Riparian damage is a different problem; many ranches still have so-called "sacrifice areas" down by the creek, where cows spend too much time. In the past decade, however, a growing riparian restoration movement has spread across Alberta, southern BC and Saskatchewan. Rather than giving their herds year-round access to creek bottoms, ranchers fence out riparian pastures and develop wells or dugouts to provide water to their herds when they are on upland areas. By grazing riparian areas only when soils and vegetation are most resistant to damage, participating ranchers restore the willow thickets, reedgrass swales and cottonwood forests that make prairie riparian areas some of prairie Canada's most productive and important habitats.

Predators remain a thorny issue. The Glaisters have lost cattle to grizzlies. Nearby ranchers report having lost stock to wolves. Those who view foothills grasslands primarily as cattle country rarely harbour warm feelings toward animals that can kill livestock. Even so, ranchers like the Glaisters value the presence of large predators, only calling in problem wildlife officers when they actually suffer livestock losses. The irony, of course, is that wolves and grizzly bears still range many parts of the Alberta foothills only because ranching – which keeps the landscape largely natural – ensures that they can find wild prey and, in the case of the bears, a diversity of plant foods. In southwestern Alberta, recently, some ranchers have begun working cooperatively with the Alberta Fish and Wildlife Division to head off predator–livestock conflicts before they happen.

Most of the environmental criticisms aimed at ranching relate to management practises that can be, and increasingly are being, remedied. Meantime, as long as ranching families like the Glaisters can keep the land intact and make a reasonable living at ranching, the last and best that remains of prairie Canada's biological diversity will have a fighting chance.

"A well-managed ranch operation," says Larry Simpson, "is a living, working model of a steady-state economy. If the entire world could be managed and kept in as good condition as many ranches, then we would be in good environmental shape."

His Royal Highness Prince Philip, the Duke of Edinburgh, was in Regina for the launch of the Prairie Conservation Plan. "There are those who know and understand the serious consequences for the future health of this planet if ecosystems are wantonly destroyed," he said, "and there are those who have the power or the influence or the resources to prevent that destruction.... The solution is to establish two-way communication between these groups."

As well-heeled urbanites and developers drive up the real estate value of Canada's best surviving grassland ecosystems, ranchers like the Glaisters are facing new struggles to protect the places they love. Larry Simpson is among those determined to ensure that they don't stand alone.

Man for the Mountains (2000)

The rain has ended. Clouds are shredding themselves against the peaks up the Waterton valley. Golden sun streams through a gap in the west and fills the valley below with emerald green, as if the land were lit from within. A lazuli bunting in a nearby aspen sings as if mesmerized by the surreal stillness of this June evening. The air smells of wild roses and new green foliage.

For a while conversation stops and the people gathered on the porch at Hawk's Nest find themselves lost together in the utter calm and glowing beauty of the moment. A dozen of us are here this evening, conservationists gathered from across the country to plan how to protect this landscape from the forces of fragmentation that have already destroyed so much of Canada's wilderness beauty. Some of the group are wealthy philanthropists determined to invest in nature's future. Others represent conservation organizations like the Nature Conservancy of Canada. A couple of us are biologists. Sitting in an old armchair at the corner of the porch, a big man with a black cowboy hat and fringed coat catches my eye and grins. He's watched this view thousands of times before. He knows that when the sun dips behind Horseshoe Ridge and the humid evening chill comes spilling out of the shadows beneath the aspens, the spell will break and the group will move indoors. In the warmth of the old hunting lodge, as owls begin to hoot outside, it will be time for another kind of magic.

For now, let the beauty of southern Alberta's grizzly country speak to the spirits of those gathered here to help protect it. Later, Andy Russell will speak to their imaginations as he has already done so many times before. That, after all, is why they are here.

There isn't a lot about Andy Russell – at least not on first appearance – to suggest that this man has become a living icon of Canada's conservation movement. His hair is silver-grey, his face tanned and chiselled with lines from wind and age, and he doesn't stand as straight as he used to. He's an old-timer now, with the slow drawl and ready laugh of a cowboy. That's what he is, after all.

But let him ease back and fix you with those hawk-like eyes, let him fish around in his mind for the right story for the occasion, and it won't take long to discover that the old man of the mountains has lost none of the wisdom, acerbity, humour and power that have made him a force to be reckoned with for more than 50 years.

Perhaps more than any 20th-century Canadian conservationist, Andy Russell helped to define both our wilderness movement, and our collective understanding and concern for wild animals and wild places. His uncanny talent for storytelling transformed the lives and minds of an entire generation by awakening them to the meaning of wilderness and challenging their complacency about its well-being. And his bull-headed passion for fairness and refusal to be intimidated won lasting changes in how governments and industry respect their obligations to the environment.

If there is hope for reconciliation between people and the places where we live in the 21st century, it will be in no small part due to Andy Russell's contribution to the century just past.

"As surely as the sun rises tomorrow morning, grizzly country is wilderness country, and he cannot live without it. Man, through most of his recent evolution from primitive to present-day civilization, has chosen to fight the wilderness blindly, attempting to break nature to his needs, at war with it, and sometimes mercilessly destroying the very things he needs the most. The grizzly can show us something of what it means to live in harmony with nature."

—Grizzly Country, *1967*

I was in Grade 10 the year that my sister Margaret gave my father a copy of Andy Russell's newly released *Grizzly Country* for Christmas. It sat on the coffee table in our Calgary home for weeks before I picked it up one day and idly flipped through it, looking at photos of grizzly bears, bighorn sheep and wild places.

Once I started reading the text, I was captured. During the following week, I read Andy Russell's book from cover to cover, twice. It was like nothing I had ever read before, a richly lived and deeply thought chronicle of adventure and discovery in the wild country of western North America. Woven through the personal anecdotes and vivid storytelling were well-researched facts about an animal that, at that time, was more a figure of fearful imagination than a real creature to most North Americans.

Until then, to a boy growing up in Calgary, the Rocky Mountains had been little more than a blue-grey wall along the western horizon. Some days, especially when a chinook arch spilled across the sky, they seemed magnified, close, crisp with detail. Other days they receded into distance, becoming vaguely unreal.

Grizzly Country – and after it, *Horns in the High Country* – had the effect of turning my face toward those mountains more than ever before. It had never occurred to me that wildness might be so close to home. Hiking the hills on the outskirts of Calgary alone, or fishing with Dad and my siblings along some quiet foothills stream, I would look west to where steep-sided valleys receded into shadows among the peaks and hear Andy Russell's stories whispering to me of what might lie just beyond. An entirely new world of wilderness had opened up for me.

What I didn't know at the time was that I was not alone in feeling the powerful effect of Andy's words. Prior to the late 1960s, few Canadians had concerned themselves about wildlife and the environment. My generation was born into one of the longest economic boom periods in the country's history. The 1950s and 1960s were an era of brash confidence and rapid development. It seemed like our natural resources could never run out.

Andy Russell's books – particularly his classic *Horns in the High Country*, *Grizzly Country* and *Trails of a Wilderness Wanderer* – played a crucial role in awakening Canadians' awareness to the costs of too much mindless exploitation. While his seemingly endless wealth of personal anecdotes awakened a fascination and longing in the hearts of many readers, he was blunt about pointing out the rate of landscape destruction and its consequences to the Rockies. His writings were distillations of nostalgia for frontier times and people, love of wild nature and urgent concern about the rate of change and loss.

Reading those books, I realized that Andy Russell was in many ways like my father. Like Dad, he'd lived through most of the changes that characterized the 20th century. He shared my father's love for fishing, hiking and hunting. So there was a kind of symmetrical rightness to the fact that my first chance to meet Andy Russell in the flesh was in 1974, when the University of Calgary honoured both him and my father with honorary doctorates – Dad for a lifetime of service to education, and Andy for his lifetime of service to conservation.

That was 26 years ago. Since then, Andy has added another lifetime of service to conservation, and he now holds three honorary doctorates.

A ndy Russell's life began as the frontier came to an end. He was born in the southern Alberta town of Lethbridge in 1915, and spent his earliest years on a ranch beside the St. Mary River. He grew up surrounded by people who had lived the beginning of the western frontier – wolfers, trappers, Blood and Stoney indigenous people, ranch hands and teamsters. When he was still a young boy, his family moved west into the foothills of the Rockies, settling near the headwaters of Drywood Creek.

Radios were rare and television undreamed of in those days. Most rural homes didn't even have electricity. Evenings were long and quiet. In the quiet glow of oil lamps, or outside around flickering campfires, conversation was the chief form of entertainment. Andy recalls sneaking into the edge of the campfire glow as a small boy and listening, spellbound, to the stories of old frontiersmen.

After dropping out of high school, Andy worked as a trapper and hunting guide in the wild and windy country along the eastern edges of the Rocky Mountains. He left his childhood home in 1936 and signed on as a packer and guide for a famous Waterton-area outfitter named Bert Riggall. He refined his storytelling art around countless campfires.

During his years with Riggall, Andy Russell travelled thousands of kilometres by pack train through the upper Oldman drainage, BC's Flathead watershed and the spectacular wilderness of the upper Castle and Waterton rivers. Alberta's oil and gas industry had not yet awakened to the possibility of petroleum beneath the mountains, so few mountain valleys had yet been marred by roads. Thousands of bighorn sheep roamed the windy ridges, grizzly bears foraged along floodplains and avalanche slopes, and growing numbers of elk ranged the open timber. The youthful Andy had all this and Bert Riggall too – an English-born botanist and photographer with a naturalist's gift for observation and interpretation. It seemed like wealth beyond all imagining, and fertile soil for the conservation activist and nature writer that still lay latent in this gangling young ranch kid with a knack for handling horses and telling stories.

Andy's boss also had two daughters. Kay, the eldest, often travelled with the pack trains, cooking and managing the camps. In 1938 Andy and Kay married, spending their honeymoon where they had spent their courtship – exploring wild country on horseback. When Bert retired in 1946, Andy and Kay took over the outfitting business. They eventually moved into a small bungalow on their ranch, just north of Waterton.

But things were changing in the backcountry. During the postwar boom years of the 1950s, the Alberta government discovered that oil development made for happy voters and flush treasuries. There was little political gain in regulating petroleum firms, so government instead put its energy into promoting development. While government engineers built new gravel roads up major river valleys, oil company bulldozers fanned out across the landscape, slicing new seismic lines into once pristine wilderness.

For Andy and Kay Russell, the new roads spelled the end of a golden era. Well-heeled clients weren't willing to pay for pack trips into country others could drive to. "I knew that outfitting was finished, at least the way I'd known it," says Andy. "We were among the top three outfits in North America at that time, but it didn't matter. I'd seen some of these other guys try to hang on, and it was just pitiable to see what happened."

Andy stopped outfitting in 1960. He retained his pack stock

and outfit, however, and put them to work for an ambitious new undertaking. After years of close observation of grizzlies, bighorns and other wildlife in their wilderness homes, Andy had decided to try his hand at creating nature movies. If he could no longer take urban people into the dwindling wilderness, perhaps he could take wilderness to them in the cities, and try to awaken popular concern over the loss of wildlife and wild places. He knew grizzlies and other wilderness animals were becoming scarce, and it troubled him that few others were aware, or cared.

His first two efforts were doomed by lack of familiarity with the business side of filmmaking. In 1961, he and his oldest sons, Dick and Charlie, headed into the high country to film a third movie, this one on grizzly bears. Working with heavy camera gear and dealing with the vagaries of weather, terrain and animal behaviour, the family crew took three years to complete their movie.

During 1962 and 1963, much of Andy's filming took place not in the Rockies but in Alaska's Denali National Park. The crew was not permitted to carry firearms for protection. A lifetime of experience with grizzlies had already taught the Russells that the bears were far less dangerous than their reputation suggested. But even Andy and his sons were surprised by how tolerant the bears were, as long as the crew paid attention to bear body language, backing off when a grizzly wanted to feed or wander through an area the crew was already occupying. Previously, with the unconscious arrogance that firearms give humans, they had not been nearly so sensitive to the signals bears gave them. It was an important lesson about the potential for peaceful coexistence between grizzlies and humans: all they needed to do was to treat the bears with humble respect.

Andy needed money to pay for the cost of production of the movie, so he came up with the idea of writing a book. He'd already written a number of magazine articles, mostly for American hunting and fishing magazines.

"I flew down to New York," he says, "and had lunch with the editor-in-chief of Alfred A. Knopf Publishing. I had about a hundred pictures that I showed him over lunch, full-frame photos of mule deer and bighorns – I had one there of just the head and shoulders of a grizzly – and he asked me how the hell I got pictures like that. I told him that was what I was there for, and I wanted to write him a book. He sent me home with a $3,000 advance."

Grizzly Country sold tens of thousands of copies and was translated into more than a dozen languages. It is still in print, more than a quarter of a century after it first came out, in 1967. Andy took the movie on the road soon after the release of his book. The book's runaway success guaranteed him sellout audiences.

At first, however, Andy faced a torrent of criticism for portraying grizzlies as peace-loving animals and describing filming them without protection. "I was condemned for that book by some people. They said I was endangering people out on the trail because they'd believe what they read and get in trouble with bears. The chief naturalist in Jasper National Park gave me hell."

Whatever the popular prejudice might have been about grizzly bears at the time – Andy recalls the curator of the New York Zoological Society describing the retiring omnivores as among the three fiercest predators in North America – the movie footage Andy took on the road told a different story in a way that was undeniable. Clearly, this animal had received a bum rap from people whose prejudices and fears got in the way of their ability to observe and think.

Andy spent 11 years showing that movie. He took it all over North America and filled big theatres everywhere he went. Some nights it was standing room only. "But it was a tough way to make a dollar, living out of a suitcase and having to deal with different strangers all the time."

Other books followed on the heels of *Grizzly Country – Trails of a Wilderness Wanderer* (1971), *Horns of the High Country* (1973), *The Rockies* (1975) and *Memoirs of a Mountain Man* (1984). In between books Andy researched, wrote and taped more than 500 episodes for a popular radio series on Alberta's history sponsored by TransAlta. He also did speaking tours, television appearances and numerous magazine articles. One way or the other, he made good and sure nobody missed hearing what he had to say.

Internationally, Andy Russell is known for his films and his books, but closer to home, he's also known for rolling up his sleeves and wading into the nearest dogfight when wildlife and the environment are threatened.

There was the coyote incident, for example. Back in the 1960s predators had even fewer friends than now. Agricultural service boards considered poisoning coyotes to be just one part of a holy war to make southern Canada safe for chickens and sheep. In waging their war, some took shortcuts. A rancher neighbour of Andy's stopped him one day in Pincher Creek to tell him about several dead coyotes he'd found around his ranch in the south Porcupine Hills. Local agricultural field agents had been lacing the carcasses of dead horses with Compound 1080 – a deadly nerve poison – and leaving them out on the range. It was a coyote-killing technique as effective as it was illegal. The rancher had complained about the illegal baits, which posed a danger not only to eagles and other wildlife but to ranch dogs and even children, but had had no success. What, he wondered, could they do to change the situation?

"I said, 'Howard, can you get us some of those coyotes?'" Andy recalls, a glint in his eye. It was May, sunny springtime in the Alberta foothills. Howard managed to retrieve ten coyotes in various states of decomposition. "Well, about ten," Andy says. "Some were just pieces. They were pretty ripe."

The friends knew that the Agricultural Service Board had a meeting scheduled the next day in Pincher Creek. Andy placed a phone call to some of his television news contacts in Lethbridge and suggested they might get some good footage if they could get a camera crew to Pincher Creek by ten that morning.

When the municipal councillors and agricultural staff arrived for their meeting, they found news cameras trained on them and several foul-smelling coyote carcasses spread out on the lawn. "Oh, man, those things stank," Andy laughs. "That air was so thick you could have cut it up and built a fence with it. They were just livid."

Overnight, says Andy, there ceased to be a problem with illegal coyote baits. And once again Andy had acquired some new friends – and new enemies.

Andy first stepped outside the calm currents of conformity and began to make waves in the cause of conservation back in the mid-1940s. He says his moment of truth came over what now seems a relatively minor issue. In those days a group of local ranchers had permits to graze several hundred head of cattle inside Waterton Lakes National Park. Elk commonly moved out of the park in winter to forage on those same ranchers' haystacks. The ranchers wanted something done about the elk, and they held a meeting in the park to discuss the problem. Andy was the secretary-treasurer of the grazing association.

"I was sitting there taking notes and listening about the elk bothering them," Andy recalls. "They weren't a bit concerned about the park grass. And I thought, Andy Russell, it is time for you to rare up." Andy asked the chairman for permission to speak. He then pointed out that it seemed a bit ridiculous for his neighbouring ranchers to be so concerned about elk coming down on their haystacks when, in his view, their cattle were eating most of the winter elk feed in the summertime.

"Oh brother! They'd like to have shot me. One of those fellows never forgave me. To the day he died, he never forgave me."

Andy's first conservation adversaries may have been his fellow ranchers, but since then he has put far more energy into protecting ranchers' interests. His most frequent adversaries, not surprisingly, have been big oil and the Alberta government (which, he points out, are pretty much the same thing). In 1957 Shell Canada discovered one of Canada's richest sour gas deposits in the mountains of southwestern Alberta. The company promptly began construction of its giant Shell-Waterton sour gas processing plant beside Drywood Creek, almost within spitting distance of the ranch where Andy grew up. Some of the most heartbreakingly beautiful country in the world – Andy's old outfitting territory – was soon defiled by roads and pipelines. Toxic chemicals from the processing plant killed fish in Drywood Creek. Sulphur dust blew from stock piles into surrounding pastures, acidifying the soil. Hydrogen sulphide gas and other contaminants spread downwind. Through the 1960s and 1970s Andy was at the forefront of repeated battles over industrial pollution and land abuse.

His running war against industrial greed came to a head in the early 1980s, when Andy and Zahava Hanan, a rancher near Millarville, took on two of the largest oil companies in the world. Esso owned an aging gas processing plant near Hanan's ranch. Shell Canada had found a large deposit of highly poisonous sour gas in the foothills to the west. The two companies applied jointly to Alberta's Energy Resources Conservation Board – the regulatory agency – for permission to run a high-pressure pipeline from Shell's Moose Mountain field to Esso's Quirk Creek plant. The plant would extract the toxic sulphur before shipping the natural gas to market.

Zahava Hanan had already documented a long series of problems with industrial pollution near her ranch. Andy Russell suspected that the aging plant would not be able to handle the increased load. One explosion or leak of the extremely lethal gas would have had devastating consequences.

But trying to stop the project would not be easy. The regulatory board received its funding in equal parts from oil companies and the government's energy department. Consequently, it had an established pattern of ruling in favour of industry, no matter how valid the concerns of local residents.

When the board convened a ten-day public hearing on the pipeline proposal, Andy and his partner intervened. In that first hearing, they faced intimidating cross-examination. "It was perfectly obvious what they were trying to do with us," says Andy. "Everybody was running from these guys and had been for years. Well, I wasn't, and I wasn't going to start either."

A hearing that was supposed to last only ten days ended up stretching on for three years – the longest hearing in the board's history. Phalanxes of well-paid lawyers and engineers faced off against the two ranchers. "They didn't know what to do with us," says Andy. "One time I was in the washroom at the Calgary courthouse at noon and I was in one of the booths. In comes Shell's lawyer and the lawyer that was working for the government. And the one guy says to the other, 'You know the trouble with Andy Russell is, he says the damnedest things and people believe him.' I had a heck of a time trying to keep from laughing in that booth."

Though Andy and Zahava Hanan hired a former Shell engineer and an up-and-coming Calgary lawyer to fight their case for them, there's no doubt that Andy's public profile also played an important role in the battle. The two ranchers eventually won. Their David-and-Goliath struggle helped change the way in which government regulated Alberta's energy industry.

Shortly afterwards, Andy Russell was on the warpath again – this time over a dam the Alberta government proposed to build on the Oldman River north of Pincher Creek. Again, he lent his name and personal credibility to a grassroots battle against overwhelming odds – in this case, a powerful alliance of government water engineers, irrigation lobbyists and private engineering companies that had already dammed most other southern Alberta rivers. Once again, power brokers were shocked out of complacency as the Friends of the Oldman River won battle after battle right up to the Supreme Court of Canada. In the end, however, the dam builders won simply by ignoring the rulings of regulatory boards and courts. Andy Russell's 1987 book, *The Life of a River*, remains a lasting indictment of the Alberta government's short-sighted obsession with resource development in the 20th century. Although the Oldman River was lost, the fight helped save Alberta's Milk and Quebec's Great Whale rivers from similar fates.

A ndy Russell's wife, Kay, died in 1984. He has lived alone for more than a decade now. He has slowed down a little and now gets as much enjoyment out of the achievements of his children and grandchildren as he once did from his own.

Two of his sons – Dick and John – have worked as wildlife biologists for decades. John, a caribou and bear biologist, lives just down the hill from Hawk's Nest. Another son, Charlie, visits from time to time when he isn't at his cabin in Russia's remote Kamchatka peninsula with artist Maureen Enns, testing their theories about peaceful coexistence between grizzly bears and humans. Two other Russell offspring – Gordon and Anne – live within a few hours of the family home. Charlie's son, Anthony – Andy's oldest grandchild – works as a Banff National Park warden. Conservation and love of wild nature run in the blood of all the Russell clan.

Even so, Andy Russell is not yet ready to sit back and leave others to do all the fighting for wild places and wild things. He continues to champion conservation causes even now, well into his ninth decade on this Earth. Lately, he has turned his attention to heading off the threat real estate development poses to the wildlife, habitat and cultural traditions of the foothills ranching landscape that gave shape and meaning to his life. The oil and gas industry has not heard the last of him either – Andy has plans to organize an investigation into several pollution sites near his home in southwestern Alberta.

I asked Andy recently whether he could see much cause for hope now as the 21st century begins. He stared off into space for a few moments before answering. "I think we're over the hump. I think we raised enough hell that they're going to be awful careful about what they'll try and pull off. I mean, some of the stuff government and the oil companies pulled off back in the late '50s and '60s and '70s was totally against the law. But now they're getting so they're having to kind of think about breaking the law. They didn't pay any attention to their own laws at all in the old days."

Almost a century ago some of Bert Riggall's regular clients built a rustic lodge on one of the highest points on his ranch, a place he called Hawk's Nest Butte after a pair of red-tailed hawks who nested regularly near its base. At first it served as a summer resort for four Minneapolis families who hired Riggall's outfitting services each summer. Later, it became a summer home for the Russell family.

From the front porch of Hawk's Nest, the view is staggering. Away south stands Chief Mountain, cliff-walled and aloof, one of the most sacred mountains in Blackfoot culture. A sweep of lesser mountains extends from the Chief in a broad arc west and then north. Beyond their peaks is the promise of remote, wilder country – the upper Castle drainage, the vast Flathead valley and, farther north, the upper Oldman. Below, a mosaic of aspen and fescue grassland sprawls peacefully down Cottonwood Creek, past century-old ranches, to the boundary of Waterton Lakes National Park. This is all grizzly country, and it's all Andy Russell country. The fact that grizzlies still survive here after having been extirpated from so much of their North American range, and the persistence here of so much wild habitat after a century of pell-mell habitat destruction, both stand as tribute to the unending energy, remarkable storytelling and determined activism of one of North America's most famous conservationists.

Andy Russell no longer stands quite as erect as he once did, and his jet-black hair has gone silver.[11] His face remains craggy, but softened with age. But his eyes still spark with humour when he holds court for the most recent visitors to Hawk's Nest. In the golden light of another spring evening, as the people gathered on the old wooden porch watch the last streak of golden sunlight fade from the ranchlands spread below, the old man for the mountains leans forward to catch what someone says.

He chuckles and shakes his head. "That reminds me of the time when old Frenchy Riviere was trapping beavers up on the Drywood," he begins, watching faces turn to him, expectant and eager. He leans back and gazes out into the far places of his memory, and chuckles again. Time for another story. Conservation, as always, will follow.

Truly Good People (1999)

Lloyd Lohr is a quiet man with a deep, abiding love of nature. A farmer who lives near Stettler, now retired, he carefully

---

11 Andy Russell died at the age of 90 on June 1, 2005.

husbanded his family farm for almost half a century before handing over the reins to the next generation. His grandfather's homestead, now grown in with aspens and wildflowers, is still visible in a half section of wooded land the Lohrs have never cleared or broken. Lloyd watches birds there in summer, and allows a few hunters at a time to pursue white-tails through the quiet woodland each fall.

Like many other farmers, Lloyd safeguards a pocket of habitat that would yield more income if developed. He does it because he loves wildlife and identifies his own well-being with the health of a landscape of which luck and good planning have made him steward. He puts up bluebird and duck boxes each year and volunteers with local and provincial natural history groups like the Federation of Alberta Naturalists.

Francis and Bonnie Gardner ranch a couple hundred kilometres southwest of Lloyd, near the headwaters of Willow Creek. Francis calls their ranch a "working wilderness." The Gardner cattle share the windy foothills ridges with bands of elk and mule deer, grizzly bears and, in recent years, wolves. Although the family has lost cattle to wolves more than once, Francis bears them no malice. When he has problems, he calls in the Alberta Fish and Wildlife Division to dispose of the offenders. When he has no problems — which is most of the time — he takes pride in the fact that, under his family's stewardship, their ranch remains so wild and healthy that even wolves and grizzly bears still survive there. Not too far away a neighbour takes this kind of thinking a step further by even refusing hunters permission to shoot wolves, coyotes or other predators.

The Gardners have won awards for their caring and progressive attitudes toward land health. Farther south, at the head of Todd Creek, Hilton and Alta Pharis have gotten their share of recognition too. Looking at the gradual degradation their cattle had wrought on the willows and other riparian vegetation along upper Todd Creek, the Pharises embarked several years ago on a determined mission to restore the health of the stream so that, as Hilton says, "we could leave things a little better than they were when we got them."

Behind the fences that now guard the most sensitive parts of their stream corridor, sedges and reedgrass grow thick and lush in the gaps among the flourishing willow stands. Cutthroat trout numbers have rebounded, and the valley looks vigorous, green and well-loved. Caring shows.

Harvey Locke and Wendy Francis don't own land that they can care for in the way that the Lohrs, Gardners and Pharises do. Nonetheless, their labour of love shows on Alberta's landscape too. Harvey was born at Lake Louise in Banff National Park. He grew up with a deep personal attachment to the mountain paradise. As years passed, however, he saw the small mountain town of Banff give itself over to uncontrolled commercial activity. Dismayed, he watched as Parks Canada seemed to make no serious effort to slow down the cancerous growth of ski hills and resorts. He determined to do whatever he could to protect Canada's first national park from greed and bungling. Wendy, his wife and a fellow lawyer, was no less committed to saving parks. She resigned from her law firm to become the conservation director of a local chapter of the Canadian Parks and Wilderness Society.

In 1997 Canada's minister of Canadian heritage released a new park management plan for Banff that was, to a large extent, the result of Harvey's and Wendy's work. Thanks to their sacrifice of countless volunteer hours, donated dollars and deferred holidays, Banff's frenzied conversion into a scenic shopping mall has been brought to a near-halt. Parks Canada is slowly putting the badly impaired Bow River valley in the heart of the park back together by pulling out unnecessary facilities and restoring damaged habitats and movement corridors.

Elliot Fox is a native of Kainaiwa – the Blood First Nation. After he graduated from Lethbridge Community College, he began talking to other tribal members about environmental problems and restoration opportunities on the Blood Reserve – Canada's largest. Building on the cultural value his people have traditionally attached to the Earth and its creatures, he and other concerned members of the tribe established an environmental organization to clean up landfills, promote better waste management and fight weed infestations. He developed a resource management plan for the tribe's timber berth to protect its wilderness qualities and vulnerable wildlife species, while allocating a controlled amount of timber for cutting. His efforts helped restore a vitally important bull trout spawning run and have put Kainawa into the front line of First Nations environmental protection.

Jan Edmonds is a biologist who lives in Edson. She spent more than a decade working with government, conservation groups, logging companies and others to try and ensure the future of west-central Alberta's beleaguered woodland caribou herds.

In spite of setbacks – like the government's allocation of virtually all the region's caribou habitat to large pulp companies and the failure of Alberta's Special Places program to deliver anything more than postage-stamp-sized pockets of partly protected habitat – Jan has persevered tirelessly. Determinedly positive, she continues to work every imaginable angle to buy time and habitat for the old-growth dependent, and too easily poached grey ghosts of the northern forest.

So too with Lorne Fitch – a senior biologist in Alberta Environmental Protection's Lethbridge office. Lorne has spent more than two decades working to protect biological diversity in the most heavily modified part of the province – the prairie south. With Barry Adams, another dedicated civil servant from Alberta Public Lands, Lorne developed the Alberta Riparian Conservation Program, or "Cows and Fish," as it has come to be known. Working with other conservationists, like the Alberta Cattle Commission's Keith Everts and Chris Mills, and Trout Unlimited's Gary Szabo – as well as a growing number of ranchers and farmers – Lorne and Barry have revitalized countless southern Alberta creek bottoms simply by rearranging the way cows use their watersheds.

From the Alberta Wilderness Association's Dianne Pachal and Cliff Wallis and the Alberta Fish and Game Association's Darryl Smith and Andy Boyd, to conservationist-historian Grant MacEwan and backyard nature expert Myrna Pearman, Alberta is full of people whose love of land and wildlife burns intensely, fuelling conservation action from Rainbow Lake to Onefour. Hunters donate their weekends to plant shrubs and trees along irrigation canals. Housewives volunteer to stuff envelopes for wilderness advocacy groups. Scout and 4-H groups do litter blitzes. Farmers leave hayfield corners uncut. None expect praise – they just want to keep things good, or make them better. They are motivated by love of the place, not greed, self-interest or political ambition.

These are truly good people. In their devotion to nurturing and restoring the ecological diversity that is Alberta, they demonstrate that the 20th century produced more than environmental harm. It also bred a new kind of native Albertan – people who choose to cherish and defend their home, rather than simply exploiting it for what they can take. These are our neighbours and friends, and they are among this province's most valuable natural resources. Their quiet dedication enriches us all.

God bless them, every one.

Conservation Officers (2012)

Al Boggs was tall and stern-looking. His face was weathered and his gaze was firm, and he did not crack a smile as he confiscated my deer.

I was newly turned 14 that winter and had spent the weeks leading up to my birthday wildly excited about the chance to join my dad, brother and uncle on a late-season deer hunt at Alberta's Wainwright military training base. We were among a hundred or so lucky hunters whose names had been drawn for the first-ever opening of this sprawling landscape of sand-hills, aspen and deer.

When we finally arrived at the camp, however, there was some confusion between the biologists and the camp commander over whether this was meant to be an either-sex season or does-only. The day of the hunt, as we joined the crowd of other hunters at the morning's orientation meeting, the officials told us to shoot only antlerless deer until they could get clarification on the rules.

Partway through the day I managed to ditch my dad and strike out on my own. Shortly later I spotted two deer – an immense mule deer buck standing up and staring back at me, and a bedded deer partly obscured by buckbrush in front of him. I made the elementary deduction that if one was a buck, the other must be a doe, and shot the second deer. It proved, however, to be a very big four-by-four buck.

Officer Boggs didn't raise his voice, but nor did he mince words. If I was going to be a hunter, he said, I was responsible for obeying the game laws and knowing what my target was before pulling the trigger. As a young hunter, I also had no business sneaking away from my dad. I had broken game laws and was lucky he had decided not to charge me. He gave me a stern lecture, seized the deer, and sent me home humbled, chagrined and very impressed with the seriousness of his message.

Two weeks later, having learned that the hunt was, indeed,

meant to be an either-sex season and that my deer had, after all, been legal, Officer Boggs turned up on the doorstep of our family home in Calgary. It was his day off, but he'd made the long drive from Edmonton to deliver the hide, head and already-butchered meat of my first deer to a grateful – albeit still mildly terrified – boy. Although I'd never have guessed it from his demeanour at the time, he'd felt awful about having to take away an eager kid's first deer.

From that day on, whenever I meet a conservation officer in the field, I am reminded of the principled professionalism and human decency of Al Boggs. And to this day, many hunting and fishing seasons later in my life, I remain convinced that one of the great things about Canada's outdoors is the uniformed men and women who devote their lives to making sure that nature stays healthy, that game and fish populations are protected from abuse and that all the things we take for granted about the wild will continue to be there for our kids. They deserve a lot more recognition than they get.

The job of conservation officer is far from easy, and there are nowhere near enough of them. Alberta, for example – the fastest-growing province in Canada, with a population of well more than three million people – currently has fewer than 120 conservation officers to cover the entire province. Of those, almost half will be eligible to retire within the next five years, and it's an open question whether those can all be replaced. Passion for the environment notwithstanding, there are lots of reasons young Albertans are more inclined to look at other options first – not the least being the boom in the oil and gas industry, where unskilled workers can take home more than $250 a day without the bother of having to invest in the minimum two years of post-secondary education required to become a much less well-paid wildlife officer.

Ironically, that same oil boom, just like previous booms in the 1970s and the 1950s, has made the job of conservation officer that much harder by riddling the landscape with thousands of kilometres of little-used roads and off-highway vehicle trails that are a poacher's paradise, not to mention the inevitable few companies and contractors who are less than diligent about cleaning up after themselves or about treating fragile trout streams, lake shores and wildlife habitat with the kind of care they deserve.

Ontario, with four times Alberta's population and many more endangered species, is proportionally worse off, with barely 280 conservation officers. It's the same story in most provinces – big landscapes, fragile habitats, vulnerable wildlife populations, people everywhere – and only a few determined, hard-working conservation officers stretching themselves thin to protect the natural world from those who abuse it.

The job of enforcing fish and wildlife laws has become more complex in recent years as new legal precedents and government policies complicate what used to be a fairly straightforward job. Court decisions that have clarified the Treaty and aboriginal rights of Canada's indigenous peoples may have righted old wrongs, but the rights affirmed by those court decisions can be abused by some, and create more grey areas for enforcement officers in the field. The duty to protect people's privacy and constitutional rights, as well as legal precedents that create complex rules of evidence, mean that a minor procedural slip by an officer can cost him or her a conviction in court after weeks – or even years – of careful, painstaking work.

On the other hand, today's conservation officer has access to investigative tools almost undreamt of by Officer Boggs and his predecessors. Advances in DNA analysis and other forensic techniques make even a scrap of hair or a drop of blood potent evidence that can clinch a case. Officers use robotic deer and elk decoys that move and blink. Specially trained dogs sniff out evidence humans would miss. Many poaching rings have been broken in recent years because of the work of undercover agents and the use of computer technology. Alberta officers recently secured convictions against a group of Quebec-based poachers by following Global Positioning System information, which the poachers had inadvertently recorded when they took digital photographs of their kills, back to isolated sites in central Alberta where remains of the poached white-tailed deer could be matched to DNA evidence.

Sometimes convictions produce particularly satisfying results. Last fall, an Ontario court found a poacher from Hamilton guilty of shooting at a decoy deer from a road. It was an old decoy – in fact, the same poacher had already been convicted once before – 11 years earlier – for shooting at the same stuffed deer. This time, his shot damaged its electronic controls. Not only did he lose his shotgun to the Crown and have to pay a fine, but the judge ordered him to buy the Ministry of Natural Resources a new deer robot decoy to replace the one he'd shot – poetic justice for a two-time loser.

Of course, conservation officers don't just enforce laws. The officer who spends her or his day investigating and charging poachers and polluters is just as likely to get called away from supper to deal with a black bear raiding someone's apple tree or to spend the weekend teaching conservation courses to hopeful hunters and anglers. The men and women who choose careers as conservation officers or park wardens mostly do so out of a passionate commitment to wild things and wild places – they certainly aren't in it for the money – and most of them work as hard for conservation during their time off as they do when they're on the clock.

We who wait impatiently through the endless days of late winter for the first fishing trip of the year, or look forward to the renewal of our hunting traditions with each golden autumn, can be confident that when the time comes we will find healthy habitat and well-managed fish and wildlife populations. And one of the main reasons for our certainty is that a small but determined army of conservation officers and park wardens is out there every day, watching out for the things we treasure about wild Canada.

A grateful angler who emailed the Ontario Conservation Officers Association's website said it for all of us: "Thanks for working hard to do a tough job, protecting our valuable natural resources from the thoughtless, stupid, and criminal. Keep up the great work."

CHAPTER *10*

Coming Home

The Once and Future Wild (1998)

The 20th century seemed to recede behind us as the current bore us steadily down into the wild Milk River canyon. Plains cottonwoods – ragged trees with massive trunks – blushed green along the river banks. Swallows skimmed between the boats. The air smelled of brown river water, sage and balsam. The canyon walls, soft curves and bleached lines, receded up toward the sky across broad sagebrush flats.

Gail dipped her paddle lazily into the gentle current. Brian, our 2-year-old, slept on her lap. Katie, bright-eyed with interest, gripped the gunwales and peered back upriver.

I glanced back too. I could see Corey, our oldest boy, perched in the bow of Ian Jack's big rowboat. Closer by, Mike McIvor – bushy-bearded and craggy-faced – pointed out a kingfisher to his wife, Diane. Ahead, two more canoes were just disappearing around a bend.

As I turned back and straightened out the canoe, an immense slab of river bank, easily eight metres high, calved off and crashed into the river right in front of us. The pool erupted in a great foam of brown water that set our canoe rocking violently. We floated over the place where the bank had disappeared, but there was no sign that anything had happened. The river had eaten several cubic metres of silt and not even burped.

Gail said, "That could have hit us!"

I nodded, shocked by the suddenness with which the bank

had collapsed, and the eerie finality with which the river had swallowed up all traces of the cave-in. It was a reminder that this place was as close to wilderness as anywhere in Canada's prairie landscape.

The Milk River canyon is in extreme southeastern Alberta – closer to Regina than Calgary. The river's tortuous meanders trace green scrollwork along the bottom of one of the deepest and broadest canyons in prairie Canada. Looming like mirages, the towering cones of Montana's Sweet Grass Hills rise above the canyon's southern rim. To the north, if one is willing to spend an hour or two hiking up eroded slopes – dodging clumps of prickly pear cactus and keeping a sharp eye out for rattlesnakes – a gently undulating expanse of mixed grassland sweeps away to the flanks of the Cypress Hills: some of the finest surviving native prairie in Canada.

Canada's prairies have lost 90 per cent of their native vegetation and contain half of the country's endangered species. Even the Milk River canyon's vast expanse of prairie, badlands and river bottom is a pale shadow of what it used to be. Bison no longer drown by the hundreds each spring when crossing the swollen river. No grizzly bears scavenge on bison carcasses in spring or fatten on chokecherries and saskatoon berries each fall in the shrubby coulees that drain down to the Milk. As shadows spill purple across the sagebrush flats and nighthawks begin to call above the cottonwoods, the scalp-tightening howl of lobo wolves no longer shocks the evening into listening stillness.

The occasional distant rumble does not herald the approach of tens of thousands of bison but merely the passage, high overhead, of another passenger jet. The scenery is spectacular, but strangely empty. Like other places modern Canadians perceive as wilderness, the Milk River canyon retains its scenic beauty but has lost much of its ecological wealth.

Canada has little of its original wilderness left. The 20th century was too brash; we were all in too much of a hurry. Even the great barren lands of the Inuit and other northern peoples are marked by abandoned camps and new diamond mines; the very permafrost is melting as the global climate warms. Other regions retain little at all of the wild – southern Ontario's Carolinian forests survive only as tiny tatters, for example. In most of Canada the wild is wounded and under threat.

With the exception of the children, all the people floating down the Milk River that June day in 1991 were experienced in the art of making do with wounded wilderness. The McIvors had spent two decades fighting to save Banff National Park's shrinking wilds from encroaching commercialism. Ian Jack had campaigned almost as long to keep BC Hydro from destroying the last undammed stretch of the Columbia River. Rob and Corlane Gardner, from Medicine Hat, Alberta, worked daily to save prairie Canada's last remnants from a host of assaults. All were familiar with the taste of defeat.

Today, we floated through a wilderness of ghosts, concentrating on that which still survived rather than letting our minds linger on what might have been. The Milk River canyon was the kind of setting that made it almost possible to forget what we all knew: that Canada's future nature would never be as wild or complete as its past.

And then we saw the elk.

It was late afternoon when the first boat swung past a logjam and slipped around a bend, dipping into a sudden riffle. Someone pointed. Paddles stilled. Everyone watched, as we floated quietly down the length of a long pool toward four elk who stood hock-deep in the tail of the pool.

They were sleek and dark in their new summer coats. For paddlers expecting to see only the usual prairie mule deer, they looked incongruously huge. The elk stood rigid, watching the approaching boats: ears cocked, eyes wide, nostrils flaring. Then the nearest cow barked and wheeled, and all four thundered up out of the river in a spray of foam. Noses held high in characteristic elk fashion, they vanished into the cottonwood forest.

We floated in close to shore. I could see water seeping into their tracks – elk tracks, beside the Milk River. Nobody spoke. None of us had imagined that elk might find their way back into this relict prairie wilderness after having been eradicated more than half a century earlier. It was a profound epiphany; all sense of loss and reluctant compromise spontaneously erased. That evening I found myself glassing the cottonwood flats and canyon slopes, half-believing I might see a grizzly digging roots.

Lately, I hear that over 200 elk now range through the Milk

River canyon. Last year, only a few kilometres away, a pair of wolves appeared out of nowhere, denned, and gave birth to a litter of pups.

Prevailing wisdom about Canada's diminishing wilds says that elk and wolves are gone from the prairies forever; but that prevailing wisdom is proving wrong. In the same way, against all hope, trumpeter swans, sandhill cranes and otters have found their way back into the windy aspen parkland of south-western Alberta where I live, and the once-endangered bald eagle and peregrine falcon again trace graceful lines across southern Ontario skies. The wild, against all logic, has begun to return.

The baby boom generation – my generation – grew up suppressing our belief that the wilderness that in so many ways defines Canada was doomed ultimately to vanish. When Kurt Vonnegut said, "Everything is going to become unimaginably worse and never get better again," we knew he was right. We knew that pulp companies, big oil, agro-industry and urbanization would win in the long run, and that wilderness, like clean air, was something we had to resign ourselves to leaving behind. We thought we would have to be content with the leavings – the little bits we could wrestle out of greed's grasp and guard for future generations who would dwell in a poorer world.

Now, at the dawn of a new millennium, I think we were wrong. Canadians have already begun to bring back the wild. Wilderness is not just our past; it will be an important part of our future. We have not surrendered hope; we are reinventing it.

That magical encounter with an animal once eradicated from Canada's prairies had a hidden significance that eluded me until much later. It wasn't until the fall of 1997, when I returned to sit on the edge of the Milk River canyon and look down at its scrolling patterns of cottonwoods, thorny buffaloberry and needlegrass meadows, that I began to see the profound significance of that brief encounter.

It was October, now. The cottonwoods were golden. Wind hissed and whispered in the grass around me as I sat on the edge of a sandstone cliff and watched my children explore the tangled shrubbery below. The far river was shrunken and pale, winking in and out of sight amid the trees. An eagle looped slowly across the sky.

Contemplating the times I'd been here before, I realized that my life had spanned most of the last half of the 20th century. The children whose happy voices lifted every so often on the wind would live most of their lives in the next. And I realized, suddenly, that I no longer felt the same deep foreboding about their future that had haunted me when we embarked on that float trip seven years earlier. During the last years of the 20th century, unimagined possibilities – once rare as prairie elk – have begun to emerge out of the gloom, offering growing hope that we can yet restore much of the wildness that Canada has lost.

Mike and Diane McIvor's tireless efforts on behalf of Canada's first national park finally bore fruit in 1995 when Canada's Minister of Environment released the report of a scientific panel that had conducted an independent review of how Parks

Canada was managing the Banff Bow valley. The Banff-Bow Valley Study proved beyond any remaining doubt that the McIvors had been right all along. Two years later, Parks Canada announced a new management plan for Banff National Park and began to tear down tourist facilities, restrict travel on some roads and trails and build bridges and underpasses to help wolves and grizzlies cross the highway.

None of us had even dared believe such a thing was possible, that day in 1990 when we all floated down the Milk River, contemplating the fate of wilderness in the 20th century. Bureaucratic rationalizing and corporate lobbying had always trumped the efforts of average Canadians who loved the dwindling wild. Nothing hinted that would ever change – but in the last years of the decade it did. The battle for the ecological health of Canada's national parks is far from over, but a new generation of park management plans modelled on Banff's shows that the tide has begun to turn.

In 1995, Rob and Corlane Gardner saw their efforts rewarded too, with the establishment of a new National Wildlife Area along the South Saskatchewan River. Against all established wisdom, the Canadian Armed Forces not only supported but actively promoted grassland protection and restoration. Elsewhere in prairie Canada ranchers, tired of criticism about the damage their cattle do to riparian areas, teamed up in the late 1990s with conservation groups and government experts to launch Cows and Fish, one of the most successful ecosystem restoration programs of the century. All across Rob and Corlane's beloved prairie landscape, new grazing strategies are bringing back willows, clean water and wildlife to once-trampled riparian areas.

Ian Jack too, after a campaign that lasted almost 30 years, finally secured protection for the last undammed reach of BC's Columbia River: 160 kilometres of cottonwood forest, cattail marsh, oxbow lakes and meandering river stretching from Invermere, BC, north to the sawmill town of Donald. He died shortly after that unimaginable victory, leaving a legacy of hope to inspire future generations after the often hopeless struggles of his own.

All this and more had happened in the few short years since we had come together to enjoy a few days together on one of Canada's last prairie wilderness rivers. There had been no lack of determination among that little group, but there had been a pronounced lack of optimism. We had become conditioned to failure.

Almost from its beginnings, Canada's conservation movement was a gloomy one, haunted by the spectres of paradises lost and driven by a kind of crisis mentality. Wilderness protection campaigns were mostly rearguard actions driven by imminent threats – a mine proposal, a tourism development scheme or a new forest allocation. To express optimism or confidence was almost considered a betrayal of values in a movement that drew its desperate energy from an underlying defeatism.

Nonetheless, a people's vision of its future is as subject to rein-terpretation as its myths about its past. In Canada, as elsewhere in the world, conservationists increasingly describe the new century in terms of ecosystem restoration and the "re-wilding" of over-exploited landscapes. Dialogue about wilderness conservation in the 21st Century is dominated no longer by the language of loss but by the language of healing and recovery.

None speak that language with more quiet passion and commitment than Dave Sheppard.

A gentle, soft-spoken former biology professor, Dave retired from the University of Saskatoon in 1977 and moved to the foothills west of Pincher Creek, Alberta. There he and his wife, Jean, began to explore the spectacular mountain landscape that lies at the head of the Castle and Carbondale rivers. Originally part of Waterton Lakes National Park, the area contains a host of rare plants; hundreds of elk, deer and bighorn sheep; vitally important habitat for grizzlies; and some of the most beautiful streams and mountains in the Canadian Rockies.

As they explored the unexpected paradise that lay just beyond their back doors, the Sheppards began to encounter others who shared their growing passion for the place. They also found a growing network of natural gas pipelines, roads and wells. Clearcut logging spread farther into the headwater basins each winter. Noisy dirt bikes and off-road vehicles penetrated everywhere in summer, even onto the summit ridges of some mountains.

Dave Sheppard teamed up in 1990 with others concerned

about the thoughtless damage they could see accumulating on the landscape, and formed an advocacy group called the Castle-Crown Wilderness Coalition. Their objective: to persuade the Alberta government to protect the high country as a wilderness park.

But it isn't wilderness, any more than the Milk River canyon is wilderness. Roads penetrate nearly to the head of every valley. Much of the old-growth timber has been clearcut. Gas wells and pumping stations extend up to timberline on some mountains.

Dave Sheppard knows all that, but it doesn't deter him. He sees it as wilderness tomorrow, even if it isn't today. He isn't prepared to settle pragmatically for the last few valleys where roads have not yet penetrated; he wants to close roads, reclaim gas well sites, start over again. He believes the land deserves no less. Already the coalition he founded has tasted the first hint of future success: the Alberta government announced in 1997 that it was restricting motor vehicle use on about 80 per cent of the woods roads in what Sheppard and others already are calling the Castle Wilderness again. It's the first sign that the tide of wilderness destruction has begun to ebb.[12]

---

12   In 2015 a newly elected Alberta NDP government announced that the entire Castle wilderness area would receive the highest level of protection in the province. Initially, the government shut down commercial logging but allowed off-highway motorized recreation to continue damaging the landscape. A 2017 draft management plan corrected that error, however, and proposed the parks be managed to some of the highest standards in Canada.

Dave Sheppard was not among the battle-weary souls who floated the Milk River with my family back in 1991. He was there, however, the next time we all met in one place. It was at the first international conference of the Yellowstone to Yukon Conservation Initiative, held in the fall of 1997 a couple hundred kilometres east of the Milk River, in Waterton Lakes National Park. Mike and Diane McIvor were among the crowd of more than 400 excited conservationists who gathered to plan the re-wilding of the entire Rocky Mountain chain. So was Rob Gardner. The talk was not about defensive tactics to save the bits that remain; it was about restoring wildness and landscape health to a vast area that suffered too much short-sighted development in the 20th century. There was new energy and new determination on the faces of those people who had met the elk that spring day on the Milk River, and seen their first clue to Canada's wilderness future.

Canada's conservationists are on the offensive at last. While saving what survives of Canada's original wilderness remains important, the emerging ecosystem restoration movement seeks also to restore wildness to places previously written off. Landscapes seemingly lost to development, in this vision, will be the wild green places of tomorrow.

When Shell Canada exhausts the last gas well in Dave Sheppard's much-loved Castle country, the Castle-Crown Wilderness Coalition he helped found will be there to ensure that the company reclaims its well roads. And then a stillness will settle on those valleys. Mystery will seep back out of the woods, and shy animals – grizzly bears, elk and wolverine –

will venture back into places they have had to avoid for half a century. Those who choose to hike up there will again be able to hear the thin tearing sound that an eagle's wings make when it banks above the whitebark pines and wheels up into the wind. Like the eagle, their eyes, again, will be full of wildness.

By the same token, when our children next paddle the Milk River, the elk they see will be come as no surprise. In the night they might even hear wolves howl. Perhaps they'll discover fresh grizzly tracks in the river mud. Why not? Why not bison too? The elk returned. Only lack of imagination and determination stands in the way of rebuilding the living diversity that we once relegated only to our past.

We cannot change our past, but we can choose our future. That future could be better, and wilder, than today. In working together to restore the wild beauty, space, freedom and wildlife that have always shaped our collective dream of Canada, we might heal not just our land but ourselves.

Healing, hope, home: in restoring the wild to our native land, we may yet find our way home at last.

᪣

Facebook Post

November 27, 2015. Bob Creek Wildland.

Yesterday a lynx strolled across the road as I was unloading my toboggan. Perfect little moments.

Recognition (1997)

I set my canoe into the silt-grey waters of the Athabasca River one evening and slipped quietly away into the gloom.

It was barely May, too early in the year for birdsong. The only sounds were the muted chuckle of the river and the occasional distant hiss and whine of passing traffic on the Yellowhead Highway. Elk watched my canoe drift past. Higher, on the open slopes of Mount Colin, a herd of bighorn sheep picked their way up a shadowed meadow. They knew where they were going. I did not.

They were at home. I was just passing by.

I had thought about doing my field work on foot with a flashlight, but common sense suggested I look for alternatives. Grizzlies haunt the river flats in early spring, avoiding the lingering snowpack of the high country while they forage on sweet vetch roots and winterkill. The thought of meeting a grizzly nose-to-nose in the dark was sufficient to make me look for other ways of counting owls.

Owls were only a few of about 250 species of vertebrate animals I was supposed to inventory for Parks Canada. Soil scientists and botanists had already mapped this part of Jasper, tracing lines around discrete ecosystems and landforms. Now it was my turn to document how many mammals, birds, reptiles and amphibians were at home in each ecosite, as we called the map units.

Owls are hard to find except in early spring, when they give their distinctive territorial calls. I had no choice but to seek them at night, which is why I was now tunnelling silently into the gloom. My canoe tipped and tilted beneath me, responding to the icy boils and back eddies of a river that, a few kilometres upstream, was glacier ice. I looked into the silt-shadowed water and shivered, contemplating the consequences of an unexpected encounter with a sweeper.

A boreal owl tootled briefly as I slipped past a large stand of old-growth white spruce. From time to time I heard the familiar hooting of a great horned owl or the monotonous high-pitched whistles of a saw-whet. Once something went crashing out of shallow water and vanished into forest gloom.

The moon rose beyond Roche Miette. It silvered the landscape, casting trees into relief and spilling a path of silver across the river's rippled surface. Navigating was easier now. The lower Athabasca River in Jasper National Park is fast-flowing but gentle. I was not too worried about swamping. Still, it was good to be able to watch out for sweepers or gravel bars in the cold glow of the moon.

The mountains silhouetted on either side stretched off to the northwest and the southeast, separated by high valleys trending in the same direction. I had seen these mountains once out the window of a commercial jet. From that elevation they looked like giant waves that had suddenly hardened in place – long lines of limestone breakers forever waiting to crash down on west-central Alberta's boreal plains.

From canoe-level I could see the way in which each range ended abruptly at the edge of the Athabasca River. Glaciers long ago shaved off and steepened the mountain ends. A few thousand years ago the glaciers melted back to where they wait, now, cupped among the highest peaks, poised to advance down-valley again when the climate cools again.

Those shrunken glaciers fed the river on which I now floated. The valley's glacial origin was obvious to me; even the mighty Athabasca River is too small to have carved the broad valley through which it flows. It was a river of ice, not water, that carved this valley.

Another owl tootled, high on the forested benchlands above the river. I backpaddled, ferrying away from a spruce sweeper and bouncing down a shallow riffle. A pair of geese began to clamour. Their long necks bobbed up and down as they paced me down the far side of a midstream island. They were still complaining when the canoe carried me around a bend.

A sudden confusion of channels glistened in the moonlight. The river widened here, slowing as it approached Jasper Lake.

A freshening breeze – spilling down the broad valley from the high country to the west – nudged the canoe gently out of the main channel. I had to paddle hard to get back into the current. The channel turned. The breeze pushed me toward the bank.

The channels widened and coalesced as the current bore me out onto the shallow waters of Jasper Lake. Twice I ran aground on silt, pushed off, drifted a few metres, and ran aground again. The water was wave-rippled, silt-laden and secret. It offered no clues as to where the deep channel had gone.

❧

Jasper Lake is only a lake for part of each year. When the glaciers melted back, they left the valleys of the Athabasca and its tributaries filled with loose gravel, silt, clay and other debris. The Snake Indian River joins the Athabasca from the northwest at the same point where the Rocky River enters from the southeast. Both rivers swept countless tons of raw sediment out of their new valleys each year for centuries, depositing it where they lost power upon entering the main Athabasca valley. Over the years, both rivers built alluvial fans that spread across the valley and joined, blocking the Athabasca and damming up Jasper Lake.

The Athabasca also carries a heavy load of sediment. Pooled behind the natural dam, the Athabasca has deposited ten centuries' worth of silt and sand in Jasper Lake. What began as a lake is now a deep deposit of fine glacial flour. Only in summer, when the Columbia Icefield and other headwater glaciers melt most feverishly, does water cover the silt flats and Jasper Lake again become worthy of the name.

❧

Tonight was a bad night to paddle Jasper Lake. The spring runoff had begun to cover the silt flats, but the resulting lake was only a few centimetres deep at best. Bit by bit, by trial and error, I found the deepwater channel, drifted farther into the lake, and ran aground again. Even when I was sure of where the channel lay, the stiffening breeze confounded me by blowing the canoe off course. Repeatedly I found the channel, only to lose it and run aground.

Finally, in frustration, I decided to wade across the moonlit lake to shore, cache my canoe beside the highway and hitch-hike home. I stepped out of the canoe, grabbed the bow rope, and began to walk. Semi-trailer truck rigs burrowed through the darkness along the south edge of the lake. I was just contemplating the shock that one of those truck drivers might experience if he or she happened to look my way and see a man walking across the surface of a lake, pulling a canoe, when I had a shock of my own: I found the missing channel.

Soaked and furious I gripped the side of the canoe and drifted until my feet found the silty bottom again. I clambered back into the canoe and began to paddle down the channel I had blundered into. The wind took control and again blew me aground in shallow water.

I sat shivering in the darkness, as exasperated as I was discouraged, watching wind ripples shudder endlessly down the long, silver reflection of the moon. Listening to the stillness, I became aware of a strange, high-pitched hiss, like vibrating power lines. There were no power lines, however. Alone in mid-lake, I listened carefully. The sound seemed to come from the canoe itself.

Leaning over, I watched the grip and scurry of water flowing along the sides of the canoe. All at once it dawned on me that what I was hearing was the saltating hiss of millions of tiny silt particles. Silt was sliding against the aluminum as the river bore it out into the lake. Glaciers had ground this flour-like silt from mountain rock. The melted waters of those same glaciers carried it in suspension down-valley to my canoe, and Jasper Lake.

As I contemplated my discovery, a low moan rose out of the darkness far across the lake and swelled into a long, resonating howl. It faded, died and was gone, leaving only a faint hissing, the tug of wind on wet clothing, and a silver line of moonlight spilling across a dark lake.

Later that night I finally made it to shore, stashed my canoe and went home to a hot bath and a dry bed. When I awoke the next day, the Athabasca valley was a place transformed.

I had thought I knew the Athabasca River: its valley-bottom forests, steep-walled mountains and wolves. I had visited the headwater glaciers. I understood the story of how they had once extended east onto the central Alberta plains. But that night in the middle of Jasper Lake, was the first time I came to see that they were not separate things; all were one.

The wind that blew my canoe aground had only recently kissed the surface of glaciers that were the source of the water on which I floated. The same west wind, year after year, had pulled moisture in off the Pacific Ocean, lifted it high into the Rockies, and shed it as snow – the snow that fed those glaciers.

Depleted of moisture, warmed by the sudden descent to low elevations, the same wind funnelled down the Athabasca valley – which those very glaciers had carved in times gone by – and swept winter snows away. In doing so, the west wind helped create a rich habitat mosaic for elk, sheep, deer and other animals upon which the wolf I had heard relied for food.

Silt ground by glacier ice from those high mountains, washed downstream by glacier meltwater, had filled Jasper Lake. Each winter, when the glaciers froze rock-hard, the lake level fell. Those same west winds swept up the silt, depositing it in dunes where those wolves denned.

Wind and ice, river and mountain, wolf and water: all were part of the same whole. All were linked by cause and effect, time and consequence. All were threads in the same landscape tapestry.

For days I gazed around me, wide-eyed, seeing the landscape in which I lived as if for the first time. My midnight awakening had opened me to discovery. Over the months and years that followed, my intimacy with this place deepened and accreted as I followed the threads of my discovery into new understandings.

৵৪

Years earlier, a friend had a similar experience. David Zieroth and I worked as park naturalists in Kootenay National Park. He was a poet by choice and a historian by training. Each summer David chose a subject about which he knew little, and forced himself to learn all he could about it. Then he sought within his imagination a way to bring it to life in the nature interpretation programs he delivered in campground theatres.

One year he decided to focus on glacial geomorphology – how glaciers change landscapes. He knew next to nothing about it. Every day he cloistered himself in the park library, poring over geography books. He poured himself into a crash course on arêtes, eskers, moraines, hanging valleys and all the various landscape features that result when ice, rock and water spend a long time in each other's company. Each evening he drove home, bemused, from the park office in Radium Hot Springs to his house on a hillside near Invermere.

By mid–May he seemed irritable and distracted. He had filled himself with facts, but nothing had gelled. He knew the details but he could not find a story, and the campgrounds would soon be open.

Then one day he flew into the office, ecstatic.

"What happened?" I asked.

"I've got it!"

"What?"

"An esker connection," he cried, grinning with relief. "I've made an esker connection."

The previous evening, driving down Highway 93 in the golden light of a spring evening, David had found himself slowing as usual where the pavement traced an elegant S-bend along the benches above Stoddart Creek.

"All at once," he said, "I realized that the S-bend was there because they built the highway right along the top of an esker. I've driven that S-bend almost every day for years. I'd never even wondered about it before. And then I looked around and I saw that the benches were kame terraces. Then I saw other eskers and drumlins in the valley bottom, and hanging valleys along the edge of the Columbia valley ..."

Deer were feeding on the sunburnt side of a kame slope. A raven drifted above the esker, looking for road kills. David came home that night through a landscape he had never truly seen before. The irony confounded him: he and his wife had built a house, started a family and spent years taking pleasure in the surroundings they had chosen for home. Yet they had never seen the eskers.

M ost animals are acutely aware of landscape. Humans, for the most part, can choose to ignore it.

We do not need to seek out sunbathed south-facing slopes on cold days in fall; we merely turn up the thermostat. We do not retreat to the shelter of old-growth forests or seek a familiar rock overhang when the rain falls; we go indoors. Engineers design our roads for speed so that we can waste as little time as possible when we travel between artificial places of our own creation. The engineers who build those highways fill valleys and carve down hills so that drivers need not notice the natural ups and downs. All the curves are smooth. Mileage signs tell us how much longer until we escape the landscape and get "home."

Ranchers, loggers and others who make their living outdoors are necessarily more aware of landscape than those who huddle in cities and towns. Hunters – true hunters who leave their vehicles behind and venture quietly into the wild – seek to become creatures of landscape much in the same way as their prey. It isn't that we don't try.

All, however, return at night to heated homes, flick on the lights, settle before the television, eat something from the fridge. All are part of a culture that assumes going home must entail turning one's back on the living landscape.

❧

There used to be people who viewed things differently. Keith Brady, a park warden, showed me one of their camps one day in Waterton Lakes National Park. It was at a place called Indian Springs for its long association with the indigenous people of the Great Plains.

The campsite filled a grassy bay where rolling fescue grassland sweeps up against an aspen-covered sidehill. I could see and hear a small spring that issued from the ground and chuckled away into the prairie.

"That spring doesn't freeze in winter," Keith said. "They would have had water all year round."

A nearby ridge gave the people who dwelt here shelter from wind too. Trees grew tall along the ridge and around a nearby wetland. Shelter from wind, in a landscape where winter winds commonly gust to hurricane intensity and last for days on end, is a vital matter to every living creature. Firewood was abundant on the hill above. The long-gone people whose campsite we had found would only have had to drag it downhill.

We sat our horses, studying the landscape. Chief Mountain, one of the most important mountains in Blackfoot mythology, stood forth from the rest of the Rockies several kilometres to the east. Closer, a complex of eskers, moraines and hollows stretched along the edge of the Waterton River valley. Wind-whipped grassland covered the knolls and ridges. A few bison fed on the crest of one hillock. They were part of a captive herd; a century ago there would have been wild bison in the same place. The Waterton valley's howling winds ensure that this eskerine complex remains snow-free – except lee slopes and hollows – through most winters.

The indigenous people who camped at Indian Springs hunted the bison by herding them down the long draws between eskers and forcing them into deep snowdrifts where they could slaughter the big animals. The people camped at the one place in the landscape where they were consistently assured of open water, shelter, firewood and proximity to good hunting. There was no need to go home after hunting. They were already there – like the bison, the aspens, the wind and the eskers.

Modern North America's landscapes are now our homes too. We just tend not to think of them that way, choosing to see them as real estate and resources instead. We drift, unanchored, into a future that frightens most of us, feeling vaguely incomplete, but unable to define what is missing. We profess concern about "the environment," but it is an objectively defined environment that lies outside our homes, and ultimately it is an abstract concern. That concern, in any case, is limited to those brief periods when other matters, concerning the world-within-a-world we have created, do not distract us.

We can always "go home" and shut the door when it all gets too much for us.

G ail and I lived briefly in a bedroom community south of Calgary. We chose Okotoks because the Calgary we had both grown up in was long gone. We hoped a small foothills town might offer some kind of link to the things of the past we most value. Reality soon disillusioned us.

All that first summer I watched over the back fence as a developer eradicated 2.5 square kilometres of foothills landscape. As the summer progressed, heavy equipment rebuilt it into a generic suburb that might have been anywhere in the Western world: a placeless colony for domesticated humans. The northwest-southeast glacial scours vanished; branching, interlinked roadways replaced them. Bulldozers and earth-movers re-contoured and dammed what had only recently been a coulee full of wild rose, birdsong and mule deer, replacing it with little ponds and terraces. The swales that once spilled spring runoff into the coulee vanished overnight. The new landscape had a new hydrology, buried in plastic pipes. Exotic shrubs and lawns of tame bluegrass replaced the native fescue, wheatgrass, silverberry and pasture sage. The very scent of the place changed: silver willow musk, wild rose and curing hay gave way to 2,4-D, dust and engine exhaust.

By the time the first snow fell, another piece of Alberta land-scape had become mere real estate. Looking around at the street where we lived, I realized that only a decade or so ago it too had been foothills prairie. Yet Gail and I, our neighbours and those hopeful young families moving into the new subdivision next door proudly declared ourselves Albertans. We professed to be at home here, amid the For Sale signs.

By the time we left, Okotoks had become a place of horrified realization for me: the flip side of David's esker connection. I had been forced to see, beneath the common and accepted urban cityscapes and pastoral farmscapes among which I grew up, the fading shadows of what could, and should, have been my habitat and home place. It was as if I had watched helplessly as vandals defaced my home – and then, as one turned, seen that he wore my face.

When we moved to Okotoks Gail and I were closer than we had been in years to the houses where we grew up and the places we had known in youth. We soon realized we were more homesick than we had ever been. We had tried to go home. We just had not known what that meant.

W e moved again, coming home to Waterton, far from the scrapers, bulldozers and landscaping companies. But they are not far behind. That dust cloud of haste and unconcern will continue to rise from the near horizon until we western Canadians succeed in redefining home and establishing a more reflective and honourable relationship with the places of which fate grants us the chance to be a part. Like the vandals in my vision, those scraper operators, catskinners and contractors wear our visages. Our eyes stare blankly from those faces, failing to focus as they sweep the living landscape. Interest flickers only when they see familiar things – bank machines, televisions, asphalt, cellphone screens; other products of artifice and desire.

What we recognize depends upon what we can see. What we see depends upon how our senses have been trained: a big part of who we are. Who we are depends, usually, on the kind of home we grew up in.

I still return to my family home at Christmas and Thanksgiving. I visit my mother in the house that has been a part of my life since the age of 4. There is a crucifix on the dining room wall; I remember holy cards tucked behind it after my First Communion and palm leaves drying behind it each spring. I know which stairs squeak, what the furnace sounds like late at night, which walls are patched, and why. Everything about that house is familiar, rich with association, memory and significance. The faces around the table are people I know and love. We have laughed together, suffered together, learned to give each other space and to take pleasure in the times when we reunite.

That house and those people are home. They matter deeply to me. I could not stand to be cut off from them. I could never bring myself to do harm to any of them. They are all inextricably bound up in how I have come to know myself.

So too, I now know, are the Athabasca River valley, the eskers and kames south of Radium, the wind-whipped aspen forests of Waterton, and the wild places and living landscapes I've come to know – however imperfectly – and grown to love through years of exploration, contemplation and growing concern about their well-being.

It is time for us to come home. It is past time. It is time to rediscover the living landscapes of the wounded West and recognize them as the home places that make us who we are –

no less than our families, the houses in which we live and the ways in which we earn our livings. It is time to seek our own esker connections – moments of epiphany that transfigure our surroundings and transform us. No matter how hard we race toward the horizon, it recedes ahead of us. Perhaps home is not beyond the horizon after all. Coming home may be a simple matter of learning to see more clearly where we are already, determining to treasure it, and choosing to stay.

༖

Facebook Post

July 18, 2016. Wolf Willow.

A magic evening on the way south through the foothills. Huge thunderstorms in all directions, with cumulus clouds towering up into the last sunlight as evening darkened their bases. I watched for tornado spouts; they seemed a virtual certainty under such dark and hostile skies. Instead, I saw lightning and dark curtains of rain spreading off across the plains.

Topping out on the divide at the north end of the Waldron Ranch on Highway 22, I dropped into mist. Drifts of hailstones along the roadside explained the sudden fog. From there down into Chaffen Creek, mist was draped in all the hollows and drifted slowly along the timber fringes. Hail lay like snow in places, etching out every wrinkle and trail along the slopes. Dark timber stood at the heads of shadowed draws. Overhead the cloud wrack lay in long strips across the sky and a full moon slid in and out of the openings. It was the kind of evening where one might expect to see caped and hooded figures emerging from the tree shadows – magic coming back into a world that has forgotten its existence.

I didn't see anything like that. Nor did I see the ordinary things I knew were there – elk and grizzly bears, grinning coyotes and skinny weasels. I wish I had, because we are given evenings like this to remind us that those ordinary things are, in fact magic.

It was dark when I got to the cabin. Sheet lightning flickered silently over the hills to the east. An owl slipped out of sight. The river was speaking quietly behind the dark trees.

Magic everywhere. It's still out there.

OUR PLACE | 397

Selected References

Annand, Amanda Dawn. 2010. "The 1910 Fires in Alberta's Foothills and Rocky Mountain Regions." Bachelor's thesis, University of Victoria.

Anonymous. 1980. *Alberta Forest Service 50th Anniversary Fact Sheet*. Alberta Provincial Archives.

Beaubien, E.G., and M. Hall-Beyer. 2003. "Plant Phenology in Western Canada: Trends and Links to the View From Space." *Environmental Monitoring and Assessment* 88, no. 1: 419–29.

Berry, Thomas. 2006. *The Dream of the Earth*. Berkeley: Counterpoint. (Orig. pub. 1988).

Bowes, Gordon E., ed. 1963. *Peace River Chronicles: Eighty-One Eye-Witness Accounts from the First Exploration of the Peace River Region of BC, including the Finlay and the Parsnip River Basins*. Vancouver: Prescott.

Bradley, Cheryl, Albert A. Einsiedel, Tim Pyrch and Kevin Van Tighem, eds. 1989. *Flowing to the Future. Proceedings of the Alberta Rivers Conference, Calgary, 1989*. Edmonton: University of Alberta Press.

Canadian Forest Service. 1990. *Forest Management in Alberta – Report of the Expert Review Panel*. Edmonton: Alberta Energy/Forestry, Lands & Wildlife.

Canoe Alberta. 1978. "Reach Reports of the Athabasca River System." Volume 3 of *Canoe Alberta: A Guide to Alberta's Rivers*, 4th Edition. Edmonton: Travel Alberta.

Cheadle, Walter. 2011. *Cheadle's Journal of Trip Across Canada, 1862–1863*. Victoria: TouchWood Editions.

Costello, Allan B. 2006. "Status of the Westslope Cutthroat Trout (*Oncorhynchus clarkii lewisii*) in Alberta." *Wildlife Status Report* no. 61. Edmonton: Alberta Sustainable Resource Development.

Craig, John R. 2006. *Ranching with Lords & Commons*. Victoria: Heritage House Books. (Orig. pub. 1903).

Crerar, A. 1983. "River Basin Management: The Alberta Experience." In *River Basin Management: Canadian Experiences*, edited by Bruce Mitchell and James S. Gardner, 271–78. Waterloo: University of Waterloo Department of Geography Publication Series No. 20.

Diettert, Gerald A. 1992. *Grinnell's Glacier: George Bird Grinnell and Glacier National Park*. Missoula: Mountain Press.

Fish and Wildlife Historical Society. 2005. *Fish, Fur and Feathers: Fish and Wildlife Conservation in Alberta, 1905–2005*. Edmonton: Federation of Alberta Naturalists.

Freedman, Bill. 2013. *A History of the Nature Conservancy of Canada*. Don Mills: Oxford University Press.

Government of Alberta. 2014. *South Saskatchewan Regional Plan 2014–2024: An Alberta Land-Use Framework Integrated Plan*. Edmonton: Government of Alberta.

———. 1979 (revised 1984). *A Policy for Resource Management on the East Slopes of Alberta*. Edmonton: Energy and Natural Resources Division, Resource Information Services.

———. 2000. *Irrigation in Alberta*. Edmonton: Deptartment of Agriculture and Food, Technology and Innovation Branch.

Hanson, W.R. 1972. "The Conservation of a Canadian Watershed: A Case Study." Paper presented on behalf of the Eastern Rockies Forest Conservation Board at the United Nations

Conference on the Human Environment, Stockholm, 1972. Alberta Provincial Archives.

Hanson, W.R., and G. Tunstell. 1962. "Forest and Water Conservation: Watershed Management on the East Slopes of the Rocky Mountains in Alberta, Canada." Paper presented at the eighth British Commonwealth Forestry Conference, East Africa, 1962. Alberta Provincial Archives.

Henday, Anthony. 2001. *A Year Inland: The Journals of a Hudson's Bay Company Winterer*. Edited by Barbara Belyea. Waterloo: Wilfrid Laurier University Press.

Hervieux, Dave, Mark Hebblewhite, Dave Stepnisky, Michelle Bacon and Stan Boutin. 2014. "Managing Wolves (*Canis lupus*) to Recover Threatened Woodland Caribou (*Rangifer tarandus caribou*) in Alberta." *Canadian Journal of Zoology* 92: 1029–37 (and supplementary tables).

Holroyd, G., and K. Van Tighem. 1982. *The Ecological (Biophysical) Land Classification of Banff and Jasper National Parks*, Volume III: The Wildlife Inventory. Edmonton: Canadian Wildlife Service.

Hood, Glynnis. 2012. *The Beaver Manifesto*. Calgary: Rocky Mountain Books.

Hunt, Constance, and Verne Huser. 1988. *Down by the River: The Impact of Federal Water Projects and Policies on Biological Diversity*. Washington: Island Press.

Hunt, Laurie. 1992. "Food Habits of Nesting Prairie Falcons in Southern Alberta, Canada." Edited by G.L. Holroyd. Proceedings of the Third Prairie Conservation and Endangered Species Workshop, Brandon, Manitoba, 1992.

Hynes, H.B.N. 1970. *The Ecology of Running Waters*. Liverpool: Liverpool University Press.

Laycock, Arleigh H. 1954. "Water Supply of the Saskatchewan River: Its Source, Use and Conservation." Unpublished report for the Eastern Rockies Forest Conservation Board, Calgary.

Leopold, Aldo. 1966. *A Sand County Almanac, with Essays on Conservation from Round River*. Toronto: Random House Books, Toronto. (*A Sand County Almanac* orig. pub. 1949; *Round River* orig. pub. 1953.)

Manning, Preston. 2010. "Canada and the Environment: A Fresh Start for a Fresh Decade." *The Globe and Mail*.

MacEwan, Grant. 1952. *Between the Red and the Rockies*. Toronto: University of Toronto Press.

————. 2002. *A Century of Grant MacEwan: Selected Writings*. Calgary: Brindle & Glass.

Masterman, Bruce A., and Jim D. Stelfox. 2009. *Looking Back: An Historical Report of Angler Experiences along the Eastern Slopes of South-Western Alberta*. Edmonton: Alberta Sustainable Resource Development, Fish & Wildlife Division.

Meredith, Duane, and Don Radford, eds. 2008. *Conservation, Pride and Passion: The Alberta Fish and Game Association, 1908–2008*. Edmonton: Edmonton Journal.

Mitchell, W.O. 1947. *Who Has Seen the Wind*. Toronto: Macmillan of Canada.

Murphy, Peter John. 2006. *The Alberta Forest Service, 1930–2005: Protection and Management of Alberta's Forests*. Edmonton: Alberta Public Affairs Bureau.

Nelson, Joseph S., and Martin Joseph Paetz. 1992. *The Fishes of Alberta*. Edmonton: University of Alberta Press.

Palmer, Tim. 1986. *Endangered Rivers and the Conservation Movement*. Oakland: University of California Press.

Patterson, Raymond M. 1961. *The Buffalo Head*. Toronto: Macmillan of Canada.

———. 1968. *Finlay's River*. Victoria: TouchWood Editions

Potyondi, Barry. 1992. *Where the Rivers Meet: A History of the Upper Oldman River Basin to 1939*. Lethbridge: Southern Alberta Water Science Society.

Rowe, Stan. 2002. *Home Place: Essays on Ecology*. Edmonton: NeWest Press.

Russell, Andy. 1967. *Grizzly Country*. New York: Alfred A. Knopf.

———. 1984. *Trails of a Wilderness Wanderer*. New York: Alfred A. Knopf.

———. 1973. *Horns in the High Country*. New York: Alfred A. Knopf.

. 1984. *Memoirs of a Mountain Man*. Toronto. Macmillan of Canada.

———. 1987. *The Life of a River*. Toronto: McClelland & Stewart.

Schäffer, Mary. 2011. *Old Indian Trails of the Canadian Rockies*. Calgary: Rocky Mountain Books.

Smedley, Harold H. 1938. *Trout of Michigan*. Self-published.

Smith, W., and R. Cheng. 2016. *Canada's Intact Forest Landscapes, Updated to 2013*. Ottawa: Global Forest Watch.

Spry, Irene Mary. 1963. *The Palliser Expedition: An Account of John Palliser's British North American Expedition, 1857–1860*. Toronto: Macmillan of Canada.

Stegner, Wallace. 1969. *The Sound of Mountain Water*. New York: Doubleday.

Stelfox, Henry. 1972. *Rambling Thoughts of a Wandering Fellow, 1903–1968*. Edited by John G. Stelfox. Self-published.

Sterling, George. 1990. "Population Dynamics of Rainbow Trout (*Onchorhynchus mykiss*) in the Tri-Creeks Experimental Watershed of West-Central Alberta: A Postlogging Evaluation." *Tri-Creeks Experimental Watershed Research Report* No. 10. Edmonton: Alberta Fish & Wildlife Division.

Tomback, Diana. 2006. "The Impact of Seed Dispersal by Clark's Nutcracker on Whitebark Pine: Multiscale Perspective on a High Mountain Mutualism." In *Mountain Ecosystems: Studies in Treeline Ecology*, edited by Gabriele Broll and Beate Keplin. Berlin: Springer Science & Business Media.

Van Herk, Aritha. 2002. *Mavericks: An Incorrigible History of Alberta*. Toronto: Penguin Canada.

Van Tighem, Kevin. 1997. *Coming West: A Natural History of Home*. Calgary: Altitude.

———. 2000. *Home Range: Writings on Conservation and Restoration*. Calgary: Altitude.

———. 2013. *The Homeward Wolf*. Calgary: Rocky Mountain Books.

———. 2015. *Heart Waters: Sources of the Bow River*. Calgary: Rocky Mountain Books.

Vonnegut, Kurt. 1970. Speech to the graduating class of Bennington College (cited in *Time*, June 29, 1970).

Wood, Kerry. 1967. *A Corner of Canada*. Self-published.

Zieroth, Dale. 1976. *Mid River*. Toronto: House of Anansi.

Also by Kevin Van Tighem

Bears Without Fear

ISBN 9781927330319 $25.00 (CAD)

Fear of bears seems almost to be part of what it is to be human. Our species emerged out of the depths of time into a world already populated by these great carnivores. Before we mastered iron and later developed firearms, we had few defences against bears—only watchful caution and elaborate ceremonies and sacrifices to ward off fear.

Where human populations grow, bears have traditionally dwindled or disappeared. But when we return to the wild, to places where bears still survive, all our primeval fears awaken again. The risk of an automobile accident on the way to bear country far outstrips the risk of a close-range encounter with a bear, but it's the bear that worries us as we hurtle down the pavement at a hundred kilometres an hour.

In this timely and sensitive book, Kevin Van Tighem calls on decades of experience, knowledge and understanding in order to enlighten readers about our relationship with and attitude toward bears. Along the way we are confronted with the realities confronting these great animals as a result of our ever-expanding human population and their ever-shrinking natural habitat. Through historical research, field observation, practical advice, personal anecdotes and an array of stunning photos, Van Tighem has written a comprehensive book that is meant to demystify bears in order to promote a deeper understanding of these powerful yet vulnerable creatures.

The Homeward Wolf

An RMB Manifesto
ISBN 9781927330838 $16.00 (CAD)

Winner! 2014 Mountain Literature / Jon Whyte Award, Banff Mountain Book and Film Festival

Wolves have become a complicated comeback story. Their tracks are once again making trails throughout western Alberta, southern British Columbia and the northwestern United States, and the lonesome howls of the legendary predator are no longer mere echoes from our frontier past: they are prophetic voices emerging from the hills of our contemporary reality.

Kevin Van Tighem's first RMB Manifesto explores the history of wolf eradication in western North America and the species' recent return to the places where humans live and play. Rich with personal anecdotes and the stories of individual wolves whose fates reflect the complexity of our relationship with these animals, The Homeward Wolf neither romanticizes nor demonizes this wide-ranging carnivore with whom we once again share our Western spaces. Instead, it argues that wolves are coming back to stay, that conflicts will continue to arise and that we will need to find new ways to manage our relationship with this formidable predator in our ever-changing world.

Heart Waters: Sources of the Bow River

by Kevin Van Tighem, photography by Brian Van Tighem
ISBN 9781771601399 $40.00 (CAD)

Shortlisted for the 2016 Banff Mountain Film and Book Festival award for Mountain & Wilderness Literature.

For more than a century the foothills and Front Range mountains of western Alberta have been recognized as being vital to the water supply for western Canada. Virtually all the water that sustains communities, ecosystems and the economy of prairie Canada comes from this narrow strip of land arrayed along the Continental Divide. For all its importance, however, water management decisions affecting this enormous region have ignored the significance of land health and focused almost exclusively on building dams.

Heart Waters delves deeply into the history and ecology of a landscape whose critical value as a watershed is matched by its sheer beauty and diversity. A rich array of stunning images by Jasper-based photographer Brian Van Tighem complements the author's well-researched explorations of the stories whispered by the living waters that drain from Banff National Park, Kananaskis Country and the famous ranchlands of the Bow River watershed.

Kevin Van Tighem's latest book is a deep exploration of place and an invitation to recognize that our water future depends upon knowing our headwaters better and caring for them more passionately — as our heart waters.

Kevin Van Tighem, a former superintendent at Banff National Park, has written more than 200 articles, stories and essays on conservation and wildlife which have garnered him many awards, including Western Magazine Awards, Outdoor Writers of Canada book and magazine awards and the Journey Award for Fiction. He is the author of *Bears Without Fear* (RMB, 2013), *The Homeward Wolf* (RMB, 2013), *Heart Waters: Sources of the Bow River* (RMB, 2015) and *Our Place: Changing the Nature of Alberta* (RMB, 2017). He lives with his wife, Gail, in Canmore, Alberta.